AN AUTOBIOGRAPHY

MY PATH

&

MY DETOURS

FRANKLIN WATTS, INC.
NEW YORK · LONDON · TORONTO · SYDNEY
1985

The photographs in this book are from Jane Russell's
private collection except as noted.

Photographic insert following page 182:
first page, Movie Star News;
sixth page (bottom), Richard Gingrich collection;
seventh page (top), Richard Gingrich collection.

Photographic insert following page 278:
first page, Richard Gingrich collection;
sixth page (bottom), Playtex and Grey Advertising.

The publishers wish to thank Buck Waterfield for
loaning the photograph of his mother
by George Hurrell for use on the jacket of this book.

Book design by Nick Krenitsky

Library of Congress Cataloging in Publication Data

Russell, Jane, 1921–
Jane Russell : my path & my detours.

Filmography: p.
Includes index.
1. Russell, Jane, 1921–   . 2. Moving-picture
actors and actresses—United States—Biography.
I. Title.
PN2287.R82A34   1985   791.43'028'0924 [B] 85-13708
ISBN 0-531-09799-4

DEDICATED TO

MY CHILDREN

WHO MORE THAN ONCE HAVE BEEN

MY REASON FOR LIVING

I WISH TO THANK

Jan and Bob Lowell for helping
me when I'd let them;
Lois Stalvey and Marjel Delauer
for giving me the
courage to go on alone;
Edith Lynch and Kevin Pines
for their objective observations;
and especially Margaret Obegi
for her on-the-spot reporting
throughout *Company;*
Pamela Russell for tying up
all the loose ends;
Christie Van Cleve for typing
my horrendous pages;
my patient editor, Jim Connor,
for cutting me down to size;
and the Lord for getting this
book off my desk.

F O R E W O R D

B Y

E D I T H   L Y N C H

Publicist for Howard Hughes and RKO
Confidante and friend for Jane

From the day Jane came to the studio to make her first RKO film, she was queen bee on the lot—never mind the other contract players. Although her contract was with Hughes personally, she was considered an RKO star.

When we met I found her to be shy, impatient, and loud—a roaring mouse. But with all that bluster, she couldn't quite hide the humor and kindness in her—an earthiness and wisdom that fascinated everyone; she was a really funny gal.

Through Jane I also met the Lord and was introduced to the intricacies of astrology. People interested Jane, and the study of human influence had her in its grip. My birth sign was okay: Gemini, praise God, just like Jane! I might not be writing this today had I been born under another sign.

I had heard, "She is religious," in that incredulous tone used to convey a horrendous affliction. "The Lord is a living doll," she had once said and was widely quoted in the press. But never mind; she had walked hand in hand with the Lord since she was a pup. Her mother's Bible study training and chapel attendance each week had made Him a part of her, like breathing.

Jane is a confusing mess of opposing traits: honest, empathetic, bright, loud, impatient, lazy (by her own admission), shy, sympathetic, bossy, disorganized, and creative. This dichotomous creature rose to film stardom and set an interesting pace for her associates. Some were scared shitless by her, but the discerning few who understood her and recognized her innate shyness, which she covered by extraordinary bluster, liked her, and she, in turn, figuratively gathered them to her ample bosom as FRIENDS FOREVER.

PREFACE

This is not the story of some-
one who found Christ in the middle of her life and therefore
found a bed of roses, perfection, and joy from that day forward. Rather, it's the story of one who found and accepted
Jesus at the age of six and then found herself on the same
long painful journey as that fellow in *Pilgrim's Progress*.
Wherever that poor Pilgrim found himself, I've been there
twice. And, unlike Pilgrim, I often fell off the path; or, as the
Lord said, "Your detours have been as in a maze." In those
times I can just see Him looking at me sadly and shaking His
head.

I've also known the joy of getting back on track and seeing
my Savior smile. And *what* He's saved me from! I couldn't
have made it this far without Him—and I don't think He intended me to. Through all my ups and downs I've never been
alone. He was there, guiding and directing, even when I
couldn't see the why or wherefore, telling me that if I could
just hold tough a little longer, I'd find myself around one more
dark corner, see one more spot of light, and have one more
drop of pure joy in this journey called life.

I have always been in love with C. S. Lewis and said he
was to be my next husband. But the darned man up and died
many years ago. Anyway, he writes in one of his books, *Mere
Christianity*, that you mustn't judge Christian crabby "Miss

Bates" with agnostic good-natured "Dick Firken." You instead have to say how much more crabby Miss Bates would be if she weren't a Christian, and how much better Firken would be if he were. In other words, imagine what a hell-raiser I might be if I didn't have the Lord! I shudder to think!

Satan is the father of liars, and, boy, has he tried to hand me a bag full of lies! But, when I listen to that still small voice, I drop that bag and run like hell!

Jane Russell Peoples
1985

O N E

It was 1940. I was nineteen years old and as I drove home in my new Ford coupe, I was ecstatic. I couldn't believe the changes that had taken place in my life in only a few months. I had had a feeling for some time that I was standing at a blind corner but that just around that corner there was something waiting—something good— and all I had to do was round that corner. But never, *never* in my wildest premonitions did I think it would be a starring role in a Howard Hughes motion picture entitled *The Outlaw*.

One simply didn't start out in this business starring in a picture! You worked, studied, and dreamed for years. If you were lucky, you might do bit parts in little theaters and slowly work your way up. But here I was, totally unprepared. Oh, sure, I had gone to a couple of dramatic schools just after high school. My mother wanted her tomboy daughter to go to finishing school. I balked at that, so she thought a dramatic school might be the answer. That's all she could afford after my dad died.

The first was the Max Reinhardt school. I started in September 1939, fresh out of high school. I never met Mr. Reinhardt or his wife. The classes they taught were for third- and fourth-term students. Most of the time I ditched classes and went to the bowling alley across Sunset Boulevard with a girl

I'd met at school. She was Betty Groblie, who later hosted a television interview show in Washington, D.C., on which I was a guest.

One day Betty and I tried out for Earl Carroll's Most Beautiful Girls in the World revue. His theater, too, was just across the street. We thought why not? It might be fun. I was picked, much to the horror of my teacher, Mr. Omed. He shouted, "Do you want to be a cheap showgirl or an actress?" I was mortified. When I found out the show was going to New York, and not staying in southern California, the thought of leaving football star Robert Waterfield, with whom I was in love, at Christmastime was unthinkable.

Since I wasn't going to be a "cheap showgirl," I gave up the Reinhardt school too. I was bored with drama school and didn't want to be an actress anyway. My mother had been an actress before she was married. Now, I love her dearly, but I didn't want her running my life. She had been quiet and subtle, saying things like, "Daughter, you can choose art, music, or drama. . . ." But I knew she secretly hoped I'd choose drama. College was out. I got C's and even D's in math and science. I decided to be a clothes designer.

I remember sitting in the corner when I was a little girl, listening as my mother taught elocution. After her student left, I repeated the piece they had been working on, word for word. I also remember my mother telling me that she had named me Jane (there had been several Janes in her mother's family) because she could see *Jane Russell* looking good in lights. Those two memories were enough for me, so off I went in search of a good dress designer school. It was Friday by the time I found one. The new semester started the next Monday. I was told to bring my check back and enroll then. However, on my way home, I passed Maria Ouspenskaya's dramatic school, where Pat Dawson, one of my best friends from Van Nuys High, was starting. I thought I'd surprise her, but when I arrived she wasn't there. I waited in the large entry hall and watched the students walk by with plays under their arms talking about diction and directors. The bug bit me again. I forgot all about not wanting to be an actress. I marched into the office right then and gave them the check that was meant for designer school.

Well, Pat was indeed surprised, and Madam Ouspenskaya actually taught for two hours every afternoon. Madam was a divine, tiny, seventy-five-year-old lady who could do a handstand and often proved it to the delight of her classes. She was a chain-smoker and always had a cigarette jammed into a long holder set between her teeth. There was always a glass of water on a table beside her from which she would occasionally sip. One day my friend Jennifer Holt, who is Jack Holt's daughter and Tim's sister, took a drink of Madam's water while she was dusting the room and discovered it was 100 proof vodka!

Years later, Madam was watching me at a television rehearsal. When I came off the stage to say hello, she said to me in her marvelous Russian accent, "You know, Jen, you could be a very good acktress, but you haff no henergy." No energy. It's true. I've watched myself too often on the screen and I seemed to be moving in slow motion.

There was a marvelous diction teacher at the school, Margaret Pendergast McLean, and a ballet class in which I was the clown. I was just awful! And by the end of six months at Maria Ouspenskaya's School of Dramatic Arts, I certainly didn't feel ready for any starring role.

Pat's mother, Mammy Dawson, had worked as a secretary for Jack Warner before she married film editor Ralph Dawson. She dragged me to Charles Feldman, one of the classiest agents in town. Although he was utterly charming, he told me that his agency handled only established stars. They simply didn't take on unknowns. But Howard Hughes was looking for a girl for a picture he was going to produce and that girl would be one in a million. The agency couldn't take the time to sort them out.

I stood up and smiled. "Let's go, Mammy. How in God's green earth can kids ever get started if they can't even get an agent until they've made it?"

Of course, much later, inevitably, I saw Charlie Feldman at a Hollywood bash. When our eyes met, he slowly drew

his finger across his throat and grinned, red faced, at me. I just laughed back.

Meanwhile, Pat Alexander, a friend from the eighth grade, was working in a diner at Hollywood and Vine when Tom Kelley, a marvelous young photographer, spotted her and asked if she would like to model.

"Sure," she quipped, "if I keep my clothes on."

Tom laughed and said he did do nude calendars, but that wasn't what he had in mind for her. He was thinking more along the line of ski clothes and other sports shots. "Don't worry, honey, my wife is always there."

Pat asked Tom whether a friend might come along. He might be interested in her, too. That was fine with him. She filled me in on all this as we drove my mom's car to his Hollywood studio. To Pat and me it was another world, and we were duly impressed.

The first thing I did was put on a bathing suit and stand on a stool. I never felt so vulnerable in my life! You see, for years I'd been so skinny that the boys in school called me "bones." Standing on that stool in a bathing suit was sheer agony.

Tom was patience itself. He showed me how to stand on my toes like swimming star Esther Williams, bend one knee in front of the other, raise my arms folded over my head, and stretch my torso. It was positively the most awkward position one could get into.

"If it's not uncomfortable, it'll be a lousy picture. Now smile!"

When I saw the shots, I was thrilled. I didn't look so skinny after all. Tom Kelley was some photographer!

Soon Tom and his wife, Natalie, became like family, and they were extremely protective of Pat and me. I was soon doing fashion shots for Nancy's of Hollywood.

Tom knew that Pat had no desire whatsoever to become an actress, but he felt that I did and he sent me to Twentieth Century-Fox for a screen test. I'll never forget it. A wardrobe test of Betty Grable was in progress, and I sat in a dark corner of the set and watched. She looked gorgeous, and I felt again that yen for this business. I thought, "Maybe some day they might do wardrobe tests of me." Ha! After Betty Grable and her crew had trouped out, the test cameraman sat me on a stool. He shot full face and both profiles, left and right, and said, "That's all." The word came back to Kelley some days later that I was unphotogenic. Tom roared with laughter. "Those dumb shits! They could have come up with anything but that! If you aren't photogenic, the sky isn't blue!" he hollered.

About this same time I met my first Hollywood "wolf." It was both sad and funny. I'll call him Mr. X. He had taken me to the Paramount studios, where I was said to be too tall.

"Well, for Alan Ladd maybe, but what about Fred MacMurray?" he asked. I was mad about Fred MacMurray. They just showed us the door.

As we walked off the lot, a little tear trickled down my cheek. My companion seized his opportunity. Did I *really* want to be in pictures? Well, he could positively get that accomplished! I was to meet him at Schwab's Drugstore on Sunset that night at five o'clock.

Since I didn't want to go all the way back to the Valley and have to turn around and drive over the hill again, I went to Pat Alexander's. Pat's mother, whom I called Ommy, listened to my story about Paramount and being too tall and what Mr. X had said. She narrowed her eyes and cautioned me about that sort of man and what he might have in mind. "Just watch him," she laughed.

I met him at Schwab's, but I insisted on taking my own car—my mother's, that is—and I followed Mr. X to a plain little house in Beverly Hills. After a rather short, serious discussion, he pulled me down on his lap and promised me the moon while trying to kiss me. Then I did the unforgivable. I laughed. I told him I was in love with a football player who was six foot one. I laughed all the way to the door. He was, by the way, the only honest-to-God Hollywood wolf I ever met.

I needed a job. Modeling wasn't all that steady. Ommy told me about a job folding small boxes in the packaging plant where she worked as a secretary and bookkeeper. I went in the next day. I folded boxes until the man in charge stopped me.

"You don't have to win any races here. Slow down and have a break."

I knew I'd go mad if I even thought about what I was doing and just the thought of doing it every day was impossible. So I folded until the bell rang at five. I told Ommy to give my regards to the man in charge, and thanks, but no thanks. She just laughed. She knew it wasn't for me.

Next I answered an ad for a doctor's assistant. He was a chiropodist. I got the job. I wore a white uniform, took the patients' shoes and socks off, and stuck their feet in pails of warm water . . . for a week! Then I gave the chiropodist my regards.

Now what? By the summer of 1940 I was really disheartened. What about all those feelings that something was about to happen? That something good was just around the corner? So much for premonitions. I needed to get away from it all. Robert was busy with football as usual at UCLA, so I borrowed Mom's car, let all my feelings slip away, and headed sixty miles out to my cousins in Fontana, California, to the most important Pat of all—my cousin, Patricia Henry.

We were the only girls among ten boys. She had six brothers and I had four. We were Geminis born one year apart and we could read each other's minds. Our mothers had been inseparable as sisters—Geraldine and Ernestine, the Jacobi girls from Grand Forks, North Dakota. Pat and I were more like sisters than cousins. I would always go to Fontana when the sky looked darkest. There I could lick my wounds.

It was so good to be back in Fontana. I knew my head would clear there, and I'd find my direction again. And then it happened! The phone rang. It was Mother. An agent, Levis Green, had called several times and wanted me to meet someone. It was terribly important. By this time I was disenchanted by people who wanted to drag me to meet someone, so I simply told Mom to tell him

I would be home in a week and he could just wait. I was going to enjoy Patricia and my cousins in Fontana.

When the week was up and I started home, I had to admit to a certain sense of anticipation as I turned into our long drive.

"That agent hasn't stopped calling, Daughter," Mother said the minute I got out of the car. A first for her. "His name is Levis Green."

I called.

"Where have you been?" he hollered into the phone. That didn't bother me; I was used to hollering. "Can you get in here right now or first thing tomorrow?"

"What's it all about?" I asked.

"Howard Hughes is going to make a picture. They're testing on Monday, and Freddy Schussler, his casting agent, wants to see you."

"Me! How did they know about me?" I thought, *"Howard Hughes!"*

"Oh, when I saw a picture of you at Tom Kelley's studio and asked him who you were—he wouldn't tell me. He calls me the Silver Fox. Anyway, he told me to lay off, that you were a nice little girl from the Valley. I swiped the picture, put it in my briefcase, and showed it to the different casting directors when I made my rounds of the studios. Nothing happened till I got to Hughes' office. Freddy took one look and said, 'She looks the type; bring her in.' Then I had to go back to Tom to get your phone number. I didn't even know your name. This has been one hell of a week."

"Okay," I said, laughing. "I'll meet you at ten tomorrow. Where's your office?"

When we met the next morning I liked him immediately. He did have silver hair, and black eyebrows over blue eyes that were set in a tanned, lined, young-looking face. He had signed Craig Stevens, Susan Peters, and Susan Ball to contracts for the agency, which was owned by Howard Lang. It was a small, personal agency, and Levis was a hustler. Obviously! He was a bachelor too, I found out.

We drove to Freddy Schussler's office, where this wiry

little man gave me a scene to learn and a costume and a wig fitting and told me to report to 7000 Romaine Street, which was the address of a large gray building that looked like a factory. It was Howard Hughes' headquarters. There, in a small office with only a desk, a davenport, and a cot in one corner, I met Howard Hawks, who was going to direct the picture for Mr. Hughes. Hawks was a tall, gray-haired man with blue, blue eyes and a gentle manner. He explained that the part was that of a girl who was half-Irish and half-Mexican. She had been raised by her Aunt Guadalupi and had an accent. Her brother had been killed by Billy the Kid, and she hated his guts. When she tries to kill him with a pitchfork, he rapes her.

"Ye gods!" I thought. "Wait till I tell Patricia!"

"We'll be testing Monday, so learn the scene, and good luck," Mr. Hawks said, patting my shoulder.

"What a nice man," I said to Levis as we left. "I can't believe all this is happening to me!"

"Well, now maybe you can understand why I was so nervous. They've been testing kids for the parts of the girl and Billy for months, and the last test is only three days away. Can you learn lines?"

"Yeah, sure, uh . . . I think so." I was finally getting very excited.

When I got home, I had a brainstorm. My friend Eloisa Pachecco was Mexican–American, so down I went to see her. We sat in the car and she read the scene over and over while I mimicked her word for word.

If Mother was on tenterhooks, she never let on. She just smiled. I studied my lines and lay awake at night thinking, "Could this be it? Could this be that corner I've been wanting to turn?" Deep inside I knew it was there waiting. Monday would tell.

It finally arrived, and so did I at 7000 Romaine. In the basement. I was in costume and the long hair fall was firmly attached. Four other girls who were finalists, I gathered, were also there. It had been a long search. We were all dressed alike. We were all brunettes and we were all nervous. Five boys were there too, all dressed alike in cowboy clothes, including boots, hats, and gun belts. One of them was Gene Fowler's son, Will. Hawks came over to me and with a big smile introduced me to the cameraman, Lucien Ballard. They were getting ready to shoot a boy and girl picked at random. The set was a barn built in one corner of the huge basement. There was the proverbial haystack with a pitchfork and leather trapping hanging from a post.

The shot, Mr. Hawks explained, was the close-up of the scene where Billy the Kid throws Rio down on the hay after she has tried to kill him. He's trying to find out why she's after him.

One couple did the scene and the rest watched. Then two more. I had given the boys a quick once-over and spotted the one I thought was the best looking. His name was Jack. I didn't get to work with him. He did his scene with someone else. Then suddenly it was my turn. Honestly, the camera didn't bother me. It was just a larger edition of Tom Kelley's, and the lights were so intense that the people standing around just faded away. It was just this boy and myself. I really wasn't nervous. After I finished, Mr. Hawks came over to me and smiled. He nodded toward a man behind him.

"That fellow back there," he said, "he told me that you speak pretty good English for a Mexican."

We both laughed. My rehearsal with Eloisa had paid off. But when we shot the picture I had no accent. Howard Hughes decided it might limit me in getting other roles.

When the tests were finished, we all went home. No decisions were made. I was just left hanging, waiting for a phone call.

A few endless days later I got a call from Levis. Mr. Hawks wanted to see me. I went over the hill to Romaine Street and up to the office. My heart was in my throat. Mr. Hawks took me to a projection room and ran the film of all the tests that were shot the day I did mine. Mine was last. I sat there, feeling like I was hooked to an electric wire, and watched each girl. I was sure which girl had it. The one in the second test. She was so good, my heart sank. Then mine came on the screen. It's hard to describe the feelings I had. It was like watching someone else, only knowing it was me. There was a softness about the girl on the screen that the others hadn't had. To see your own likeness and feel it isn't you, to see beauty when you feel so unbeautiful, so plain, so average (as most teenagers do) was a shock. I could feel Mr. Hawks smiling at me.

He didn't say a word, but took me back up to the office. The boy I'd picked as the cute one was there. His name was Jack Beutel. He was sitting on the davenport, so I sat on the cot. Mr. Hawks sat behind his desk and just looked at us, his blue eyes twinkling. Then, in his slow quiet way, he said, "Well, you two kids have the parts. Mr. Hughes has been looking at all the tests over and over and you're our decision."

Jack grinned from ear to ear, and I flopped back flat on the cot and threw my hands over my head. We were too dumbfounded to speak.

"Now that's just the kind of thing I want you kids to do," Mr. Hawks said, "be spontaneous and natural."

It's a shame we didn't get to work with him all through the picture. As it turned out, the shooting of *The Outlaw* was interminable, and Jack and I didn't have a spontaneous move in the whole picture.

We were to sign stock contracts at $50 a week, but if the picture was successful, they would be torn up and new ones signed, Mr. Hawks assured us.

As Jack and I were leaving Mr. Hawks' office with our contracts under our arms, we noticed a man waiting to go in. A little way down the hall Jack punched me and we stopped.

"I think that's him," he said.

"Who?" I asked.

"Howard Hughes!"

"Where?"

"Back there, outside Hawks' office."

I turned and saw a tall, lanky man leaning on the wall with his hat on the back of his head, a white shirt open at the neck, and dark trousers. He was just standing there watching us go down the hall. (He was not wearing sneakers, and I never saw him in any in all the years I knew him.)

"Hi," Jack said to him with a smile, and I ventured a little wave.

He smiled shyly, gave a little nod, and went into Mr. Hawks' office.

That was it. That was all there was to our first encounter with Howard Hughes. He wanted to see his two handpicked choices in the flesh, but not in the office, just casually in passing. It sent chills up our spines. I didn't see him again until we came home from that first, strange new experience, shooting on location in Arizona.

When I got downstairs Levis and his boss, Howard Lang, were there waiting with their agency contracts for me to sign. "Boy," I thought, "they sure aren't wasting any time." When I got home with my contracts, my mother just said very calmly, "Well, praise the Lord."

Later, when Howard Hawks gave a party at the Mocambo nightclub, I didn't know what in the world I was going to wear. I didn't own an evening gown, and that's what you wore to a party at the Mocambo. At last I found a long-sleeved, high-necked, beige jersey dress with beige and turquoise silk fringe that hung from the hip line to the floor. I had to have it. It was smashing! Mother's eyes popped when I told her the price, but she loved it. The gown was awfully expensive, but I can't remember now just what it cost.

When Mother dropped me off at Hawks' house, I was greeted by his red setters. They had a ball trying to catch the fringe hanging from my skirt. Jack Beutel and Gary Cooper and his wife, Rocky, were also there. Hawks served drinks and then we went on to the Mocambo.

This was the Sunset Strip at its prime. Beautiful nightclubs and restaurants lined the street: Ciro's, the Trocadero, the Players, and the Mocambo, to name but a few. There were chic boutiques, couturiers, and beauty shops. It was probably the most expensive piece of property in California.

The Mocambo was the first nightclub I'd ever been to. It was beautiful—soft lights, soft music, and wine served in long-stemmed glasses. Jack Beutel sat across from me, next to Rocky Cooper, and Gary Cooper was on my right. When Cooper asked me to dance, I could hardly get up. He was very kind and even better looking than on the screen. He was the most handsome man I'd ever seen, with a deep tan set off by just a sprinkling of gray at his temples. He was so tall! It was wonderful. Mr. Hawks just kept watching us and smiling. I was suddenly very glad Mother had taught me to be a lady. Jack and I were thrilled to death with the whole evening and kept grinning at each other across the table.

The next day I bought my first car, a brand new 1940 Ford coupe. I had wanted a convertible, but they were just too expensive. Right now I needed wheels: a publicity campaign, fittings, and all sorts of exciting things were starting to happen, and I couldn't keep borrowing Mom's car. I went directly to the hospital to meet a friend of Mr. Hawks, "Slim," who was there with a broken leg. She was a stunning ex-model who knew a lot about clothes. Mr. Hawks wanted me to have a wardrobe when we went on location.

Slim was absolutely charming, and later became Mrs. Hawks. She called a buyer at I. Magnin's and I went down and was fitted with what I called my Elizabeth Fish wardrobe. (Every time Mother saw a picture of a young English society girl named Elizabeth Fish in a magazine, she would show it to me. She was always hoping I'd get a taste for something besides jeans.) Now I had soft cashmere dresses, a camel hair coat, and a tan suit, all simply tailored and stunning.

Then Mr. Hawks took me to Nudie's, the cowboy turned tailor, where I was fitted with a tailored beige western outfit—boots, hat, the works—all very subdued and beautifully cut.

I was on cloud nine. I was nineteen years old; I had a new car, a beautiful new wardrobe, a contract to star in a motion picture, and a wonderful director I could trust. I thought I was in heaven.

As I drove through the gates of La Posada, the seven and a half acres I'd called home since I'd been twelve, I felt the joy I'd always felt living in this beautiful place. The cast iron gates swung open to a curved driveway that was lined with white bridal bushes and tall palms. White pasture fences led up to the sprawling Mexican hacienda my mother had dreamed about and architect Kemper Nomland had built. The depression hadn't hurt the Russells; on the contrary: My dad, Roy Russell, had been promoted to general manager of the Andrew Jergens Company's West Coast factory. No way did we suffer like the Henrys. True, the hired couple, the palomino horses, and the luxuries were gone, but the fruit trees, pines, and eucalyptus were all still there, and everything was paid for. The alfalfa fields on either side of the drive were still flourishing, and Mary, the cow, still gave the richest milk in the Valley. Dad had left us very blessed, considering he was only forty-seven years old when he died.

When I pulled up in my new Ford, my brothers, Tommy (sixteen), Ken (fifteen), Jamie (thirteen), and Wally (twelve), came whooping and hollering from every direction, yelling, "You're gonna be a MOOVIE star! Woo, Woo!" "Hey, Daughter, where'd you get the car?" "Can I borrow it?" No dignity, no respect! That bunch thought the whole thing was a hoot! I bubbled over with excitement telling Mom all about what had happened. She just beamed and blessed me on my way. She was going to have her actress after all.

It wasn't so easy with my football player. Robert Waterfield wasn't so sure about any of it. When I'd been picked for Earl Carroll's Most Beautiful Girls, a fellow UCLA player had said to him, "Hey, Waterfield, you'd better throw in the towel." Well, he didn't, and we managed through that; but pictures, that was something else. That could really be the beginning of the end. I knew it wasn't, and I did everything I could to reassure him. At last he decided to ignore the whole thing. When we were together, we didn't discuss anything that happened over the hill in Hollywood. Everything was the way it had been with us for the last two years. That was the way we both wanted it. It was safer.

The Outlaw started location shooting near Tuba City, Arizona. Pillars of stone stood against the sky like huge sentinels across the stark, high desert. There stunt men, grips, prop men, hairdressers, makeup and wardrobe people, the director, and the actors lived in a city of tents set up next to an Indian village built of adobe. A huge center tent served as the dining room. All our food was trucked in because we were so far from town. On Saturday nights we'd pile into buses and ride forever, it seemed, to Flagstaff to bum around. Everybody got loaded and we sang all the way back.

The company—consisting of Hawks, the director; Lucien Ballard, the cameraman; Jack Beutel, "Billy the Kid"; Walter Huston, "Doc Holiday"; and Thomas Mitchell, "Pat Garrett"—were all shooting in the Indian village throughout the week. I wasn't used in the first part of shooting, but I was kept busy all day long with photographers and publicity. This campaign was masterminded by Russell Birdwell, the famous publicist. I was posed with an Indian brave high on a cliff, with Walter Huston (whom I idolized), and with Jack whenever he had the time. I was photographed running, standing, walking, and on an Indian porch, always in my *Outlaw* costume. The wardrobe department had made more than half a dozen of the two outfits I wore in the picture. I had brought all my beautiful clothes with me but never got to wear them in a photograph.

One weekend *Look, Pic, Life, Photoplay, Peek*—you name it—every magazine in the country, it seemed, sent photographers out to take pictures of me doing everything.

"Janie, dear, walk up and down the hill for us."

"Honey, just pick up those two pails."

"Now, hold it. Don't actually pick them up. That's right."

Tom Kelley had always destroyed anything that looked awkward or showed too much skin. He was very protective. But I had no training in self-protection. I trusted everybody. It just never occurred to me that there were bastards out there who would use anything they could get. My boobs were bulging out over the top of my blouse every time I picked up those pails. But I didn't know it until I saw myself on the covers and centerfolds of practically every magazine on the newsstands. One weekend was all it took. Those pictures came out for the next five years.

Later that same week, the publicity man on the picture and a photographer wanted me to get into a nightgown and jump on the bed for some pictures. Well, even though co-operation was my middle name, I knew something was wrong with this setup. When they left, I put on my robe and went to see father Hawks. I was crying and told him what had happened. To my surprise and utter gratitude he didn't comfort me.

"Look," he said, "you're a big girl now, and you've got to protect yourself. If someone asks you to do *anything* that's against your better judgment, say NO! Loud and clear. There can't always be a Tom Kelley there to assure good taste. That's up to you. You're in charge of you. No one else."

The publicity man was fired, and the pictures were never published, thanks to Howard Hawks. And I learned to say NO! I had to do it often until the word got out. Layouts were canceled until they finally got the message. I'd warned them ahead of time, but if the camera was on a balcony above me or I was to bend over, I would just turn my back or stand and glare. I learned every trick in the book, fast. Then they'd fold up their gear and leave. They only wanted a peep show, and if they couldn't get it, they left disgruntled.

I honestly feel sorry if *The Outlaw* publicity campaign was responsible for the young girls who decided that the only way to make it in show business was to shove out their bosom or take their clothes off altogether.

I wasn't used in the picture on location, and therefore, I didn't get to work with Howard Hawks. All the film was sent back to Hollywood to Howard Hughes, and apparently there were long and heated conversations on the phone. At any rate, one day Jack and I were told that Hawks was leaving the picture and that Lucien Ballard was going with him. We went to Mr. Hawks at once.

"Yes," he said, "I'm leaving. We just can't agree on how the picture should be done. I told Howard he'd better do it himself, because *no one* tells *me* how to shoot a picture. Don't worry," he said, smiling at our two downcast faces, "we'll work together again someday. If you like, you can fly home with me."

Well, Jack and I were in shock. We walked back to our tents to find they were already being taken down.

"Home? Where?" Jack said. "I don't know whether to go to Hollywood or back to Dallas."

Then we saw the separation of the Hawks people from the Hughes people. Cliff Broughton, who was the unit manager, took Jack and me in tow. This was my first taste of what loyalty meant to Howard Hughes. I learned how terribly important it was to him.

"You two are under contract to Howard Hughes," Cliff said. "He's the boss, and he wouldn't like it one bit if you went home with Howard Hawks. You're going to fly home with me." And we did, in a daze.

Was the picture finished? Would it ever continue? What was to be our future? I didn't have answers to any of these questions. I simply went home to my terrific family, my wonderful friends, my love, Robert Waterfield, and waited.

T W O

Robert Waterfield used to say, "You and your goddamned family!" Well, we were pretty hard to separate—a wild mixture of English, Irish, Scottish, and German, with a dash of French, that had come together in Grand Forks, North Dakota. My father's side came from a dour Scot from Inverness named Russell, and my mother's side from another Scot, Jock Stevenson. My great-great-grandfather was Otto Reinhold Jacobi, a Prussian-born court painter and friend of William I. There was also the French ancestor who hid her English captain under her hoop skirts during one of the wars between France and England! The Lord alone knows what draws certain people together, but without these flamboyant characters there would have been no Jane Russell.

My mother's predecessors weren't exactly pioneers seeking their fortune when they landed in Canada but, rather, two families who had already earned theirs and, owing to circumstance, were intensely interested in the New World and ready to make a new start. Jock Stevenson, a Scotsman, was the chief coast guard officer in Ireland for the British navy to whom Queen Victoria awarded a thousand-acre land grant in any colony of his choosing when he retired. His wife, Ellen, the daughter of the French lady, had been raised in a Church of England convent. Her eight children dared not disturb her at her prayers. For two hours a day in her bed-room she prayed aloud for the whole household to hear. She prayed that her children could be raised someplace besides where they lived in Kellbegs, Ireland. Her sons loved to sneak into the Irish wakes, where there was always plenty of drink. At last Captain Jock came home to his praying wife and shouted, "Get off your knees, woman! We're going to Can-ada!" He had chosen Lake Malcolm, Ontario, where they found it wild indeed, but beautiful beyond description. The log cabin was comfortable and the Indians were friendly. The year was 1860.

My other great-great-grandfather, Otto Jacobi, was an artist who painted royalty and counted many aristocrats among his closest friends. His landscapes in watercolor are highly val-ued even today. It was rumored that he was commissioned to restore the Sistine Chapel in the middle 1800s, but when an epidemic of smallpox broke out, Otto was stricken. He surely would have died if it hadn't been for a little country girl, Sibilla Reuter, who nursed him back to health. He mar-ried her, and they had four children. Their eldest son died at sixteen, and when war clouds began to gather, Otto feared for his only other son, Ernest. His dear friends the Duke and Duchess of Nassau counseled him to leave his house and af-fairs just as they were so as not to arouse suspicion, and they provided Otto with a handsome sum of money and transport to Canada.

Otto had a studio in Montreal and later in Toronto. He was one of the founding members of the Royal Canadian Academy and president from 1890 to 1893. But the lure of the "backwoods," as eastern Ontario was called, was too much for his painter's heart, so with young Ernest he went in search of the perfect spot. That's right, they found it at Lake Malcolm. The only non-Indian neighbors were the Steven-sons across the lake. So the Jacobi family settled in, and Er-nest, now an engineer, fell in love with young Ellen Steven-son and James Stevenson fell in love with Ernest's little sister, Louisa Jacobi.

Ernest and Ellen had four children: Ernest Junior, Gus-tave (my grandfather), Lillian (Aunt Dove), and Isabelle (Aunt

Bella). Grandpa Gus was a giant of a man, and so were all his children. I got my height from him.

The U.S. government was giving land grants to those brave souls who would go west and stake claims in North Dakota. So the Jacobis and the Stevensons moved southwest into the United States and founded Ardock, North Dakota. They practically *were* Ardock. Mother said it was like heaven when she was a girl. One uncle had the post office, another had the grocery store. One aunt had a furniture store plus caskets! Still another was the druggist. All of them a Stevenson or Jacobi. In my day it was Henrys and Russells. To me it's the most natural thing in the world to be surrounded by family.

In Ardock Gustave met eighteen-year-old Amelia Hyatt, who had come to visit a friend. Amelia Hyatt jumped at the chance to marry Gustave Reinhold Jacobi. Their first two children, my mother, Geraldine, and my aunt Ernestine, were born in Ardock. Then the family moved to Grand Forks, where they opened a bank. There the rest of the children were born: Reinhold, Ruth, Jack, and Kenneth. No one would even consider having a social without inviting the Jacobi girls. They were rich and beautiful. Along with their brothers, they were nicknamed the "lawless Jacobis."

Amelia Hyatt Jacobi was proper beyond belief. Everything had to be just so. But, thank God, the children were more like their father than their mother. When the staunch Episcopalian family would start out for church or even to go to town, Grandma would look them over from head to foot.

"Ruthie, you can't go looking like that!" she'd fume.

"Hell, Mother, they're lucky to know us!" little Ruthie would say. It's been a family saying ever since. I've even heard my grandnieces and grandnephews say it.

Uncle Reinhold was captain of the football team, and Ruthie adored him. Once he was in a fight with another boy and Ruthie picked up a rake and split the poor kid's skull.

Ernestine was a beauty, but just as bad as Pat and me in Fontana. When the girls went riding in the snow sleigh, they had a wonderful time singing and laughing, but they were forbidden to go down Main Street. So just as they neared

Main, Ernie would snuggle up to the driver, grab the reins out of his hands, and whip the horses down Main Street. There they were hit by snowballs and whistled and hooted at, much to the chagrin of my mother. But she was no better. When she and Ernie were shopping in East Grand Forks one day, they saw some ladies from their church coming down the street toward them. Mother pulled Ernie into the entrance of a saloon, gave the doors a push as though they had just come out, and waltzed tipsily down the street to the shocked stares of Grandma's friends.

Grandpa Gus marched the entire family to church in the rain, the snow, or a blizzard. Once it looked almost impossible.

"We will be the only ones there. God must not come to an empty church," he said. And they went.

Grandpa was a very popular fellow and loved to drink with his Shriner buddies. They were all hard drinkers. Later, when Mother and Ernie were married and had found the Lord, they all started to pray for him. I remember thinking as a child that it was pretty silly to try to pray him out of all his fun with the boys. But the Lord was faithful, and Grandpa finally "laid it down" and became a teetotaler. But he never lost his descriptive vocabulary.

My mother was the real actress in the family. She was always whipping up shows for the Shriners, and she'd make her sisters act in them. My mother went to Emerson College in Boston, Massachusetts, then called Emerson's School of Oratory. She loved it! As a sophomore she played a lady-in-waiting to George Arliss' Disraeli. Alexander Knox's aunt, Agnes Knox Black, coached Mother in a one-woman recital of the play that she performed as a benefit for the Montreal Art Gallery. She was introduced as the great-granddaughter of Otto Reinhold Jacobi, who had been president of the Royal Canadian Academy many years before. Another recital was given for the Belgian Relief Fund in the grand ballroom of the Ritz Carlton Hotel.

Mother went to New York, pounded the pavement from one casting director's office to another, and did all the things I never had to do to become an actress. She worked in Gimbels' basement until she became a part of the road company of *Daddy Longlegs*, in which she eventually played the older lady as well as the ingenue, running like mad to change between scenes! Pictures of Mother in those days make me look like chopped liver!

Around the same time, she sat for artist Mary B. Titcomb. The picture was called *A Portrait of Geraldine J.* Later at an exhibition President Woodrow Wilson bought it and took it to the White House. Now it's called *The Girl in the Blue Hat* and hangs in his restored Washington home for all to see.

Mother found her high school sweetheart again when the *Daddy Longlegs* company played in Michigan, where Roy Russell was stationed during World War I. He had been captain of the football team when she was just a freshman, and she hadn't seen him in seven years. When she did, he was standing there in his uniform, and she fainted. He was staring at her on the bed as she came to.

"I'm not letting you get away again," he said. "We're getting married right now. Tonight." And that's just what they did. But right after the ceremony he had duty, and she had to leave for another town with the company.

It's a funny thing about the Russells; they're a tight-lipped, silent breed. After seven years, not even an "I love you" was uttered.

Grandpa Gus didn't approve of the marriage. Roy Russell's father was in the "liquor business" and Grandpa was a banker. Of course, Dad's mother didn't approve either: her fine son marrying a socialite—and in show business to boot! But soon the war was over and Mother became pregnant. Her first son, Billy—her only blonde, blue-eyed child—died at fifteen months. Aunt Ernie had also lost a child, and it was then, Mother said, that they had both begun to wonder about life after death and to become more interested in the Almighty and His purpose for their lives. Mother told me that as she had walked around the yard, holding her dead baby, feeling devastated, suddenly a deep peace came over her. "It was as though all the leaves on the trees were saying to me 'It's all right. It's all right.' Only the Lord knew," she said, "there were five more peaches on the tree."

THREE

I was born angry—mad as a wet hen. It had been a hell of a struggle getting this trip over with. The light hurt my eyes and I just wanted all the people to go away and let me sleep. I was tired and hysterical. Oh God, if I could just rest and sleep. It was June 21, 1921—the longest day of the year at that hospital in Bemidji, Minnesota, my grandparents' summer home.

I discovered this in 1950, when my friends and I were experimenting with Dianetics. Each of us had gone to a past trauma. I went with a splitting headache directly to my birth. I've seldom been that frustrated in my life, and I still find frustration very hard to deal with. If I'm very tired, I will blow sky high. Those who know me will testify they'd rather meet a bear with a sore tail than me without nine hours' sleep.

"Bed is your best friend. That's where the Lord heals you," my mother always told us. And all the Russells are sleepers. Mom is ninety-four now and has never missed a daily nap in as many years. My sisters-in-law will attest that my four brothers like nothing better than to sack out. But something besides sleep must have gone on, because Mom had twenty-one grandchildren and twenty-eight great-grandchildren at the last count.

I left Bemidji when I was nine days old. Mother and I returned to Canada, where my father was working. When I was nine months old, we moved to Glendale, California, to follow Aunt Ernie and her husband Uncle Bob Henry to the land of oranges, milk, and honey. Uncle Bob was in real estate. Dad was looking for a job, and he finally landed one as office manager with the Andrew Jergens Company, makers of Woodbury soap. Mother had $5,000 tucked away to find a house, which she did—and just what we needed—at 1018 North Angelino, at the foot of the mountains in beautiful downtown Burbank. It was a brown shake house with a big front porch with a swinging divan. The large backyard was divided in two: The front part was grass and flowers with live oaks clustered on one side that reminded Mother of Bemidji, and the back part was a play yard. When our piano arrived, the top of its packing box was taken off and, with a door cut in the bottom, served as our playhouse. In it there were a small wicker chair (which we smoked when we grew older) and some orange crates for cupboards and beds. It was the start of my mania for houses. Other girls played dolls. I played houses.

Mother, it seems, lived in the kitchen. She would brush my naturally curly hair around her finger every morning while I stood eating cereal. After we had left for school, she would sit and read her Bible at the kitchen table among used cereal bowls and nurse the baby. There was always a baby. Tom was born in 1924, Ken in 1925, Jamie in 1927, and Wally in 1929.

The garage was turned into a theater with costumes from an old trunk that Mother let us play with. I was the producer, director, and probably the star. The boys played men and women, with makeup and all—whatever was needed. A few neighborhood kids participated, and we nagged our parents to pay money, drink lukewarm lemonade, and applaud our drama.

It's no wonder that my kindergarten teacher called Mother to school to ask her what went on at home. Apparently I was constantly leaving my seat to instruct the other children with "Not that way, dearie, like this." If I started out putting diapers on the baby at five and trying to be the teacher at school, what else but producer and director at age seven or eight?

When Kenny was about to be born, Mom took my cousin Pat Henry, Tommy, and me back to Bemidji. Grandma Amelia and Grandpa Gus had one of the first cottages built on Lake Bemidji. This was Paul Bunyan country, and this giant wooden man still stands in the forests. Mother's brothers and sisters all spent summers there and would return to Grand Forks for the winters.

We adored being on the lake. Our cousin, six-year-old Bud Jacobi (Uncle Reinhold's son), showed us how to climb in the boat and where the blueberries grew. I can remember the cottage in detail, with pods strung with beads hanging down the stairs, the sun porch, and the double beds upstairs hung from the ceiling by chains. We slept in these, and they literally rocked us to sleep.

Once Bud, Pat, and I were playing with the boat. Mother had told us that the Mississippi flowed through the lake and how they'd gone in canoes up the river toward the mouth when she was younger. We were playing explorers and trying to drag the boat up on the beach, yelling, "Help! Help!" at the top of our lungs. When Grandpa saw that we weren't in trouble, but only playing, he came out and beat our butts.

Grandma Jacobi took Pat and me back to Grand Forks before we were to leave for home. She loved me, but Pat was obviously her favorite. I was melancholy as I wandered around that big house and suddenly started to cry. Grandma was very concerned, but try as she would, I wanted to go to Grandma Russell's house, so finally she took me. There I was perfectly happy. To that little Polish–German lady and Scottish grandpa I was the only child in the world.

My favorite game was playing in the middle of the bed with Grandma's box of jewelry. I didn't even care if Mama came to pick me up or not. But she finally did, and with Kenny, the new baby, we took the train home to our lonesome Daddy. He might have been grumpy, but he sure loved his family. That summer he'd written me the only letter I ever got from him. It was full of love, so you know he was desperate. He even hugged Mom for ten minutes, right in front of us. He'd written Mom a letter that said, "I'm not going to tell you I love you, I'm painting it on the wall." The ceiling and living room walls above the wainscoting had been freshly painted nile green.

Grandma and Grandpa Jacobi finally moved out to California to join their daughters and grandchildren. Grandpa was a marvelous storyteller who didn't give a damn about propriety. He was his own man! We can all remember him acting out Bible stories like a real jackass, and we'd laugh until we cried. When he told us the Midianites got hemorrhoids as a punishment from God for stealing the Ark, they *really* got hemorrhoids! He would jump up and down, grab his fanny, and scream, "Oh God, they hurt, they hurt!" Every Bible character came to life, and we all knew them intimately—David, Goliath, Samuel, Saul, Jezebel, Gideon and his fleece. I've put out about a hundred fleeces in my time, and the Lord has always honored them.

Grandma nearly went mad with him. I can still hear her saying, "Father! Father! Father!" as he roared, "That so-and-so had blue mud up his ass."

If I talk like a sailor—and I do—I come by it naturally. I can be a perfect lady when I choose, but if I'm irritated with a situation or, especially, at myself, the air can turn blue with my vocabulary.

Mother and Aunt Ernie had been going to church as they had done all their lives. They knew *about* God but, as they put it, they didn't *know* Him. One night someone took them to the Angels Temple to hear Aimee Semple McPherson, the famous evangelist. Mother had been suffering badly from ulcers and said she would rather be dead than in the state she was. That night she looked up to see the inscription written across the top of the platform: JESUS CHRIST, THE SAME YESTERDAY, TODAY, AND FOREVER.

"That's all very nice," she thought, "but it's just not so. When Jesus was here, he healed the sick." Well, the Lord went through a great deal of trouble to teach her that He was still the same.

It was there that Mother heard about glossolalia (the gift of tongues), interpretation, prophecy, and the other gifts of the Holy Spirit for the first time. Mother and Aunt Ernie were invited to come and tarry with the congregation if they were interested. Well, they thought they were; at least they were curious enough to go to the tarry room and find out. Mother looked astounded as different people raised their arms and praised God, their faces shining. She saw and heard several people start speaking in tongues with tears pouring down their happy faces. Her Episcopalian back was up, yet she was envious, and so she joined in. Finally it was time to go and nothing had happened to either her or Aunt Ernie. One helper came over to them.

"I think you two are just about ready to receive, so why don't you go and join the group for members? They're still going strong," she said.

They did and as soon as they got there, Mother raised her arms, praised the Lord, and felt as if she had grabbed a hot wire. She let out a shriek. Immediately someone was at her side.

"Sister, please! We must be more quiet."

Well, both she and Aunt Ernie got a beautiful baptism of the Holy Spirit. They each spoke in a new tongue and stayed until after midnight. They both said they have never had such a glorious experience.

The Bible came off the shelf permanently and was read constantly. At a prayer meeting in Burbank, especially for healing, Mother was prayed for and she soon felt something like invisible electric fingers scurrying across her stomach. It continued as she walked home. All night she had the same strange feeling. In the morning she had no pain at all and has eaten everything but tin cans ever since. The doctor could find no ulcer.

That was the end of doctors in our house till we were grown. Uncle Bob joined the two women, but my father thought they were mad. Mother said, "Dear, if you want a doctor, that's fine, but the Lord is our doctor." If there was ever anything wrong, from a scratch to much more serious things, we went to her and said, "Mama, pray." We had mumps, measles, whooping cough, lice, the seven-year itch, you name it. All five of us had them, and all of us at once!

Poor Mother. But the Lord healed them all. Then Tommy got scarlet fever and was left quite deaf. Dad would stand a few yards away and yell at him, but Tommy couldn't hear anything. It frustrated my father so, he'd turn purple. Finally he told my mother she was a damn fool, and that if she and her "long-haired friends" (his name for the Bible bunch) wanted to ruin their lives by waiting for divine healing, they bloody well could, but they weren't ruining his son's ears and she'd sure as hell better get him to a doctor. The doctor said there was no hope but perhaps a hearing aid would help.

Well, she kept praying and had everyone else praying. One morning, very discouraged, she sat at the breakfast table after we'd left.

"Lord, I know You can heal this boy," she prayed. "What's wrong?"

Then it came to her: "This kind goeth not out without fasting and prayer."

She pushed her breakfast away and said, "Thank you, Lord."

She fasted and prayed and a few days later, as she lay down beside Tommy to take their nap, he said, "Mama, I can't sleep 'cause that clock's ticking so loud." My dad, the doctor, and everyone were astounded.

I had my first boyfriend when I was in first grade. He had red hair and chased me to the sandbox. The girls were safe there, but we'd sneak out of the sandbox the next available instant.

In second grade my second love wrote, "I love you," on a scrap of paper and dropped it on my desk as he passed by. He was very shy and sullen. When he moved to another school at the end of the term, I was heartsick. I thought about him all summer. But I learned then that we do outgrow people and our tastes do change. One should not marry until one is older. At least ten.

In the sixth grade it was Don Ben I loved. He never looked at girls, had sulky eyes and a face like a blond Burt Reynolds. That was for me. I followed, needled, and teased him at every opportunity, but all I'd get was a shove or a "Oh, go on."

One day as I was looking out the window I saw that a new family was moving in next door, and they had six children! My poor father nearly had a heart attack—five kids across the street, five at home, and now six next door. My father came from a very small family and did not like noise or confusion. It was going to be bedlam. But not for me: One of the kids was my new love, Don Ben. I couldn't believe it. He acted horrified, but I knew he wasn't. Now I had him at home as well as at school. The poor boy didn't have a chance.

The only proof I had that my feelings were returned was one day, when mother was curling my hair, she told me that Don's mother had said that he liked me. *Like* was a strong word; it meant everything. It was as much love as any I've known.

If his family hadn't moved away, and if we hadn't moved to Van Nuys and the ranch, I'm sure I would have married him. You see, I was born married. It was all I waited for.

In 1933, when I was twelve, the Henrys moved to Fontana and the Russells to Van Nuys, "way out in the San Fernando Valley." Today it is a valley jammed with tract houses and apartments, but in those days it was lush with green fields and orchards and ranch-style houses with horses and dogs. It was easy "blue jean and T-shirt" informal country, where most people knew each other a little and no one paid much attention to movie stars.

Andy Devine, Clark Gable, Buck Jones, Harry Carey, John Ford, Raoul Walsh, Jack Oakie, Lucille Ball, and Desi Arnaz were just some of the old-time residents of the Valley. There's a definite gap between the Beverly Hills folk and the Valleyites, and neither would trade their way of life for the other's.

The stables at La Posada, our ranch, sheltered four horses and Mary the cow. Flash and Silver were the palominos. Dad and I took turns riding Silver, and Mom and Tommy rode Flash. Tom, an Indian pony with one blue eye, and a black mare, Patsy, were ridden by Ken and Wally. And Jamie rode Mary the cow, whom he loved and kissed, and slid off her rump. He called her "Maryeee, me coo," and talked his own animal language to her. The boys learned to milk her and brought in buckets of milk with gorgeous cream that rose to the top of the milk pans in the fridge.

In the summer, the boys slept out under the trees. Mary would come and lick Tom's face when she needed milking. Mom made enough bread to last a week, and our favorite snack was a large slice of wheat bread with cream and honey spooned on top in a soup bowl. It was the best thing Mom made, aside from grapefruit and avocado salad with peanut butter dressing or Swiss steak. No, for a cook, Mom was a great gardener. I never did learn to cook, probably because of that, but then I never learned to garden either.

The wash behind the house was a marvelous place to ride. You could go for miles in both directions, and we did. Mother and Dad always rode alone. He said it was the only time he had Mother to himself.

Inside the living room were huge beams, Mexican tile, and a fireplace. A great window looked across the lawn, out the gate, and two miles down the road. French doors looked out the back to the patio.

The boys had their bedrooms in one wing off the kitchen. Grandpa Russell (who had come to live with us when Grandma died), Mom, Dad, and myself were in the other wing. The hired couple had a room off the three-car garage. My room was all white with red trim and had a corner fireplace. French doors opened to the patio, where midnight blooming jasmine lulled me to sleep—and Mom awakened me to the sounds of Ella Fitzgerald, Count Basie, Benny Goodman, or Duke Ellington. I hated waking up. Still do. So I put a nail polish dot on the volume dial of the radio, and all Mom had to do was sneak in and turn the knob to the dot, leave my orange juice, which was fresh off the trees, and go. If she didn't, I woke up like the bear that I am and roared.

My poor mother had a knack for getting me upset almost every morning before I went to school. I later did the same thing to my children, so I know how it happens. My kids used to say to me, "Mom, if you'd just stay in bed, we'd be so much happier." So I stayed in bed.

My dad was five foot seven, a very bright, nervous man with a caustic sense of humor. He looked like a cross between Humphrey Bogart and Rudolph Valentino. His sign was Capricorn. It was difficult for him to show affection, but I always knew it was there. A slap on the behind or a quick kiss on the cheek was about as far as he could go with his daughter.

Dad loved to play touch football with the boys on the big front lawn. Ken, I think, was his favorite, because he was such a little smart ass. He always had an answer, and Dad would try to hide the smile that curled around his mouth, but his dark eyes would dance as he'd verbally put him down.

We all had to stay in our place and were usually shuttled off to our rooms or outside when Dad came home. "Daddy's home and he's had a hard day at the office and needs some peace and quiet."

I remember Dad getting angry at Mother, and could he ever be sarcastic! Finally, when she wouldn't fight back, he'd go into a black sulk for three days and not speak to her. Mother never fought with Dad. Her own father and mother fought until the day they died, and she swore if she couldn't live with a man, she'd leave him—but never fight.

When Uncle Ken, Mom's baby brother, married a darling redhead named Irene from North Dakota, she first met Uncle Bob Henry, who said very politely, as he shook her hand, "How do you do, Mrs. Jacobi. I'm so glad to meet you." When Irene got out of the car at our house, Daddy was poking in the roses. He looked up and said, "Hi, Red." She loved him for it. She'd fight or banter with him. He could expel some of his nasty humor on her and she'd come right back.

I remember one day saying to Mom, "Why don't you fight with Dad? I'm sure he'd be much happier. He loves a good scrap. You shouldn't let him get away with talking to you like that." She looked at me and said, "Why, dear, he just reminds me of a banty rooster crowing on top of a manure pile. I can't fight with him." Too bad he didn't live longer. He'd have had a daughter who would have fought with him plenty when she grew up.

A new school was really a new experience for me. I started the last half of seventh grade at Van Nuys High School. Mother dressed me the first day in a yellow organdy dress with black patent leather pumps.

"Oh, what an adorable little girl!" I overheard an older girl say. I never felt so out of place in my life. Skirts and sweaters were worn at Van Nuys High School. The boys wore jeans, white T-shirts, and crimson and gray school sweaters.

I took my family, and especially my mother, for granted, an unconscious pleasure. My friends were another matter. Unlike a family, they could accept or reject you, and one could accept or reject them. So most of my energy was directed toward my friends, and most of my conscious pleasure was derived from them.

There were friends in grammar school, of course, but most of the ones I've really kept in touch with I met in junior high school and we have remained friends to this day.

One of my first friends at Van Nuys High School was Kathryn Smithers, a Lutheran, whose mother strongly disapproved of my rambunctious ways. She felt I maneuvered my mother, and she certainly wasn't going to have that happen to her.

Years later, after *The Outlaw* had come out, I went to visit Kathryn at a Lutheran Bible school meeting. I was glad to see my old friend again, but when the meeting was over, her friends were damn well going to prove to me that I wasn't a Christian and was working for the devil. I should get down on my knees, repent, and never go near show business again.

I couldn't believe my ears. These accusing faces had not a drop of love in them—just condemnation. I finally tore myself away and prayed as I hurried down the street to my car, "Dear God, save me from the zealots, the self-righteous churchy bigots. Help them to know You as You are. Thank heaven I know You're guiding me."

Pat Alexander and I found each other in the ninth grade. We were the same height and coloring and thought we were twins or something. We talked on the phone each morning to decide what color sweater, skirt, and socks we'd wear (they had to be identical). The rest of the uniform was unchanging: white shirts and shoes. I loved her mother and called her Ommy, and her older sister Eleanore became "Baggy Lady." Eleanore was a totally feminine, sixteen-year-old lady who played and sang operettas at the piano. Pat and I were fourteen-year-old tomboys who nearly drove her mad.

The two of us would hike all over the Hollywood hills, swiping milk that we would find sitting on the porch of some hideaway cabin. Or we would get into a house through a window and leave something awry so that people would know someone had been there. Never anything terrible—just foolish kid pranks.

We ditched school once in a while and went to Hollywood to the movies. We'd come out of one and go into another. We often saw three double features in a day. One Sunday afternoon we climbed the wall from the cemetery into the RKO studios. After we wandered around and saw a few empty stages, a studio cop caught us and escorted us out. Little did I know that one day I'd call that place my home away from home.

When we were freshmen Pat started going with a second-year letterman, Charlie Bach. So I naturally knew a lot of older fellows, but I couldn't go out on dates yet. One night, though, we did go to a party where the seniors were. I was spending the night with Pat, and Ommy trusted us as long as we were with Chuck. The party was at some boy's house, and they were drinking home brew that his dad had made in the cellar. There were no parents, natch, and kids wandered in and out of the bedrooms and the cars.

One very quiet, stealthy "cat" was leaning in the doorway. I watched four different girls meander up to him one at a time. The two of them would disappear outside for a while, and then he was back to his post by the door. When I asked his name, I was told it was Bob Waterfield. I'd heard girls at school talk about him and I'd seen his low-cut car with the hand-tooled dashboard cruising past, but I'd never seen him or been able to watch him in action before. It sent gooseflesh up my spine. I felt like I was in Sin City. I was really a fish out of water. Then a boy tried to kiss me. I froze and said I wanted to go home. Chuck, Pat, and I left.

One incident that occurred shortly after this was a bit unnerving to me but typical of Waterfield's cat-and-mouse game. I was blithely walking down the hall and was stopped by the hall monitor—him. My heart stopped.

"Where's your pass?" Robert said.

"Here," I said.

"Oh." Pause. "How about a date?"

"That depends." My mouth was getting dry.

"On what?"

"On where, when, and why?"

"Oh," Robert said.

He just stood there and eyed me with a smirk on his face, so I gulped and walked away wondering what I should have said. Then, glad that I had done what I did, I dismissed the whole thing. I surely didn't want to be one of those broads whom I'd seen at the party taken outside and dumped back.

Anyway, Mother and Dad would never let me go out with a senior. They felt parties on Saturday night that were chaperoned were fine, but I wasn't even allowed to go to the school dances. They were on Friday night and that was the Sabbath. I can't tell you how I resented that. I was dying to dance. I would stand outside the door and watch, but I never went in.

Very soon after that Pat Alexander moved, and I felt utterly lost. That's when Mother suggested I go to Fontana to stay with Pat Henry for a while. She felt the country would be healthy and she knew Aunt Ernie would treat me exactly as she would herself. There'd be no seniors there to deal with.

Uncle Bob had traded his house in Glendale during the depression for five acres in windblown Fontana. The six Henry boys called it the "rock pile," and their father the "warden." But here they could grow fruit and vegetables, raise chickens and turkeys, and have a cow. They traded eggs for flour and fed themselves off the land. The boys all had plenty of chores to do while Pat and I made lunch, did the dishes, and washed the clothes the hard way, with a hand wringer.

Aunt Ernestine was an incredibly beautiful woman. She was a magnificent cook who candled turkey eggs until midnight and then crawled out of bed at six in the morning to bake bread and cook for the ten of us. She was the most aware adult I've ever met. Aunt Ernie always knew when the "right" boy called. She got his name and told me the minute I walked through the door. My mother, on the other hand, might re-member that "somebody" called a couple of days ago. His name? She hadn't asked. A message? Forget it! I could have killed her. But then, so could Aunt Ernie most of the time. Mother would pass it off, clowning with what we called her phony, poor pitiful Pearl act. She'd mutter, with her finger in the corner of her mouth, and with quivering chin say, "I never do anything right." Actually, she just didn't give a damn. She had more important things on her mind.

When I got back to Van Nuys in 1937 after six months in Fontana, Grandpa was probably the happiest to see me come home. Mother, when she was going through her "We don't go to the movies" period, had always let me go to the movies with Grandpa, because he was lonely and I was his pet. We saw Katharine Hepburn in *Little Women,* and the kids at school all started calling me Jo. I was thrilled to pieces. I even wrote Hepburn my one and only fan letter, inviting her to go horseback riding in the country "away from the crowd." Mother warned me not to be too disappointed if I didn't hear from her, which of course I didn't. Grandpa started teaching me to drive too. We spent many happy hours to-gether.

That summer was lovely. Riding up the wash with the boys, seeing Mother and Dad ride off by themselves, watch-ing my dad drive in and out in his immaculate steel gray Cadillac. I don't ever remember riding in that car. We kids rode in the family car, which was for sticky fingers and dogs. I ate dinner with Mother, Daddy, and Grandpa in the dining room, because Mother had decided it was time for me to learn to be a lady and not fight with the boys, who were rowdy and ate in the large breakfast room.

After dinner I'd lie on my back on the lawn and watch for the first star so I could say to myself, "Star light, star bright, first star I've seen tonight, wish I may, wish I might, get the wish I wish tonight." It was always for my own, my very own

fellah. I was in love with my father, but was never able to get any physical holding from him, so I had to find my own love. Evening was a bittersweet, "glad to be unhappy" sort of time for me. It was to stay this way until I finally got married.

Daddy developed gallstones and had to have an operation. Before he went to the hospital he sat down and told my mother just how much money she would get from his insurance if anything happened. She wanted to hear how much he loved her, but he was concerned about his responsibility, like a good Capricorn.

As he was wheeled into the operating room he said to her, "Kiddie, I'm too young to die. The Lord heals you and the kids, but not me. But pray."

After the operation he was doing very well. We were all allowed to go in his room and say hello. I got a kiss on the cheek and "Hello, brat." I adored him!

Mother went to hear a sermon about that time and the subject was "let God be King in your life." So she had prayed, "Oh Lord, please be King in my life." That night Dad had a stroke—he died in her arms. Her high school sweetheart was dead at forty-seven. Mother was forty-six and I was fifteen. She sat, stunned. God was King! But she didn't cry. Although it was the middle of the night, she drove to a Christian friend's house. "Roy's dead," she said. "Please pray." Then she went on to her parents' home. "Roy's dead." They were terribly upset. They had become very fond of their son-in-law. Then Mother came home to us all. We were still sound asleep.

She gathered us in the living room and said, "Children, I have something to tell you. Daddy passed away last night." Well, the boys kept shoving and giggling and Jamie said, "Passed away? What's passed away?" He was only ten. I couldn't stand it another minute and I yelled, "He's dead, you fool!" Well, that stopped them in their tracks. Years later, when going through counseling, every one of them remembered that incident vividly.

Our lives were totally different from that minute on. God was King, and Mother Queen. I only saw her break twice.

We went to Hollywood Presbyterian Church and as we were all standing singing, I watched her crumple to the seat, her face in her hands.

After the funeral I called Charlie Bach, Pat Alexander's ex-boyfriend and still a very close friend, and asked him to go riding with me. I couldn't bear to go by myself. We rode for hours without a word. The huge full moon did its best to throw a silver sheen on the black landscape, but to me everything seemed dark with grief.

A friend of Mother's was furious with me, saying that I should have been at home comforting my mother and not out riding with a boyfriend. But Mother said, "I understand perfectly. If you weren't here, Mildred, I'd probably do the same thing."

Now she was a widow with five children to feed and clothe on $125 a month. The ranch was paid for, thank God. There was all the wonderful fruit and Mary the cow would keep us in milk, but we'd certainly have to tighten our belts.

The first thing to go was the hired couple, and then, of course, the horses. I was there the day the trailers pulled out with Flash and Silver. Mother went into the tack room and put her head on Dad's saddle and wept.

F O U R

Mother hung on to the ranch for quite a few years. We just couldn't bear to give it up. With the help gone, I did the washing in two tubs with a wringer and then hung it out to dry. No magic washers and dryers then. I did get to sit down at an automatic ironer, however, but remember, there were seven of us, including Grandpa Russell. It took one whole day of my precious weekends to wash. My training in Fontana came in very handy. The boys helped Grandpa with the outside chores.

Jamie was the family clown. He was gorgeous and stubborn as a mule. At the dinner table he had his best audience. He would be eating and then suddenly fall out of his chair to the floor and grab his throat. Twisting and writhing, he'd gasp, "They got me! I've been poisoned!" We'd just laugh or kick him, but Mother, without ever looking at him, would simply say, "Jamie, get up."

Tommy, the eldest of the boys, always stuck up for Wally, the youngest. Mother told him when he was five that the new baby who slept in the wicker cradle was his. And he took her at her word. Ken and Jamie, the hell raisers in the middle, were the antagonists, and to them Wally was fair game. Tom would answer Wally's cries by taking on the culprit. Once when I felt Ken and Jamie were getting the worst of it, I interfered verbally and Tom took after me with a butcher

knife that got stuck in the door when I slammed it in his face. I guess I really do have a nasty mouth! The next day I found him washing my car. It was his way of apologizing. We never stayed mad for long.

When the boys were little, I could physically cuff them if they didn't do what I told them. They would run to Mother with, "Daughter won't let me, Daughter hit me." They got nowhere with her. But after they grew up a bit and I found myself on the ground a couple of times, I quickly changed my tactics. I became totally female. I'd plead sweetly, "Buddy, would you help me do such and such?" It worked just as well.

In high school I was in love with Edward Earl Watson and we went steady for a year and a half. Also in high school I found the friends who have lasted all my life. We were, I believe, a unique bunch. Although we all came from totally different backgrounds and were in different grades, we had many things in common—questioning minds, art, music, writing, armchair psychology, and a dash of malicious humor throughout.

Three girls besides myself were at the core of this group, which started in the eleventh grade. I was sixteen. Pat Dawson was an attractive girl with a disarming personality who had taken the school by storm when she first arrived. Alberta Williams was a short-haired blonde with a Betty Boop face and body, and the most stinging delivery I've ever heard come out of a mouth. Margaret Obegi was a small, alabaster-skinned Syrian who got straight A's and edited the school paper.

We tried to please our parents as much as possible, but not to the detriment of our own wills. Nothing was said behind anyone's back; we just let it all hang out and dealt with it openly. We acted as each other's psychologist for years and still do. Any problem was discussed, dissected, analyzed, and faced from this tightly woven fabric of friendship. It wasn't that we always had an answer, but regardless of the problem, there was never any condemnation. Often an understanding ear and some honest advice are all one needs to crawl out of a problem or depression.

We thirsted for literature, poetry, music, and painting. Pat wanted to be an actress more than anything. She adored Bette Davis, and I still think of Pat when I watch one of Bette's movies. Alberta was on a head trip—psychology. I was into designing houses, clothes, anything artistic.

David Martinez, a beautiful aesthetic Irish–Mexican boy, was our mentor, teacher, and the only male allowed a part in our artistic pursuits. Davey was quite a bit older.

Alberta's house became our meeting place. There Davey played Rachmaninoff, Tchaikovsky, Glière. We drank Cokes (sometimes wine) and talked for hours. I don't know how we made school in the mornings, but we did. We all took turns at writing poetry and have continued through the years. I saved every scrap. Pat dragged us to plays. Margaret introduced us to Thomas Wolfe, Aldous Huxley, T. S. Eliot, Salinger. Davey took us to museums and art galleries, and I went around redoing everybody and everything.

Davey, probably more than anyone else, was responsible for our late teen education. He introduced us not only to the arts, but also to the philosophy of "anything you do is okay as long as you don't hurt anyone." This was in direct conflict to everything I had believed in since I was a small child. Mother, Aunt Ernie, and Uncle Bob taught me that God was our Heavenly Father and that He was running the show; His Ten Commandments were rules to be obeyed to protect us. "Anything" might very well not be in His plan.

It was a very exciting but confusing time for me. I felt pulled in several directions, and for a few years we adopted Davey's philosophy. How did this make me feel? I was enthralled with our bittersweet existence. Edna St. Vincent Millay's poem became our theme: "High upon the solid rock the ugly houses stand, come and see my shining palace built upon the sand."

Sundays, after hanging the wash out, I got the boys together, picked up Pat Dawson, and headed for Santa Monica Beach. It was called Muscle Beach because all the kids from the various gym teams around

the city worked out there on bars and rings. It was also the best beach on the coast for body surfing. Van Nuys High had a big gym team, so you saw everybody from school there. It was a blast.

One Sunday, three months before graduation, as I walked past the bars and rings on my way to the blanket area, who did I run into but the green-eyed cat who'd stopped me in the hall, Bob Waterfield. I hadn't seen him for two years, and he had graduated and was now going to UCLA. He hadn't changed any. But I guess I had—from a skinny fifteen-year-old to a well-stacked seventeen-year-old was quite a change. He must have taken notice, because he and his buddy Chuck Farerro soon found our blanket.

My heart jumped into my throat, so I got up and went for a swim. Afterward I lay down on my stomach. Bob lay down beside me, picked up a wet strand of my hair, and turned my head around to face him. I felt like a bird hypnotized by a green-eyed snake, and the snake won.

On the way home a huge orange moon was climbing out of the east, and I was in a total dither. I knew I couldn't stay home that night. Mother wasn't home, so I left my diary open with a note saying I knew it was church night, that I'd met ''B. W.'' from way back in my diary, and I had to go out. Please understand.

Off we went to the beach again, but this time north to the cliffs where kids parked above and built bonfires on the sand below. Chuck and Pat took a blanket and went down on the beach to be alone. Robert and I just sat in the car. He put his arm across the back of the seat and then took it away. Back and forth, his cat-and-mouse game. We both said very little.

I was terribly attracted to him, but he was cool and detached. He was, as far as I was concerned, challenge personified, and I was scared to death.

After what seemed an eternity, he made his move. That first kiss was perhaps the most exciting moment I've ever experienced. The sensation it produced stayed with me for more than twenty years, and had things been a little different, it might have stayed with me for the rest of my life.

Mother said she knew she'd come up against something to reckon with that night. I'd never broken her rules before.

The next few nights Robert and I missed each other. Then one night he called and said, "Do you love me?"

"Yes."

"Will you marry me?"

"Yes."

"Will you go steady with me?"

"Yes!"

This last question was the most thrilling of all, because it fell in the realm of possibility. A total affair was still a definite no for me, and Robert wasn't used to that at all. Kissing and petting were as far as I was prepared to go with him. I was a virgin, and in spite of our passion, and we were like two lit torches, a virgin I was determined to stay.

He always came back, but I eventually found out he was seeing an ex-girlfriend after his dates with me. Things finally came to an abrupt halt.

One Sunday I was hurrying my chores so I could go to the beach with Robert when Chuck told me Robert was already there and that Jackie, his ex-girlfriend, was with him. I froze. Then I called Pat, gathered the boys, and went straight to the beach.

Robert was working out on the rings. I saw Jackie wearing *my* terry cloth top which matched Robert's. (I always left it in his car.) Then Robert got kicked in the chin by spotting a boy doing doubles off the rings and had to have first aid. He came over to me later and said, "Aren't you even sorry I got clobbered?" I ignored him. Even the summer sun couldn't melt the ice. He eventually left and Pat and the boys and I went home. I felt absolutely ill.

Patricia and I talked for a long time about what to do. I was ready to sink to the bottom of the well. She told me what she had done in a similar situation, and I agreed to try. I was desperate.

When Robert came over that night I was very gay and very phony. I kept this up for about an hour, while he tried to tell me how it happened. Each time I turned him off with some flip remark until he finally said, "Honey, please, I'll

grovel in the gravel, I'll do anything if you'll just stop this."
I turned, looked him straight in the eye, and told him to bring
me his pin, his gold football, his letterman sweater, and his
graduation picture, and not to come back until then.

He hung his head and said, "That's going to be tough."

He was not unkind when it came to leaving someone,
but I was like a stone. The next time he came over he had
everything, and we were over that hurdle. But hurdles we
had by the hundreds.

About a month before graduation I wanted to meet Robert's mother. She was a very popular lady with the younger
generation. Robert's father had died when he was very young,
and she had gone back to nursing. I kept telling him I wanted
to meet her, but nothing happened. So one day after school
I called her from Pat's when I knew she had gotten off work
and said I'd like to come out and talk to her. All she said
was, "Why, are you in trouble?" I was taken back about five
laps and then managed, "No, oh no! I just would like to meet
you. I thought we might have some tea or something."

"Well, I just got home but, okay, come on out."

About half an hour later, I met Frances Waterfield, the
no-nonsense lady I loved and adored until the day she died.
She was the spitting image of her son, except for a shock of
prematurely pure white hair, and brown eyes, instead of his
green. I have never seen anyone so devoted to her son. He
was her reason for living. She was very reserved, and you
kept your distance until you were okayed. But once in, you
were in, even if you were wrong. If she didn't like you, God
help you. You could "grovel in the gravel," as Robert would
say, and she'd step right over you. By the time I left, I was
in.

I think being a nurse kept Frances from getting old in her
attitudes. She was an avid reader of many subjects, including poetry, and was up on politics and the latest news. She
was a great believer in people's privacy, and through the years
she never interfered in the spats or quarrels Robert and I had.

I have always thought my mother a little square, but
Frances didn't have a square bone in her body. She never
missed a football game and was seen more than once giving

the good old Van Nuys sign ("the finger") to a carload of kids on their way to a game. Naturally they returned it with large grins, and it's no wonder they adored her.

I'd never really fought with anyone, so I was ill equipped to handle Robert. Our family was an explosive one. Except for Mother, we got it all out and then forgot it, and most of the time we got along very well. Perhaps the boys felt a competitive drive among themselves, but I was three years older and never felt I had to get the best of them. So with Robert, I was prone to get hurt or cry rather than fight dirty.

It was a game with him. Life was a constant contest or it was boring. If I objected to something he was doing, he'd pull the car over to the side of the road and say, "You don't like it, get out and walk." He was terribly spoiled. It was impossible to discuss a difference of opinion. He just wouldn't, or I should say, he couldn't.

Much later, when I was going to a psychiatrist, the doctor explained, "Well, he's a quarterback, isn't he? He's the best in the business. A quarterback's whole strategy is to throw the opposition off guard. Never let them know what your plan is. Your best defense is a good offense. Attack!"

About two months after we started going together we went to a party with his old gang, the same crew at the party where I'd first seen him standing by the door. I didn't really know any of them well, except Bobby Jackson, his best friend from grammar school and who'd just come home from the navy.

Robert's ex-girlfriend, Jackie, was there. I felt very strange and the atmosphere was charged. I sat down next to two of my classmates (with whom I had a nodding acquaintance) when one of the girls suddenly dumped her beer on my white sharkskin pants. Loyalty to Jackie, I was sure. I went into the kitchen for a towel and a boy that Robert didn't like started talking to me. When Robert came through the kitchen door and saw me talking to this fellah, he turned on his heel and left. I followed, looking for Robert. I didn't have to look far. There he was, sitting on the edge of a table, with both hands holding Jackie's fanny.

I ran out the front door and cried. If I'd had a car, I'd have split, but I was trapped. Robert never came out, but

Jackson found me and started the first of many lectures he has given me throughout the years. He said, "Look, if the big dog gets nasty, and he can be a bastard, don't ever cry or let him see you're hurt. He'll only get meaner. Tell him to go to hell, and you'll get a lot more respect from him. The only time I saw him really nice to Jackie was when she gave him both barrels."

But I knew that if I told him off that would be the end of it. He'd never come back, and I was madly in love. His sense of humor was dry and marvelous and there were times he could be so tender and sweet. I truly believed I should be married a virgin. And Robert, though only one year older, was way down the line when it came to experience. How could I expect him to stay with me if I wouldn't make love the way he was used to?

At any rate, I held out for three months with nightly pressures of all kinds. When he was sweet it was, "Well, don't worry honey, time and tide will take their toll," and when he was acid, the gravel flew as he roared out the driveway. Finally, on my graduation night I made the decision. I told Robert to drive to the dairy next to our ranch where my brothers and I had slid down the haystacks for years. There we made love. His way. My first. It was my eighteenth birthday.

And don't you know, my mother knew. The Lord had told her in no uncertain terms, "She's married." That was when she stopped fretting. Even though Robert and I were to break up and I was to become engaged to someone else first, the Lord knew whom I was to marry five years later.

Though I'd hoped it would, having sex didn't alter Robert's humor any. I was his possession, and I was to obey his rules. Suddenly going to the beach, which I adored, was like going to jail. I hadn't done anything, and yet I felt I was always being punished. I couldn't seem to please him, and I was getting awfully tired of trying. If I was going to spend the rest of my life like this, I'd go bananas. I decided what I was going to do, and the thought of the look he was going to have on his face made me laugh. Usually at the beach I got the blanket and towels and my suitcase and purse and walked behind him like a squaw. This time I jumped up, got my case, threw my sweater over one shoulder, and sashayed up the beach, gaily saying hello to every kid I knew all the way to the car. Robert had to get the blanket and towels and follow me, and he was livid. He never said a word and drove like a madman all the way home.

When I got out of the car, I turned to him in front of his buddies and said very sweetly, "Did you have a good time at the beach today, dear?"

"Yes, I did!" he shouted.

Sweeter than ever, I said, "Well, you can have all the good times you want from now on, because I'm all through."

With that he snarled, "All right," gave me the Van Nuys sign, and burned rubber all the way to the corner.

Later that night the phone rang. It couldn't possibly be Robert. As far as I was concerned, I had alienated Mr. Waterfield for all time. When I said, "Hello," I heard, "You big baby, are you still mad?" He was actually purring. I couldn't believe it. He wanted me to fight back.

I started learning how to fight, but very slowly. My father and grandfather were cut of the same cloth and my mother never fought with them, so I really had no pattern to follow. I understood how to be malleable and tractable, even patient, but to lash back was something I really had to learn. But I *did* learn.

Always after a fight he was darling. We went to the beach, the movies, ate at the Chili Burger restaurant: nothing fancy, because there was neither the desire nor the money, but we were in love and life was sweet.

After my graduation, Mother decided I should go and visit my godfather, John Errol Sydie, in Canada. The Sydies were very kind and dear to me, but I missed Robert's stone face and piercing green eyes and I wanted to go home. I had to. Our reunions were always superb.

I had dated some boys in Canada, which I dutifully noted in my diary. Robert came in one night, saw the diary open on my desk, and read it. He turned icy and told me he had dated a girl from school while I was gone. He knew how to get even. With that we continued as before; however, I discontinued my diary.

Mom was still dragging us to church on Sunday nights, though Friday and Saturday nights were now okay for dates. It was rather out of her control. By now I wasn't interested in church at all and just went to please her. Robert would pick me up afterward. One night the service wasn't over, and I heard his pipes growl outside. I turned to my mother and said, "Mom, I'm through with this farce," and got up and left.

I had developed the old "do anything you want to, as long as you don't hurt anyone" philosophy.

She said, "Lord, you go with her." He certainly did, but I didn't know it for quite a while.

Maxine West, née George, was one of the Van Nuys group. She knew some Hollywood people over the hill and asked me to go with her to a party one night. So I sneaked away from Robert. We met Jackie Coogan and ended up back in the Valley at Jerry Colonna's house. You had to walk past the horse stalls to get to his lovely ranch house. I met Bob Hope for the first time that night, and a lot of people I didn't know. Maxine and I had been drinking before we got there, so instead of being impressed with the people, I got bored and wandered out to the horses. I went in one stall that held a beautiful palomino and sat down in the hay and talked to him. I could hear Jackie and Maxine calling me, but I wouldn't move. Pretty soon half the party was looking for me. When they found me, they couldn't believe it: Here was this pie-eyed dame, all dressed up, sitting in a horse stall talking to a horse!

That was my only Hollywood party before I started working in pictures. Jerry Colonna reminded me of it years later when we were sitting next to each other at a banquet.

That fall of 1940 Robert went back to UCLA and football. He graduated from high school at sixteen, but he was not big enough yet to play much football. He was a sensational gymnast, however, and performed doubles off the high bar and rings. There wasn't anyplace he couldn't do a one-arm handstand. I remember seeing him poised on the corner of a three-story building at Muscle Beach in Santa Monica. I was terrified.

That was the same fall when I went to the two drama schools and worked for Tom Kelley until the fateful day Levis Green called about *The Outlaw*.

F I V E

That was the kind of life I returned home to from location. If the picture had never continued, it wouldn't have been a bad life. I certainly wasn't dying from ambition. Something interesting would happen, something would turn up. Now it wasn't God, you see, it was fate. Ah, sweet, ignorant youth.

The only thing to change our lives was the covers of the fan magazines. Jane Russell was plastered all over them. Robert and I were like a pair of ostriches. We buried our heads in the sand and tried to ignore the whole thing. After my brothers had given me a good razzing, they ignored it too. Only Mom kept a scrapbook.

Several months passed before I got a call from the boss, Howard Hughes, asking that I come to 7000 Romaine to meet with him. Could I?

I found my way to an even more obscure office than the one Howard Hawks had. There was a desk, a phone, and one old chair on which I sat and observed closely for the first time the man to whom I was under contract.

He looked the same—white shirt, dark trousers, and dark shoes on his lanky, thin body. His eyes were as I remembered from the quick glimpse in the hall: dark brown and kind. He had a bit of a Texas whine to his voice and spoke softly, even apologetically, as he explained that he and

Howard Hawks had totally disagreed on the way the picture should be shot.

Hawks was spending far too much money with his tent city on location—it wasn't necessary, Hughes thought. And Jack Beutel was too cocky in the part of Billy. Hughes didn't see Billy that way at all and so had decided to direct the picture himself. He wanted to shoot late afternoons and nights. Was that okay with me? He hoped it wouldn't interfere with my football player. I loved the idea of not having to get up early, but I could see problems ahead with Robert. He wouldn't like me gone at night one bit. Well, like Scarlett O'Hara, I'd face that tomorrow.

It was a short meeting. But brief as it was, when I left I knew I liked the man and could see why Cliff Broughton, the unit man, and a few others I'd met who worked for him affectionately called him "the boss." I felt at ease and totally at home with him. He was rather like a Texas cousin.

I was too ignorant to realize Hughes had never directed a picture—produced, yes, but with Hawks directing; pictures like _Scarface_ and _Hell's Angels_. Since I had never acted in anything, not even a play, I simply didn't know any better.

We started shooting on the Goldwyn lot. For Jack and myself this was a first. We had nothing to compare it with. The fact that we started shooting at three in the afternoon and continued until late at night and that we took dozens of takes instead of three or four made no difference to us. Howard was always very kind and soft-spoken, but he always wanted one more take. "Jack, you lifted your left eyebrow," he'd say. "I'd like to try it without that. It may give Billy a smart aleck attitude." Over and over we did it until, instead of just concentrating on lines and intent in a scene, we were both thinking of eyebrows. Don't move your left thumb, don't lean too far to the right, and on and on. We were like wooden dummies. But we didn't know there was another way.

Walter Huston and Thomas Mitchell did, however, both being screen veterans. Walter, playing Doc Holiday, made up his mind he was not going to let it get him; it was just a game. He just smiled and said, "Fine, Howard," each time he was asked to do it again. He was always fresh, even when there were thirty or forty takes. His long years of stage experience came to his rescue. But Tommy Mitchell, playing Pat Garrett, got exasperated. One day he glared at Howard, stormed up and down, and swore a blue streak. He finally threw his hat down and stomped on it and turned back to glare at Howard again. That clever, darling man just sat looking at his shoes as he slumped in his chair, hat on the back of his head and coat draped over his shoulders. Finally, when Tommy stopped stomping and everyone was looking at him, Howard glanced up innocently and said, "Oh, Tommy, did you say something?" Howard was hard of hearing from working around plane engines, but you knew he had heard every word Tommy said. Tommy picked up his hat, threw his arms out and his eyes heavenward, and walked away, muttering, "What the hell's the use?" I glanced over to Walter Huston, and he was shaking with laughter.

So we filmed scenes again and again. Howard knew what he wanted, but he couldn't explain it from a motivation viewpoint. So he just did it over and over until he had one he liked out of thirty or forty takes. He screened all this film over and over again every night after we were through, until dawn if necessary. He was single-minded, persistent, and never lost his temper. He was patience personified and, in his own kind way, wore us down. In one scene, where Billy was talking beside Doc's grave, we did 103 takes! Howard might have used the third one, but he felt it was an important scene, so he wanted a hundred more for a choice. Jack never blew one line.

Today, I would have lost my mind, but then I didn't know any better. I was an observer as well as a participant. I could have died when I finally saw the picture several years later. Jack wasn't good, but I was terrible.

Gregg Toland, a sweet, talented man, was the cameraman. His lighting was as in a Rembrandt painting. It fit the music of Tchaikovsky, which underscored the picture instead of the usual western music. Everything about *The Outlaw* was different. It was probably the first western ever to focus on five characters at close range, instead of huge scenes of cowboys and Indians.

I know now that Howard patterned Billy after himself to a large degree. He always came out on top, but he was really an innocent who was pushed into tight spots through no fault of his own—the antihero in fashion today.

Jean Harlow, who starred in Howard's production of *Hell's Angels,* was notorious for going braless. But this star was one who couldn't and wouldn't. From the time I was sixteen I had bras custom-made for me by a small shop in Hollywood. Bras sold over the counter were skinny-strapped torture racks.

Howard then decided it wouldn't be any harder to design a bra than it would be to design an airplane. He tried. When I went into the dressing room with my wardrobe girl and tried it on, I found it uncomfortable and ridiculous. Obviously he wanted today's seamless bra, which didn't exist then. It was a good idea—as usual, he was way ahead of his time—but I wasn't doing 103 takes on this subject. So I put on my own bra, covered the seams with tissue, pulled the straps over to the side, put on my blouse, and started out. Emily, my wardrobe girl, was terrified. What if they found out? I assured her they'd never find out from me. Everybody behind the camera stared, and Howard finally nodded okay and filming proceeded.

I *never* wore his bra, and believe me, he could design planes, but a Mr. Playtex he wasn't. Oh, I suppose given several years and a willing model he would have conquered the problem, but fortunately he had a picture to worry about just then. He was so picayune about details, he drove me crazy.

Mom came to visit the set one day. They wanted to get a picture of us together. As she walked in, she saw Walter Huston and, thinking he was an old friend, smiled, "Hello." He understood completely and smiled right back with, "Hello, yourself." He said that happened to him all the time. Later when she made the same mistake with Thomas Mitchell, he just scowled and threw her a look as if to say, "Who's that crazy woman? I don't know her." It's amazing how many different types the dear Lord put on this earth.

Each night I was driven home, since Howard didn't want me driving that late alone. I got the driver to go about ten miles out of our way to stop at Robert's house. I'd go to his window and scratch on the screen to wake him up. It was very difficult for him. He never came on the set, and his imagination conjured up all sorts of things. I tried my best to keep him cheered up until the Sundays, when we would be together. In those days you worked six days straight. It was tough. Very tough.

All in all, it was an interesting experience. Most pictures were made in six to eight weeks. We worked on *The Outlaw* for nine months, and I'm sure it cost more than Hawks would have spent in eight weeks.

When the picture was finished, I started posing for publicity stills every weekday from nine to five. I did that for two years. It was arranged from Russell Birdwell's posh Beverly Hills office. I felt that Birdwell, whom I'd only met briefly, was selling me like a can of tomatoes. He slapped a label on me and didn't know me at all. Pictures were taken every place you could think of, even at La Posada (but never showing our beautiful ranch house). It was me fighting with one of my brothers, me sitting on the fence talking to Mary the cow, me at the beach, in the water, climbing the rocks, visiting the pier, riding the roller coaster. . . .

I was supposed to be a poor Cinderella who had been lifted out of poverty to become a movie star and was helping to support her mother and four brothers. Little did the public know that I could barely make my car payments and eat on $50 a week, let alone support anyone.

Fortunately a great guy, Dale Armstrong, was in charge of the Russell shoot, so I had a friend with me everywhere I went. Bob Landry and Johnny Floria, *Life* and *Look* photographers, were used most frequently and became my buddies, too. But there were many others. Sittings were set up with George Hurrell at his studio on Sunset Boulevard. When I first arrived, there was a mound of hay set up in the middle

of the room, another time a white bearskin rug. Glamour shots were his forte, and he was the best.

Now and then a fashion sitting was arranged, but something happened when my hair was pulled up and I had on a hat, veil, gloves, and a black dress. It just wasn't me. For myself, I preferred shorts, jeans, sandals, slacks, sweaters, or long exotic clothes and chandelier earrings. Nothing in-between. I don't think I've ever had a house dress on in my life. Southern California is far more relaxed than other parts of the country, and I was spoiled.

At last *The Outlaw* was ready to be shown, but Howard couldn't get a release from the Hays office. It seems that when we shot the scene of me beside the bed when Billy was so cold and I tried to pull the covers up tight around his chin, the camera was opposite me, by the bed, and you could see way too much cleavage to make the censors happy.

I remembered that scene, and that Gregg Toland had told Howard he'd better redo it from a different angle, and we did. But Howard was trying to get the first angle passed, and that is exactly the reason *The Outlaw* was held up for so many years. He was stubborn and knew damn well that people would die to see something they were told they couldn't.

The attack on Pearl Harbor changed the direction of the publicity campaign. Now it was aimed at the army, navy, and marines.

Like most people, I worried about my own—Robert and my brothers. When would they have to go? Robert was in the ROTC at the university, and my three eldest brothers eventually went: Tom to the air force band, Ken to the navy, and Jamie to the merchant marine.

Every day I saw young kids at the various military bases heading overseas. I posed with planes and tanks. I posed aboard ships and draped over huge guns. One air force outfit even called themselves Russell's Raiders. Joe E. Brown's son escorted me all over that base, flew out shortly thereafter, and never came back. It was a sad time.

Someone once said that if all the pictures taken of Jane Russell were laid out end to end, they'd reach around the world. I wouldn't doubt it.

Besides doing publicity, I was tutored by Florence Enright, a marvelous drama coach who taught all the girls who were under contract to Howard. With her we learned lines and then how to put them into action. She'd say, "Now, I want you to light a cigarette, open the window, arrange the magazines, and take your shoes off and stretch during this dialogue." You had to remember every-thing and use this business to accentuate the lines. We learned a great deal from that little lady.

Sooner or later I met Jane Greer, Ursula Thiess, Faith Domergue, and many of the other girls under contract. One beautiful blonde girl and I became very close. Her name was Carol Gallagher and she looked a lot like a tall Lana Turner. She was everything I was not: silk stockinged, high heeled, blue eyed, and beautifully dressed. She was very shy and cool with females, but utterly devastating to men. She knew her way around the Beverly Hills restaurants and shops.

Since I was now living with the belief that anything you did was okay as long as you didn't hurt anyone (and what Robert didn't know wouldn't hurt him), I dated other fellows when he wasn't around. One was Bobby Robertson, a quar-terback for USC. I had first met him on a publicity date, and we had dated several times since. Mother came into my room one Sunday with the sports section of the *Los Angeles Times*. The entire page pictured two quarterbacks, one passing through a hole in a picture of USC and one kicking through a hole in UCLA. She said, "Well now, Daughter, which quarterback do you root for?" I threw my shoe at her. At that particular game I was standing in the parking lot with Rob-ert's mother, Frances, whom I took to every game, when Bobby Robertson came by. He just stopped and sadly stared. There I was with the UCLA quarterback's mother!

"Hi," he said.

"Hi," I smiled back, "Good luck, but I hope we win," I said clutching Frances' arm.

UCLA won 14–7. It was the most exciting game I ever saw. It was the first Bruin win over Troy in eight chances. That was the year they went to the Rose Bowl—but I didn't.

Jack Beutel knew John Payne. I wanted to meet him, so

Jack arranged it. Carol was with Victor Mature. We all got separated and I ended up talking to Payne way into the night. I liked him enormously. He was ten years older than I was and I found him to be a highly intelligent human being.

Carol and I decided to live together, since we both wanted to be on our own. Her grandmother owned a second house in the hills overlooking Barham Boulevard in Hollywood that we could rent.

She took me to her dressmaker, and pretty soon startled passersby in Beverly Hills would see these two tall females dressed in identical gorgeous suits and dresses—one blonde and all in beige and the other brunette in turquoise or all white. We both had long hair but added falls of false hair down our backs. What a sight we must have been! We probably looked like a pair of hookers, but we thought we were the livin' end. Our house usually had dirty dishes in the sink and nothing dusted, but we were done up to the teeth.

Carol was mad about Howard Hughes. She said that on most of the dates they'd had, she merely sat in the projection room while he ran film from *The Outlaw*. She was sick of the sight of me.

One night she persuaded me to call him and say we were bored. She wanted to see him in the worst way. He said, "Well, I have a general in town, and I'm taking him to dinner down the coast. Why don't you girls come along?" We did, had dinner, and then took the general back to his hotel. Then Howard brought us home. End of evening.

Later I thought how innocent that was when Howard appeared before a Senate investigating committee, where they accused him of getting dates for the Washington brass to ensure defense contracts. If the so-called dates were anything like that evening, it was ludicrous. I realized while I was watching it all on television that that was as angry as I ever saw Howard get.

From my free and easy life, leaving God out of things, I suddenly found myself to be quite pregnant. I was terrified. In those days no "nice girl" got pregnant. There was no such thing as keeping a child out of wedlock in 1942. The only solution was to find a quack and get an abortion. I didn't know anything about who to go to. Finally, after talking to an older girl I'd known at school (who knew her way around), I got the name of a doctor.

Robert drove me over to a small clean enough building in Glendale somewhere, and I went cold turkey—no anesthetic—into hell. I've never had anything hurt like that since. I suppose Robert thought it was his. I wasn't that sure. But he was still in school and marriage was out of the question.

The abortion didn't take and I had to go back with Carol. It was the same horror all over again. When we got to our house, I found myself very sick for the first time in my life.

I had a raging fever and a terrified Carol called our doctor, who rushed me to the hospital. As he gave me my first anesthesia, he swore at the butcher who had done this, and I went out. When I came to, I asked Carol whether Robert had called. He hadn't. I said, "You'd better take me home to Mother."

Mom had to be upset but, as usual, she was her totally calm self. She prayed for me and read the Bible. Every morning as I looked out on her beautiful garden, all I could see was the good Lord and how much He loved me in spite of myself. Mother said, "Daughter, the Ten Commandments are like the guardrails on the mountain passes. The Lord puts those white guardrails there to protect you, not to restrict you. Now if you crash through, you go over the side, but if you give Him *all* the pieces, He'll put you back together." I did, and He slowly healed me. I had an infection and went for treatment every morning. Then I spent the rest of the day in bed. No one, but no one, could ever tell me again that there wasn't a God and that I didn't need Him.

Robert came by almost every day, but only for about ten minutes, and always with a buddy. He couldn't stand being around anyone who was sick.

John Payne, whom I had met only that one time, heard I was sick and called from Santa Monica every night. We would talk sometimes for two hours. I'd try to tell him it was costing too much, but he wouldn't listen. He told me what to read, to stop reading the heavy stuff I was into, and to read light, happy things. He wanted to come out, to send flowers, but I was still engaged and I could see the scene if Robert found out. But I did know from just observing the two of them, and their totally different behaviors, the scale was very unbalanced in John's favor.

When I finally got well and moved back in with Carol, I gave Robert back his ring. He was shocked and very hurt. I felt sorry for him, but I knew it was something I had to do. I told him then that we had nothing in common. He loved football, hunting, and fishing, while I loved more artistic things—music, reading, talking. He took the ring and hocked it.

When I found out he had been spending his nights with some broad who had a hamburger stand during the time I had been sick, I stopped feeling too sorry for him.

I called John and told him that I had broken up with Robert. That was the start of a very serious affair. It was altogether different from my romance with Robert. Johnny Payne was a thinker, a reader, a writer. He wrote songs and loved music of all kinds. He loved to analyze people as I did, and we spent hours and hours talking. We'd be yakking away and sharing thoughts and suddenly realize it was three in the morning.

He was working at Twentieth Century-Fox at the time and investing in land along the Malibu coastline. The war had started, but it hadn't touched any of us yet. We went to Fieldsie and Walter Lang's house for small, exquisitely served dinners. Clark Gable and Cesar Romero, two beautiful men, were often there. Fieldsie had been one of Carole Lombard's best friends and was a charming no-nonsense lady. Walter directed many of John's pictures. We went to Lew and Eddie Wasserman's home, to the Ice Follies, to dinner in Beverly Hills, and other parties, but most of the time we stayed home, at his place or mine. Carol was going with Dick Foran at the time (whom she later married), so we passed each other now and then, but we were in constant touch.

Later John took an apartment across from the Garden of Allah. I, too, was thinking of taking one, but Lew Wasserman, my agent, didn't think it was a good idea. In those days people didn't just live together. We talked of getting married and laughed about my becoming Jane Payne. I've often wondered how different my life would have been if I had done so.

Howard summoned me, so back I went to that small office. Why, he wondered, had I broken up with that nice football player and was now going out with Hollywood wolves? I assured him there was no one but John Payne, who certainly wasn't a wolf. My, how the news flies in Hollywood. Howard went on to say he certainly didn't want me circulating and making the mistake so many other girls had made in Hollywood. I laughed and said, "No chance!"

I found out later that Howard's bachelor friends, like Johnny Meyers, Greg Bautzer, and Pat Decico, played their favorite game of trading girls, much as Robert and Jackson had done in high school. Howard was terrified of having anyone under contract to him becoming one of those girls.

The girls who were under contract to Howard were provided with a house and a couple for companionship plus a driver to take them shopping. They were asked to live that way for just those reasons. I met two who practically never heard from Howard—and were in no way mistresses—even though some wished they were. They were simply being kept from the "wolves." That wouldn't have been a lifestyle for me—I'm much too independent. But if ever a mother wanted her little girl to be safe, this was among the safest situations in Hollywood. One could die from boredom, but not from harassment. I honestly think sometimes Howard forgot where these girls were. I preferred my heavenly guardian and being on my own.

There's one thing I must say for old Jane: She never threw pearls before swine. I have a never-erring built-in radar system that tells me exactly how important I am to someone, and I've never gone out on a limb yet. My heart's been broken, but never from unrequited love.

One night I went home alone to talk to Carol and found Robert sitting in front of our house. He was still sad and wanted to know how I was. Football season was starting again, and he asked me if I would please still take his mother to the games. He'd take her home, but she still loved me, and he'd feel so much better if I would. So from then on, every Saturday at noon I'd pick up Frances and go to the games. That neat lady never said anything to me about breaking her son's heart—hard to imagine from a mother who was mad about her kid, but absolutely true. We'd watch the game, I'd give her to Robert, then I'd go and meet Johnny Payne.

I met John's mother, who came from Roanoke, Virginia. John had bought me a huge topaz ring but, no fool, he didn't give it to me just then. Carol had talked with him, and they felt I still hadn't gotten Robert completely out of my system.

I said to my childhood friend Lorraine Harris, "Fix Robert up with your sister Sally." I didn't like the broads he was dating and knew Sal had always had a crush on him. Lorraine set it up, and from then on Robert was always with Sally. I'd see them after the games and turn Frances over to Sally, who was busy getting autographs for kids surrounding Robert. Sally's dad told her one day on the way home, "Jane's not through with Bob, so take it easy, honey." It seems everyone knew but me.

One night John and I went to a party. We'd both had quite a bit to drink and didn't feel red hot the next morning. He was going to get a steam bath and then go see Julie, his daughter. He really tried to get me to go along, but I didn't want to. After he left I wandered around for a while. Then I finally picked up the phone and called Frances, who asked me if I could come to dinner. We'd always had rabbit for Sunday night dinner, and she was a great cook. I said, "No, I can't, but I'm sorry." I sat and stared at the wall, wandered some more, tried to read but couldn't, and about an hour later I called back. "Frances, I'm coming to dinner if that's okay."

I then called John and told him I felt homesick and was going to the Valley. He wanted me to wait until he got there, but I said, "No, I'll be all right." I was so screwed up I didn't know what was wrong with me. But he did.

When I arrived at the Waterfields, it was like going home. I didn't intend to stay, but when Robert and I went into the living room alone, I started to cry. Robert said, "What's the matter, isn't that guy being good to you?" I said, "Oh no, he's a doll. I don't know what's wrong." With that Frances summoned us to dinner, but when we sat down at the kitchen table, neither one of us could eat. Finally Frances said, "Oh, for heaven's sake, you two get the hell out of here—you're ruining my good dinner." We went out to the swing in the garden, and I don't think we said a word. But we both knew I was home for good.

S I X

F inally, after waiting for two more years for the seal of approval from the Hays office censors, *The Outlaw* was to open in San Francisco on February 5, 1943. Jack and I were to make public appearances on the stage in conjunction with the movie, but doing what? Some idiot convinced Howard that an added scene done "in person" was the answer. We got together. It was great to see Jack again. He was always fun to work with, and we were good buddies. Well, we started rehearsing a playlet on the Goldwyn lot. The rehearsal went on for weeks—we were rehearsed out, but no Howard. I tricked the studio cop into telling me where his latest office was. (There were times when even *I* had a hard time getting to see him.) Howard's offices were usually tiny little rooms like storerooms, tucked away somewhere up stairs and down long halls. But I found it and knocked on the door.

When Howard opened it, I went in and glared at him.

"When the devil are you going to see this fiasco?" I fumed. "It's been ready for a week and a half!"

"But, I thought that's what you did with plays, rehearse."

"For a play, yes. But forever on one scene? Come on!"

So he came down to the rehearsal hall, made some changes, and we went on rehearsing. The next time I went looking for him was a little easier. I found his shade-covered

window and threw pebbles at it. He stuck his head out, and I yelled, "How do I get up there?"

"Oh, it's you. Come to that door, and I'll let you in."

The same thing happened as before, and if the picture hadn't had an opening date, I think we'd still be rehearsing. A fantastic curtain of leaves and net made to look like a forest was our set. It must have cost a fortune. Then, at last, they took us—and the curtain—to San Francisco.

Birdwell was still manning the publicity for *The Outlaw*, so I was properly attired with a complete wardrobe. I took Pat Henry with me. The press was flown up *en masse* at Mr. Hughes' expense and put up in the finest hotels. I would have hated to pay the bills for the phone calls, let alone the booze, food, and the rest.

Pat and I had a gorgeous suite at the Fairmont Hotel on Nob Hill that overlooked all of San Francisco and the bay. Jack and his wife, Ceretha, an adorable blue-eyed blonde whom nobody knew he had hidden away in Texas, were in the suite below us, and Howard was in the suite above. We were to be there for nine weeks.

To hail the long-awaited opening, a monstrous painting was erected on a billboard outside the theatre. It displayed me in an exceedingly languorous pose with a caption proclaiming, "Sex has not been rationed," and in slightly smaller print, "The picture that couldn't be stopped."

The over-rehearsed scene on stage was to be added to the overly long movie. The special net curtain was ready. I stood nervously in the wings in my *Outlaw* costume. The Geary Theater audience hushed, the curtain rose, and Jack walked on to start the scene, but only his legs appeared. The curtain was stuck about four feet up. This fabulous, terribly expensive, frigging curtain was stuck! The audience started to titter, then laugh, then roar. Every press person, every invited star, the entourage that had been flown in to this fabulous world premiere screamed. Somehow they got that damned curtain up, lowered the screen, and started the movie.

None of us backstage got to see it. Instead of going to the party to meet the press, Howard took us out the stage door and we boarded one of San Francisco's famous cable cars. He stood on the step, hanging on, and we went for-lornly back to the hotel. In his suite he ordered champagne, trying to pick us all up, himself included. I sat on the edge of his chair and tried to comfort him. I don't know what happened at the big bash, but I heard later that everyone got smashed. The next day, the papers crucified us and that was the end of the stage play.

Howard Greer flew up with a full-length beaded dress for me to wear on stage. Frank McHugh, the comedian, arrived the next day and Jack and I were given straight lines to set up his laughs, and that's what preceded the picture for the rest of the run. There was a newsreel, a cartoon, the stage bit, and the picture, which in spite of bad reviews, showed nine times a day for nine weeks to packed houses. We had little time between shows, but we did manage to eat three meals and rest until the last show. Then we'd head for the hotel and have a ball for a couple of hours, either in my suite or Jack's.

No one seemed to care that Jack and I hadn't seen *The Outlaw*. We had worked on it for three years and hadn't seen a foot of it. Opening night had been such a fiasco that we weren't allowed out from backstage. One night we'd had it, so we sneaked out into the lobby and up the stairs to the balcony. The place was packed, as usual, and there wasn't an empty seat. We sat on the steps and watched. An usher came over and tried to throw us out.

"You can't sit there!" he said. "Don't you have seats?"

"Shhhhhhh," I said, "It's Jack and Jane."

He almost fell off the balcony rail, but he let us stay. That's how we finally saw the picture.

Howard was still busy cutting the film and flying in and out, so we rarely saw him. One night, though, he wanted to see me about a tour to open the picture one city at a time, his fight with the censors, my argument against this and the huge billboards of me half-clothed, and the ruckus it was causing. We were up late arguing, and I was exhausted the next day. The next time he called, I said I couldn't stay up and had to get my sleep, but he came knocking on the door anyway. I told Pat to do something—I knew what it would be like. He was a night person who worked all night and went to bed at dawn. Pat opened the door a crack and said, "Mr. Hughes, you hired me to see that Jane isn't bothered and that she gets her rest and that's exactly what I'm doing."

"But I'm the one paying you," he complained in his Texas drawl, "It doesn't mean me."

"But I'm doing what I'm paid to do—seeing that she gets her sleep," she answered. "You can't come in. I'm sorry."

Since he had no legitimate answer to Pat's reasoning, he meekly gave in like the lamb he was. Then Pat and I popped down to Jack and Ceretha's for a couple of hours. We were brats!

Robert came up to see me only once. He felt uncomfortable. I didn't feel right about him staying all night, and we got into quite a fight. He finally left, and there was nothing but phone calls until I went home.

Pat was having a ball in the big city. I had her made up, her hair fixed, and into my clothes. She'd never had anything to drink, but one night we went to a bar with the group. I wasn't paying much attention to her, but when we got home she dumped her purse on the bed. It must have contained forty or fifty dollars. I said, "Where the hell did you get that?"

"Well, the guys all down that long bar kept leaving money on it, so I just walked along and picked it up. What'll we do?" She giggled, stone drunk.

We could never return the money in a hundred weeks, since we didn't know any of the guys so we decided to buy a pair of lounging pajamas or something.

Aunt Ernie came up to see us. She took one look at those billboards and said, "I want to see Howard Hughes." And she did.

I would have loved to have been a mouse in the corner at that meeting!

"Mr. Hughes," she said, "You're selling my niece as though she were some cheap stripper, and I don't think that's right."

"Well, you know, Mrs. Henry," he replied, "I can't very well sell her like Shirley Temple."

Aunt Ernie didn't give me all the details, but what she told me was very interesting.

"I found Mr. Hughes to be very nice, Jane," she said. "He's got problems that you and I can't even guess at. His judgment may differ from ours, but he honestly believes that this is the best way to sell his picture. We have to realize that not only is it his picture, but it's his time, his energy, and his money and we shouldn't be angry at him for not seeing things as we do." He'd gotten her on his side too! But, I'll bet he never forgot her.

Mother came up to catch the show and liked it. She did a funny thing the second day there. She went to an Episcopalian church on Sunday morning and invited the two ministers to have tea with Pat and me in our suite at the hotel. She told me afterward that a lump came into her throat when she had to mention my by now "infamous" name. When they recovered from the shock, they accepted. I'm sure they probably expected to see me walk in with a naked man slung over each shoulder. Instead, they got the especially well-behaved daughters of the Jacobi sisters. I don't know whether they were disappointed or not.

Finally Lew Wasserman arrived. He was a tall, sweet, extremely bright man who was about to become the head of the Music Corporation of America. Levis had been sold to MCA along with the stable of young contractees, Gig Young, Susan Ball, and Craig Stevens among them. I was still with Levis, but now under MCA. Lew Wasserman brought muscle. The agency wanted me to break my contract with Howard. I'd been promised a new one when I'd signed the first time. Lew took me aside.

"Look, honey," he said, "I know all about you and Bob Waterfield. Why don't you go home and get married. So they put you on suspension, so what. We've got excellent lawyers and we'll break this contract. After all this time, you're still making peanuts. Hughes is exploiting you."

Wasserman was very persuasive.

"I'll even loan you my car to go to Las Vegas to get married."

I was getting mighty weary, and I wanted nothing more but to go home to Robert and leave this whole mess behind. The Catholic Church was now excommunicating anyone who saw the picture, and every pulpit sermonized about the evils of the picture. Apparently it wasn't just the cleavage that got them. It was the idea that I had crawled naked under the blanket with Jack. It was never seen. It never happened, but it was implied and that was enough. When Howard Hawks was still directing the picture, he had prepared me for that scene. He said that if I was the least bit embarrassed while playing it, it would fall flat. So he told me this story.

A man and a woman he knew had been on a fishing trip. The man fell overboard and by the time he was rescued, he was half frozen. The woman wrapped him in blankets, but he was still cold, so she slid under the blankets with him. Her own body heat undoubtedly saved the man's life.

It sounded logical to me. Billy was dying and I saved his life. I didn't take my clothes off. I just started to undo my belt and the scene went dark. But in the mind of the Church, they could see the whole thing. It was too awful.

Howard was gone somewhere, so I talked to his man in charge and told him I was through. No more tour! I didn't want to sue; I just wanted to quit. I was tired and I just wanted to go home and get married and live happily ever after. He gave me a paper to sign that said I wouldn't work for any other studio, and I went home.

Poor Lew. He just threw up his hands when he heard about that paper I'd signed. That was the end of suing anybody. I was glad.

On my way to the airport I saw this huge billboard with a picture of me standing in front of a haystack, legs planted firmly apart and a pistol in each hand. Under it it read, "Mean, Moody and Magnificent." The Church may have been upset, but I thought it was hysterical!

When I got home, I told Robert of Lew's offer to lend us his car to go to Vegas. Did he or didn't he want to get married? It had been four years since we had been seeing each other. I'd wanted to get married when we'd gotten back together, but he wanted to wait a year. He didn't trust me. It wasn't a year yet, but I knew it was time now to do it or to forget the whole thing.

He agreed, so we gathered up George Robotham, a UCLA football buddy, and his girl, Jean Willis, and started out for Las Vegas. I sat in the back seat, asleep, with Jean, and George and Robert were in the front. It couldn't have been less romantic.

When we arrived at Rancho Vegas, Robert, in his usual dry tone, said, "Let's get it over with first so we can enjoy our dinner." I'd spotted a church being decorated for Easter Sunday (which was the next day) and asked the minister if he'd marry us. He seemed flustered but agreed. So off we went to the church in our rather normal dresses. My wedding dress was royal blue crepe. The church looked lovely and the ceremony was brief. Miss Willies, as we called Jean, cried and after it was over she said, "Robert, if you dare say you're hungry, I'll kill you."

He laughed and said, "Let's eat."

After dinner Robert started wondering about George and Jean. They weren't married and we'd booked only two double rooms.

"So?" I asked coolly.

"Maybe . . . ," he began, "we ought to split up."

"Split up how?"

"George and I in one, and you and Jean in the other."

I thought that a lousy idea and said so. Loud. "Hell," I said, my voice a little lower, "those two have been sleeping together for months, so what's the difference?"

"I know, but how will it look here? I mean in a hotel?"

I stared at him as though he'd gone batty. "How will it look," I asked coolly, "if I murder you on your wedding night? In a hotel."

We went to the room and then back out for a midnight buffet, just the two of us, with nothing to say. When we were back in the room, trying to go to sleep, my mind was whirling. I vowed I would be a faithful wife.

I said, "Robert, if you ever meet anyone really important to you, have an affair if you must, but please let's don't ever break our vows over something unimportant. No chippying, okay?"

"Oh, shut up," he said.

I remember crying myself to sleep. It was a swell wedding. It was Easter 1943.

Things picked up considerably when we got home to his mother's. I began to realize that this husband of mine was only comfortable in familiar surroundings. Las Vegas and getting married made him nervous. He hated change of any kind.

Suddenly we learned that Robert's ROTC class was to be sent to Fort Benning, Georgia, to Officer's Training School. I had a nightmare that night about him being in the war and wounded. I woke up crying with Robert shaking me. "What's the matter, honey?" I told him about the dream, and he laughed and hugged and kissed me. I think we were as close then as we ever could be. I was in love and married!

S E V E N

When the time came for Robert to leave for Fort Benning, I saw him hug his mother for the first time. They weren't very demonstrative, even though their love for each other was deep. Robert was a great deal like my father. It was hard for either of them to show emotion.

Jackson and I took him to the train, and neither of us could help but smile as he marched away. He looked so miserable. Jackson said, "Well the big dog is finally having to join the ranks. What a sight." After he arrived in Georgia we would get frantic phone calls: "Get me out of here, get me into the air force, anything, I can't stand this."

I finally decided to go to Fort Benning. I could be a lot more help there, even though I couldn't see Robert often. I went alone. My cousin Pat would follow. As I boarded the train, Charlie Guest from the Hughes office arrived and handed me my suspension papers. No more money.

A cute, very young paratrooper sat beside me on the train. I wasn't in a drawing room, but a regular car loaded with servicemen, wives, and crying babies. Total strangers slept on each other's shoulders without even knowing it, they were so tired. One couldn't get to the diner, so box lunches and cold drinks were sold from time to time. Everybody was friendly, trying to make the best of it.

When we arrived in Columbus, the young paratrooper helped me carry my luggage to Traveler's Aid. I left my bags there until I could find a room. I was in the most idiotic outfit you can imagine for such a hot, humid, impossible situation: a black taffeta dress and high heels with ankle straps. I looked like I was going to a cocktail party.

The only accommodations I could find were in a visitors' barracks for only three days in the Harmony Church area, where Robert was. The town was jammed. The Harmony Church guest barracks was a long building with a row of cubicles and one bath at the end of the hall. But, with special permission, your husband could spend the night with you there.

I had just gotten out of the shower and was trying to find something cool to put on when Robert came through the door. His face was as wet as mine from sweat and tears, and his uniform was soaked, but we locked together in one long hug.

The next day I went back to Columbus to look for a place for us. On the third day I finally found a room in a three-bedroom house with one bath and "kitchen privileges." Robert could only get to town one night a week, so on other evenings I'd ride the bus to Harmony Church, where we'd sit on a log while he cried from frustration. He'd tell me about crawling through the mud and how ignorant this whole thing was.

Jobs were scarce, but $21 a month wasn't going far, so I looked for a job. I finally talked a beauty shop owner into letting me do makeups. I wasn't fit for much else. Of course, in that heat, makeup just ran off. That job lasted only for a couple of weeks.

By then Pat Henry arrived, and that helped. But we made the mistake of picking up a stray kitten that promptly got diarrhea all over the bed and rug. We were out of our cherished room at the end of the week.

No one in town knew me from Adam, but I was walking down the street one day and heard my name. I turned and saw Kenny Morgan, Lucille Ball's brother-in-law, grinning from ear to ear. He was wearing captain's bars. Kenny was into publicity and later became the head of publicity for Desilu. The next thing I knew, a newspaperman was getting a story and pictures of Jane Russell, the "movie star war bride." I was annoyed at the time, but it certainly taught me the value of the red carpet treatment. I received a phone call the next day and suddenly we had two bedrooms, a bath, a living room, and a kitchen all furnished and to ourselves. Praise the Lord and Kenny Morgan.

Pat got a job selling war bonds in a wooden tank in the middle of Main Street, and soon I joined her. There we saw all of Columbus pass by. It was July and August and there was no air conditioning, just a fan to blow the hot sticky air around. When you stepped out, your heels sank in the tar of the street. Ugh!

But our duplex apartment was away from downtown, with a huge green field, and now and then we could feel a breeze. It became the headquarters for all of Robert's buddies when they got off. Lonnie Lee had come from UCLA with Robert, and Nick the Greek, as he was called, stuck close by.

Every night I went to Harmony Church from the bond tank to see Robert. But Pat, being single, could go to the officers' clubs with anyone she liked. We looked very alike, wore our hair the same way and each other's clothes, so soon word got out that I was having a ball while my poor husband was sweating out OCS. Then a girl turned up from San Francisco who looked so much like me I thought I was looking in a mirror. She was living with a captain at the time, so Jane Russell had a three-way reputation going like wildfire. That plus the magazines and the *Outlaw* publicity was more than that post or town could handle. That rotten Pat used to go into a ladies' room and when someone would say, "Aren't you Jane Russell?" she'd whirl on them with an indignant glare and say, "Heavens, no!" Then they'd backtrack with, "Oh, of course, you're not, anyone can see that you're a nice girl. You know I hear she's shacking up with a captain." Do you know that bitch would never let on who she was. She just couldn't wait until she got home to laugh and slap her thighs while she told me the story. But I learned very early not to pay any attention to what people said about me.

Working in the bond tanks was boring, so we took turns going to the air-conditioned movies. I also simply couldn't keep the books straight—no mathematician I. I had the flu

one day and was home in bed. Pat called and told me to get on the bus and come down. We went to the office and were fired. I didn't mind getting fired, but why get out of bed for it? I think they thought we were stealing.

During this time I had no word from Howard Hughes or Lew Wasserman. I wrote Mother about the situation and she sent me a scripture: "He that sweareth to his own hurt, and changeth not . . . shall never be moved" (Psalms 15:4–5). In other words, keep your word if it kills you and you won't stand on shifting sand. She also pointed out that I had had thousands of dollars worth of publicity that no one could buy, and that it was Howard Hawks, not Howard Hughes, who had promised a new contract.

I sat down and wrote Howard that I signed a deal for seven years and I felt obligated to fulfill it if he wanted me to. I enclosed the scripture. A few days later Charlie Guest called me to say as soon as I came back to Los Angeles I was to get in touch. Howard wanted to see me.

After three months Robert made second lieutenant. Hoorah! We could finally go home for a brief ten days. Then Robert and Lonnie Lee were to be stationed at Fort Benning for a time. We split up the next morning and the guys went out on an army plane, and me on a commercial flight. I got bumped in Dallas and spent forty-eight hours there, sleeping on a bench all night in the terminal.

I called Charlie Guest and told him my predicament. He said, "Honey, we have no juice in the south yet. If you can get to Albuquerque, we can get you on TWA. I'll have a hotel room for you there." Even the red carpet treatment got me home three days late, but I was glad to think the guys had gotten home. Not so. They had their troubles too, and we all arrived within a couple of hours of each other. It was great to see Frances. She wrote almost every day to us and to all of Robert's buddies, wherever they were, all through the war.

It was heaven to be home. I ran to see everybody—Mom, Pat, Margaret, Alberta. Then I went to see Howard. It was in another dumb office. I was glad to see him, but when I started toward him he backed around behind his desk. I had to chase him around the desk to finally give him a huge bear hug. He simply didn't know what to make of me.

I told him that Robert was to be stationed in Georgia for a time and then would probably go overseas. I wanted to stay with him as long as he was in the States. Howard said that would be fine. I was put back on salary with a bonus for the time I had been off salary. What a cute man.

Robert and Lonnie went back in ten days, but I stayed on for about a month. Part of that time I spent at home with Mother. The three eldest boys were already away, and they had a rough time because of my publicity. When we were all home it was a big joke. Occasionally, to be a smart ass, I'd say in my haughtiest voice, "That has to be done *my* way and not *yours* because I'm Jane Russell! I'm a movie star!" Then the fur would fly and they'd beat me down to the floor and pile on top.

But imagine what it must have been like for them to be Jane Russell's brothers at the time when I was being hailed as the "sexpot of the century," with my photographs plastered all over the country in newspapers and magazines. I was being included in the list of things that represented "home" to our GIs. Along with Mom, apple pie, and Betty Grable's legs, there was also Jane Russell.

My brothers were fed up because they just couldn't avoid getting involved. It was Ken who said, "You can keep your mouth shut for just so long." Then pow! It happened when a shipmate of his came back from leave in Los Angeles and told a wild story about dating Jane Russell and, as he put it, "making out" with her.

Well, that was too much for Ken, and he lost his temper. There was no way he could explain to those sailors that any resemblance between his sister and all that publicity was so much crap, so he wound up fighting.

Tom solved the problem by not telling anyone that I was his sister. If anyone questioned the similarity of names, he said it was a coincidence. He didn't care if they believed him or not, as long as they left him alone.

Jamie told me about the time he was standing watch on his ship, and word got around that he was my brother. He swears that before his four hours of duty were up, every man aboard sauntered by Station Two and stared at him. It was the most uncomfortable four hours of his life, having to listen to crude remarks being made on my physical attributes and bawdy speculations as to my virtue. My brothers had more to put up with than most. Mom used to say that her boys were fighting in two wars: one for Democracy and one for Daughter.

Mom finally had to sell the ranch. We all hated to see that house go. She kept two acres on one end where she had planted fruit trees and planned to build a little house for herself after the war. Then she and Wally went out to Aunt Ernie's and Uncle Bob's in Fontana to wait out the war.

When I returned to Georgia, Pat decided to join the WAF. She learned to fly at an air base on the California border, where she met and married Master Sergeant Nelson Kayser. They eventually had four gorgeous daughters.

Now, thank God, Robert, Lonnie, and I could go to the officers' club and partake of some of the social life on the post. Robert and Lonnie were immediately put on the basketball team and later, of course, Robert played football on the post.

The 176th won the football championship, but Robert hurt his knee. When it swelled up to twice its normal size, he was sent to a hospital in Atlanta. He had seen so many guys with stiff knees he decided not to have an operation. I spent a couple of weeks in a rented room there while he waited to see what his next move would be—a desk job or an honorable discharge. We both felt suspended in midair being away from home. At last the day arrived when he would go before the hospital board to get their decision. I was holding my breath. As Robert walked up the drive, I couldn't read his stone face. He simply said, as he reached me, "Let's go home."

When we got back to our beloved Valley we lived with Frances, and Robert went back to get his degree in physical education at UCLA. He definitely wanted to graduate. I got to see all my buddies. Margaret and Davey had gotten married some time before and had a baby girl. They had an old house on Van Nuys Boulevard, and the entire living room was turned into a studio. There we all started to paint, some still life, but mostly we painted each other. David was really talented and his work was dark and intriguing, full of color and depth. We had the record player going full blast, playing symphonies, a coffee pot on the stove at all times, and half-gallons of red wine. If we ran out of paint, we used house paint—whatever. Whoever said the hippies were only for the sixties?

Robert was moving ahead much more rapidly in his career than I was. His knee finally became totally well, and he was again playing for dear old UCLA. When the best football players in the country were picked for the 1944 All Star Game, he was chosen as quarterback and as Most Valuable Player of that game. That's like winning an Academy Award.

At the end of this very exciting game, we met a small gray-haired man who was a scout for the Cleveland Rams, one of the pro teams. All of the scouts were looking for players, but in those days the boys did their own negotiations. Today, lawyers and business managers make the deals in five and six figures. Robert was very pleased, but the stone face said, "I'll think about it." When he did sign, it was for more than any other new player was getting at the time, but nothing like today's salaries. These were the days of Sid Luckman and Sammy Baugh, two of the greatest quarterbacks that have ever played football.

The big time meant being away from home again. We weren't thrilled about that. Cleveland was as cold as Georgia was hot. The other players' wives and I would sit in the stands, bundled up from head to toe and keeping warm with the help of something from a flask, and root for our guys, who were slipping and sliding around on the ice. This was a new experience for Californians.

We found a one-room apartment in an old building on Euclid Street with a pull-down Murphy bed and a tiny stove on top of the fridge. It was grim, but it became the hangout again. The rookies, who became buddies during training camp, played hearts or gin rummy in our funny little apartment.

I made friends with some of the wives, and we would shop for groceries or have coffee when the boys were at practice. I also studied the Bible a lot and got into Paul's Epistles. Once, when the team was playing out of town, we gals went to a special Italian restaurant that was our local hangout and where we knew the owners and waitresses. Someone suggested a party, so we piled into cars and went. Afterward, when I got into the same car to go home, I was suddenly alone with the driver, whom I'll call Vito, one of the regulars. When I asked where the others were, he said, "Oh, I wanted to take you home," and drove on, but not to Euclid Street. He took me to a huge dark park where no one was around. I started praying to myself and talking fast about his mother, how it would break her heart if she could see him now. I wondered how he dared! Those Rams would have creamed him if they found out. I guess I hit a cord with the mother bit, because he finally did just drive me home. The next day we found out Vito started a jail sentence that morning. That's how he dared. The Rams couldn't get him in jail. I guess he figured he'd have one last fling before he started doing time.

I took my first trip to New York to meet the U.S.S. *Portland,* which was rumored to be in drydock. I was dying to see my brother Ken, who was aboard. I stayed in a hotel across from the depot and I didn't dare get off Forty-second Street for fear of getting lost. Sometimes I took walks, but mostly I stayed by the phone. What a way to see New York for the first time!

Finally, since I was going a little batty, I called Birdwell's New York office and told him I was in town. He immediately sent over a publicity woman and a photographer to pose me with his other clients at various restaurants during the afternoon, but then I was dumped back at that dreary hotel. I ended up in tears and told them to get lost. The "can of tomatoes" again.

I never did find Kenny, so I went back to Cleveland. I was really homesick, and Robert was very occupied with the team. The guys played hard on and off the field. It was hard to tell the married ones from the bachelors. I was disillusioned and depressed.

One night I was left in a booth in a club all night talking to an old doctor friend of the team while Robert sat at the bar with a buddy and his girl. I was miserable. But when we got back to the hotel, there stood Ken. He had come to Cleveland to find me. I threw my arms around him and cried and cried. Both guys were amazed. This wasn't like old Jane at all. I decided right then and there to go home for Christmas and let Robert do his thing. The Lord could take care of him, and my fears and insecurities weren't doing me anything but harm.

Robert was doing fantastically on the field, however, using the "T" formation. Jim Benton, the famous end, and Riley Matheson, guard, decided to talk to the new rookie. Jim seemed to be lying on the air to catch those passes that were laid right out in front of him. Riley got the line to protect their new quarterback with their lives. Robert led them to the NFL Championship in his rookie season.

I watched that championship game on television with Frances and a gang of friends. When Robert kicked the field goal that balanced on the crossbar and fell into the end zone, putting them in the lead 9 to 7 at the half, we lost our minds. We could be heard for blocks when they won. Robert was made Rookie of the Year; another Academy Award.

He and center Bob Delauer drove night and day and made it home on Christmas Eve. Years earlier, when only Frances had been working, she would borrow money for Christmas, bring home lots of one-dollar bills, and throw them up in the air. Whatever you could grab was yours to buy presents with. The tree was always green, and we would decorate it until it damn near fell over.

Shopping, secrets, carols, and the crackling fire turned us all into children again. Frances was Christmas. My mom gave me my present in a brown paper bag with love. She had had it with "Ho! Ho! Ho!" and five kids for years! But Frances never gave up. I think 1945 was perhaps the best Christmas we ever had.

My dad, Roy William Russell. Mom, Geraldine Jacobi Russell.

Herself—in the mud as usual.

Grandpa J. as Grand Fork's Shrine Potentate.

Mother's little darling "Daughter."

Babysitting Jamie, Tommy, and Kenny.

Grammar school graduate.

The photo that started it all.

Howard Hughes on *The Outlaw* set. A sweet, quiet man.

You can take the hay out of the girl, but . . .

Probably winter, but smile, girl, smile.

Jack and Jane in San Francisco

for *The Outlaw* premiere.

Mom and I hit London.

Family portrait at La Posada:
(back row: Wally, Lois, Ken, Cousin Dave Henry, Mom, Jamie, Tom.
Robert and I kneeling in front).

E I G H T

After five years, for some strange reason, Howard agreed to loan me to Hunt Stromberg for *The Young Widow*. Interestingly, though, he refused to loan Jack Beutel to Howard Hawks for *Red River*, so Montgomery Clift became a star. Not that he wouldn't have anyway, but what a raw deal for Jack.

Louis Hayward, my co-star, was an absolute charmer, and I was "in love again." I often got crushes on my leading men. Hayward played an aggressive, brash young man in the movies, but he wasn't like that at all in person. He was a Pisces—a very sensuous and sensitive man. A perfect gentleman. He spent hours talking to everyone on the set to avoid me because of our vibes. I had a crush on him, and it was mutual.

Penny Singleton (well known for her Blondie role) saved the day for me. I was supposed to be down in the picture, and she was so up. I'll never forget one long and emotional scene that she got through beautifully, crying real tears, only to have me bang my suitcase on the door and screw it up. I've never felt so embarrassed in my life. Since then I've had it done to me a few times, and I always knew how the other person felt.

The worst part of that movie was the fact that I had three directors who were all totally different. The first was William

Dieterle, a dark moody European who had me weeping over flowers and kissing one in a particularly symbolic way that sent Louie's eyes heavenward with an "I say, isn't that a bit much." Dieterle was off the picture.

Next was André "Bundy" de Toth, who was marvelous! But he hated the project almost as much as I did, so he finally managed to escape. He directed most of it, though, and during his stay I met his secretary, Portia Nelson, who became a lifelong friend.

The third director drove me mad. He was one of those raving perfectionists who insisted that every jot and tittle of that terrible script was gospel, and you didn't dare leave out an *if, and,* or *but,* which made the damn thing wooden and mechanical. I was also supposed to smile all the time. He said my somber face "only lit up when I smiled." Dear God! The young widow should have died with her husband and that gruesome story need never have been told.

The best thing to come to me from this experience happened by accident. (The Lord is sneaky.) Between takes, while the camera crew was relighting a set—which can take forever—I went through to the next set to doodle around on a piano. I took lessons as a kid, but now I preferred playing by ear. I liked all the obscure songs with minor chord changes. Portia happened by one day, listened, and we got to talking about songs we liked. I'm sure if there had been one other soul there, we would never have gotten to know each other so well. We are both Gemini, shy, private people. At any rate, she mentioned a song I loved but couldn't play, so she sat down and played it so much better than I could, I wanted to slap her. I sang it and she said, "You know, you're very good." Finally, and I mean finally, she sang a song and it was beautiful. She had a high, clear voice, unlike the husky pop voices of the day, with such intonation and shading! Her lyrics were sung with such understanding that you felt you'd heard a poem sung. Barbra Streisand has that today. I was flabbergasted and asked, "What the hell are you doing pounding a typewriter? You should be singing." We made each other promise to sing. No more being a straight man for a comedian on personal appearances for me, and no more secretarial jobs for her.

Portia met the Van Nuys gang and went to Bible study with us and became like family. Her last job as a secretary was with Bundy de Toth and his wife, actress Veronica Lake.

Mother finally started building her small house on the two acres she had left after selling La Posada and found she was landlocked! The fellow who bought the five and a half acres had said that she could use the front gate to the property, but afterward reneged. Mother was beside herself, saying, "Lord, you promised to be a husband to the widow, and father to the fatherless, now *do* something." A few weeks later at a landowners' meeting she was told there was a road being put in at the opposite end of the two acres that came right to her property line. The Lord had it on the planning boards all the while she was yelling.

As my brothers came out of the armed services, they got married, and Mom cut off a chunk of land and put it in their names.

Ken learned the building business from his father-in-law and then got Tom started. They eventually built four houses on Mom's two acres. So Mom had the boys, their wives, Lois, Pamela, Nola, and Mary Lou, and twenty-one grandchildren around her.

My sister-in-law Pamela laughingly said, "The Russells have had every kind of wedding there is: Jane and Bob eloped (three children), Lois and Ken had a garden wedding (four children), Tom and Nola had a small church wedding (three children), Wally and Mary Lou a large church wedding (four children), and Jamie and I had a shotgun wedding (six children)!"

My sisters-in-law got along beautifully, and whichever child misbehaved in their yard got spanked. It didn't matter which mother it was. If the kids were hungry, they were fed, and if they were dirty, they were washed.

One friend visiting the property once said, "My God, it's like walking into a rabbit hutch!" It was!

My four sisters-in-law once went to see *A Streetcar Named Desire*. They had heard so much about Marlon Brando's awful character Stanley and were bursting with curiosity to see what he was all about. When they came out of the theater they were more than a little disappointed. Their conversation, as I recall it, went something like this:

Tom's wife, Nola: "He wasn't so terrible at all. He was no different than any of the Russell boys."

Wally's wife, Mary Lou: "I thought he was charming. I never felt more at home with an actor on the screen. It was like being in our own living room."

Ken's wife, Lois: "I can see Kenny knocking all his dishes off the table and saying 'Okay, I cleared my side, now you clear yours.' "

Jamie's wife, Pamela: "Or Jamie yanking everything off the table, tablecloth and all, then rolling on the floor and clutching his throat, screaming."

We had Bible study in Mom's kitchen. It was just like the days when we were kids and Mother read to us from the Bible under the trees. People came and went as they pleased—no formalities, no rituals.

Then Mother discovered a little church in Pasadena and its darling Irish preacher named Thomas Lennon. She kept nagging, so finally we went. For the first time in years I heard not only tongues spoken, but also interpretation and prophecy. The church was nondenominational, and like Mom, Lennon saw many things in the Bible that weren't being taught in churches, for instance, restitution of *all* things. Jesus died for *all* men and *none* would be lost. This message was kindling a flame in all of us.

During the service many times someone in the congregation would get a message in tongues. Brother Lennon waited quietly for the interpretation. It was always an explanation of his preaching—the Lord clarifying the message, so to speak. I used to feel self-conscious about going up to the front to pray. And then, one night as I was whispering, praying, all of a sudden my tongue got thick, and I couldn't control it to speak English. I was thrilled to my toes and remembered this exact feeling from my childhood. The memory of baptism that

Pat Henry and I had received when we were eleven or twelve years old returned, and I had thought I had made it all up. I hadn't imagined it! It had really happened then and was happening now. Soon the stuttering settled down to a clear language, but one I couldn't understand. It was the Holy Spirit speaking one of His 800,000 languages, praying the prayer I didn't know how to pray. I went home on cloud nine. From then on there were three carloads of young people driving an hour each way every Sunday night to church.

Dan Reeves moved the Rams to Los Angeles in 1946. We were thrilled. The press said it was my fault: "If Dan Reeves wanted Robert Waterfield, and he did, he'd have to please his wife, Jane Russell, and bring the team to Los Angeles." That would be the day!

By this time Howard had made a deal with United Artists to distribute *The Young Widow,* with *The Outlaw* as part of the package. *The Outlaw* would open at the Oriental Theatre in Chicago after many more battles with the censors. That meant more personal appearances. This time I was determined to sing, or I wouldn't go. People were expecting something, and Howard was afraid I couldn't cut the mustard. He was being protective.

Without my knowing it, Howard had Portia picked up in the middle of the night by a big black limousine and brought to a sound stage at Goldwyn studios where he was waiting. "Well," he asked, "can she sing?" Portia answered, "Yes, she can sing and it's a damn sight better to let her sing than let your star go on stage and be made a fool of by some comic. Yes. Yes, she can sing."

Howard thought about this for a few minutes and then said, "Okay, I'll figure out some way for the comedy and the singing to be tied together."

He laid his problems in Preston Sturges' lap. Sturges was directing a picture for him at the time, so Howard felt he could ask him a favor. Preston knew a sweet little comedian named Jimmy Connally, who clowned around, hit wrong notes, and literally broke up the piano while his wife tried to sing. When she finally managed to sing one chorus people applauded,

relieved that she got through it. It didn't matter whether she could sing or not, so they figured that was safe. Now I'd play the wife.

Portia went with me for moral support. My wardrobe for nine shows a day consisted of one crepe dress with a few sequins splashed down one side. The theater manager finally bought me another dress.

Beatrice Kaye, a well-known vaudeville headliner, was already booked in at a percentage of the house. She was delighted the film turned out to be *The Outlaw,* for with nine shows a day for nine weeks and crowds lined up around the block, she could retire! I could have, anyway.

The first show Jimmy tore up the piano and I finally got through one chorus. When I got to my dressing room, the manager wanted to know if I knew any other songs. I said, "Sure, lots of them." I hadn't listened to all that jazz for nothing. We picked out some tunes and some keys, and it was decided that I would sing three or four songs, depending on whether or not there was an encore. What about Jimmy? They sent him home on the train for Los Angeles. Never in his life, said the manager, had he seen a star introduced in such a disgusting manner. It was shocking.

I thought, "Well, why not. It can't be any worse than it is. If I fall down, I'll get up and go again." The next show I sang four songs with no arrangements. The band faked it. Portia, who felt responsible for talking me into singing, was so nervous that when I got off the stage she ran for the bathroom and threw up. I felt wonderful. I had no nerves at all, and that was the start of my singing career. But once more I was shoved into something without any preparation.

It was wintertime, and I was freezing my ass off in my only California coat. I called Howard and said I would pay for half of a fur coat if he would pay for the other half. He said no, and this really burned me up. Portia told me that Universal had supplied an entire wardrobe for their singing star, Susanna Foster, plus a fur coat when she made personal appearances. I was furious, so I marched down to Marshall Field and started in the lingerie department with new underwear, nightgowns, and robes. Then I worked my way through suits, cocktail dresses, shoes, bags, and costume jewelry. I finally wound up with two good warm coats. I put all of this on the hotel tab. The entire wardrobe was paid for and not one word was said, but I'll bet it would have been cheaper if Howard had paid for half a fur coat.

Robert and some of his teammates came through Chicago. That was wonderful. He said it was time I had a wedding ring, so we went to a jeweler and I designed a ring to match a wide gold bracelet watch with J. W. R. engraved on the top of each. I ended up eventually getting three different rings from the same jeweler. The ring was so wide that soap got under it when I washed my hands, so I would take it off and, while I would be drying my hands, it would inevitably get picked up. I finally went through the last ten years of my marriage to Robert without a ring. Now I put rings in my mouth.

After Robert left, Portia and I found a church in Chicago where they spoke in tongues. The church had benches that were rounded on top and a bit off the floor so your toe didn't get bent as you knelt. There was also a long pad on the bench for your knees. I memorized those benches so the boys could build them when we found a place of our own at home. We very much wanted a chapel for all our black sheep.

When the show was over, I bought a new Packard, and Portia and I drove home nonstop. We made it in fifty-two hours.

A few years later, when I was a guest at the Ambassador East, the Rams were in Chicago preparing for a big game with the Bears. Some of the braver wives came along. Husbands, however, were "incarcerated" at the Ambassador West. God forbid that the wives should be under the same roof as their husbands! The guys weren't allowed to break training with anything even faintly resembling sex, especially after Wednesday night.

Now, there happens to be a tunnel between both Ambassadors for the convenience of guests who want to go from one hotel to the other without having to go outside. Well, I found out about that tunnel, and I was fed up to the teeth

about no fraternization between married couples, so I decided to take advantage of this "convenience." With my fur coat over my pink flannel nightie, I took the elevator down to the tunnel level, strolled westward ho! into the Ambassador West, and took the elevator to Robert's room.

Don Paul, Robert's roommate, opened the door and his eyes practically popped out of his head.

"You're not supposed to be here," he gasped.

"Get out, Don," I practically hissed. "Go east to my room and visit your wife. I'm sleeping here tonight."

We beat the Bears anyway that game.

Following Chicago, *The Outlaw* opened in Atlantic City and eventually went on to Boston, where we were invited to a luncheon with Billy Graham. I thought, "Billy Graham and *The Outlaw?*" The Lord said in so many words that we were all working for Him, but He had many roads to travel, and ours was a different path. I'll bet Billy was glad of that.

After Boston, we went to New York for some publicity, but mainly to see the new Broadway shows and to go to all the small, charming nightclubs, like the Blue Angel, to hear Mabel Mercer, and The Living Room, where Joe Bushkin was playing. Those were the days when New York was beautiful, clean, and chic.

Now that I'd sung in public, I wanted to get Portia started in singing. I left her in New York to eat bread and cheese if necessary, but to sing. We had met three gals from UCLA who were there to seek their fortune and who shared an apartment. Portia stayed with them. Two slept in the bed, one on two chairs pushed together, and one even slept in the bathtub for a short time.

At the Blue Angel I told the owner, a Mr. Jacoby, that he should have Portia in his show. He looked rather amused, said maybe he could hear her some time, and wandered off.

Portia wrote a lovely song, "It's as Simple as That," which Jo Stafford recorded, but that's about all she accomplished that trip. Her time was yet to come.

N I N E

As long as Robert and I were both earning money, I wanted desperately to build our own house. My mom had saved a chunk of land that looked out across the wash, but Robert would have none of it. He wasn't going to get suckered up in that rat's nest of a big family.

I started looking for the right lot. Every time I found something I thought might do, he'd eventually go and look at it and say no. It was a terrible strain on me, but I kept looking. Finally, I found a perfect lot high up on a mountain in Sherman Oaks. The view was breathtaking: The whole valley spread out like a blanket in front of you. At night it was a sea of lights. The mountains across the Valley looked like a movie backdrop. There was not much smog then. I prayed, "Lord, I'm putting out a fleece like Gideon in the Bible. Robert always says no because of his fear of change. If you want us to have this lot, cause him to say yes."

My mother had always told me to feed a man before you confronted him with a decision. But dinner wasn't ready, and I couldn't wait. Robert and I drove up and I explained what I wanted to do.

"Okay, buy it. Now let's go home and eat," he said. I was ecstatic. Praise the Lord! I couldn't sleep for planning.

I went up the mountain every day during the nine months it took to build the house. If I was working, I'd go at night in the dark with Robert, or with Portia, if he was on the road. I had dozens and dozens of Deadar trees planted all around the property line. Junipers lined the driveway and ivy covered the steep slopes from the road up to the pool yard. It was hell trying to water them, but well worth it. Eventually, it was like being at Lake Arrowhead, but only five minutes from town.

I was enjoying my house, swimming at the beach, my friends, and just playing when I got a call from Levis. I was to meet him at Paramount studios. I arrived in a pair of wild African print shorts with a skirt that matched the top, buttoned at the waist only, black sandals, and my hair flying. Robert had bought me a new black Cadillac convertible for Christmas, and I had the top down.

"What are you doing dressed like that?"

"That's the way I was dressed when I got your message to hurry and see you," I said. "So here I am."

"Oh, all right," he said. "He's waiting."

"Who is?"

"Who" was producer Bob Welch. He didn't mind my outfit, and he loved me. Finally, after we'd chatted, I found out I was wanted for a picture called *The Paleface* playing opposite Bob Hope. Wow!

Paramount was the first "family" lot I'd worked on. It was a big studio with all the executive buildings and stars' dressing rooms circling a little park. My dressing room was next to Bob Hope's. I was sent to wardrobe and fitted for period dresses plus a buckskin suit with Indian beads and fringes. Heaven! Also a corset and pantaloons. Ugh!

The script by Frank Tashlin was a delight, and I discovered that my role was like a "female Bob Waterfield"—dry and flat. When the critics later said I was "expressionless," I knew I managed to hit it: a stone face.

Bob Hope was a ball, another Gemini. He's even funnier off screen than on, and everything's relaxed except his chocolate eyes, which never stop darting, never missing a thing. His name for me was "Lumpy."

The director, Norman McLeod, a dear, easygoing man, had his own brand of quiet humor. One early afternoon when the lights had to be changed, which took a bit of time, Bob said, "Well, I think we'll get this tomorrow; there's still time to get in a few holes of golf. I'll see you later." And he walked off the huge sound stage. When he got to the door Norman stomped his foot and said softly, "Bob, you come back here." Bob, of course, was gone. We all broke up laughing and went home.

This picture was a complete package—no lines were changed, one director, always on schedule, and no sweat. What a pleasure! I thought, "So this is how movies are made? I can't believe it." It was fun from morning till night.

I guess one of the best things that happened to me on that picture was meeting Carmen Cabeen. She was to be my stand-in and best friend from then on. She was a fabulous-looking girl with thick dark hair, dark eyes, and Elizabeth Taylor eyebrows and lashes. Her husband, Boyd Cabeen, who looked like David Soul, was Bob Mitchum's stand-in until the studio had to separate them. Together they were "Peck's bad boys." At the moment, Carmen and Boyd were separated. When Portia and I talked about the Lord, Carmen was glued to the conversation—starving, not just hungry. She ended up in Mom's kitchen and Brother Lennon's, and with her baptism a beautiful gift of prophecy.

Right after *The Paleface*, I was put into a film about which the less said the better. I was loaned to Republic Pictures for *Montana Belle*, another western. I played Calamity Jane. I ran a dance hall and George Brent was my lover. As the leader of a gang, I robbed trains and banks by night, with me masquerading as one of the guys. This epic was over so fast that I barely remember making it, which is just as well.

Allen Dwan, an old pro, directed it, and he was a doll. He even let me sing. I figured that since Calamity Jane was posing as a dance hall dame, why not let her sing. I even suggested the song she should do. It was "The Gilded Lily," written by my dear friend Portia Nelson. It was thrilling to hear an honest-to-God orchestra play her song. I sashayed around that barroom floor chucking old grizzled cowboys under their chins while I sang it.

Singing, I discovered, was what I really enjoyed, and luck had it that when Kay Kyser lost his radio show vocalist, Ginny Simms, he substituted with guest singers. I was one of them. What a break! Portia and I knew several of the guys—Barclay Allen on piano, Rock Hillman, my neighbor, on guitar, and Jerry Fielding, the arranger. Kay Kyser sent me to Sandy Oliver because he wanted more vibrato in my voice. I learned from listening to jazz singers on the radio, so I had a straight tone, which I wasn't about to lose. Sandy taught me, among other things, to keep my hands off the microphone.

Sandy, who was a great, wacky dame, made me relax until I was roaring around doing anything that came into my head, no matter how silly, until it became natural to move gracefully while singing. I never considered myself a dancer—and still don't—but I do have a natural sense of rhythm. After working with Sandy Oliver, I was able to move around on a stage without looking like a klutz.

Kay Kyser seemed pleased with the results and signed me to a twelve-week stint on his program. At the same time I recorded a single for Columbia Records and an album of eight torch-type ballads for the same label. The album was called "Let's Put Out the Lights."

Each year at the Press Photographer's ball at Ciro's every star in the industry who could entertain did so and those who couldn't sat in the audience. All the agents attended too. That year they asked me to sing, so Sandy Oliver wrote some special material for me and played piano on stage to give me moral support. I was scared to death—not of singing in public, but of performing before my peers of the industry.

My first song was "Look What They Done to Me." It was a spoof on the way I got into pictures, with lines like, "They put me in a picture that my ma won't let me see—look what they done to me." The next was a minor folk ballad to the tune of "Poor Wayfarin' Stranger":

> Hush, kiddies, go outside and play,
> Ma's just been dropped by MCA.

They say she hasn't got the drag
To bring the payin' customers inside.
Time was when Ma had lots of talent
and, oh, then MCA was gallant.
They toasted her with gold and wine,
It's us, it's you and Jules Stein . . . .

Well, they all screamed, and Hedda Hopper reported the next day that I would be a nightclub entertainer to reckon with in the future. Later, I sang the song for Jules Stein, the powerful head of the Music Corporation of America agency in New York. He wanted me to record it so he could send it to all the MCA people for Christmas, but I never did.

I suppose from Hedda's item plus my recordings, I got an offer for twice the amount of money usually paid to actors to appear at the Latin Quarter in Miami Beach. I talked it over with Robert, and he agreed to go with me—for that kind of money, why not? Barclay Allen, the pianist with Kay Kyser, came to accompany and conduct. It was another challenge for which I wasn't really prepared. But when had I ever really been prepared for the steps I took?

The day we arrived, Robert, Barclay, and I were sitting in the bar of our hotel with the Ritz Brothers when I was asked to award the winner of the beauty contest that was taking place outside on the patio. Harry Ritz said, "Go on, honey, do it. She'll get a kick out of that." So I did. There was an audience of about 200 people out there. The next night I opened at the Latin Quarter. The show was produced by Lou Walters, and he was the only one I had any dealings with; we all worked very hard. I wore a white satin strapless gown, and the show went fine. Not great, but fine.

The following day the club owner, whom I never met, went to New York and the next thing I knew, the papers said I was being sued by the Latin Quarter for appearing in a street dress. Naturally this kind of news was the kiss of death as far as ever working in other clubs was concerned. The owners are constantly aware of how entertainers are doing.

I was being sued for appearing in public (in a street dress) at the beauty contest before the opening at the club. The management had been counting on people flocking to the

club out of curiosity, and to them I'd blown it. There was nothing in my contract like that and Harry Ritz hollered, "What the hell do they expect you to do—hide in the john till you go on stage?"

They lost the suit but the damage was done. As far as I was concerned, I vowed never to work for Lou Walters again, although for years the only offers I ever got for club work were from the Latin Quarter—about one a year.

About a year earlier in 1947 on Christmas Eve Howard phoned just after dinner, apologized for disturbing me, and asked if I could come over to his house. He had to see me about the new contract he was contemplating. My first seven years were ending. Robert and I were still at his mother's at the time, and I promised to be back as soon as I could.

When I walked into Howard's Bel Air house I was appalled. It resembled a mausoleum, all marble and cold, with white sheets covering all the furniture. The frustrated decorator in me itched to get my hands on the place. His Japanese houseman led me up the stairs to a small den where Howard lived. It looked just like his office, except it had a bed.

"What," I yelled, "are you doing in such a horrible house? It's god-awful! Why the hell don't you buy something cozy? Something at least livable?"

He shrugged in a weak sort of defense. "Well, you know, Jane, I don't pay much attention to such things."

"Well, it's about time you started."

After getting that out of my system, we settled down and started talking about the new contract conditions. He proposed certain ones and I counterproposed; he had questions and I had some. This went on until I got the vague feeling that we were getting nowhere. It was as though he didn't want me to leave.

When it got to be ten o'clock, I decided it was time to go home. After all, it was Christmas Eve and my husband and mother-in-law were waiting for me. Howard got the message and said good night at my car and warned me to be careful driving home.

It wasn't until some time later that I discovered what that evening was all about. It was Howard's birthday and he didn't want to spend it alone, yet he couldn't let me know his need. If he had, I would have baked him a cake or at least have hugged him. But if I did, he would have died of embarrassment. Anyway, I was his for another seven years.

The following year when Robert was on the road with the Rams and I was home alone, Howard phoned.

"I moved," he said. "I got out of that house you hated so much. Would you like to see the new one?"

I was dying to see his new house. He was seeing Ava Gardner then and told me that they were going out to dinner along with Johnny Myers, Faye Emerson, Elliott Roosevelt, and a wealthy Brazilian, George Guinle, who wanted to meet me. After dinner, the plan was for all of us to troop up to the new house and be given the grand tour.

After dinner we went back to the new house and it was really lovely—Old English and as warm and cozy as the other was cold and stark.

"Well, this looks like someone lives here!" I exclaimed. Howard seemed pleased that I was pleased.

Howard, Johnny Myers, his right-hand man, and Ava wound up at the bar after the tour of the house, while I sat in the living room with Faye, Elliott, and the Brazilian zillionaire. After an hour or so, Ava, who was always full of energy, decided she wanted to go dancing. Howard didn't want to go and he asked Johnny to take her, the Brazilian, and me while he stayed home with the Roosevelts. I was enjoying my night out, so off we went to the Mocambo, where we danced until closing time. We were still there when the band went home, because Johnny and Ava wanted to sit around some more. I went out and phoned Howard, who wanted to know when we were coming back. The others had left and he sounded sad.

"We're coming back," I told him. After all, Ava was his girl and there he was sitting home alone. I felt it wasn't fair. So back we went and spent some more time drinking and talking until it was getting light outside.

I thought it was time we broke it up, and Howard said he would drive Ava home. I suggested that I go home with

her and pick up my car the next day. I didn't particularly relish the idea of driving back that late and then spending all the next day alone. But Howard objected, loudly.

"No, no, no," he said suddenly. "You won't get any sleep if you stay at Ava's. You two will talk all night." I laughed to myself. He sure didn't want Ava and me comparing notes.

"And I don't want you driving home alone at this hour. It's not safe. And you've all been drinking," he continued. "You can stay here. You'll have the middle bedroom."

"Well, why not?" I thought. I was dead tired and bed was all I was interested in. I certainly had nothing to worry about. Howard was totally convinced that if I drove home I would crash the car and get myself killed. He was always worried about people: If we crossed the street alone we were sure to get hit by a car, or if we went skiing we'd break a leg. He worried like a mother hen. I didn't have the heart to upset him.

Howard took me upstairs to a guest room and told me to be sure to lock the door. He left with Ava, and I locked my door and climbed into bed. Before I could count to ten, I was fast asleep.

I don't know how long I slept—it could have been minutes or it could have been an hour—but suddenly I was jolted awake by a loud pounding on the door. I sat up, flipped on a light, and said sleepily, "Who's there?" It was Johnny Myers. I thought, "Oh, God, Howard's wrecked his car or got hit while crossing the street or broken his leg skiing." I leaped out of bed and opened the door. Johnny came roaring in, drunk as a skunk, and proceeded to chase me around the room.

I screamed at him, "What the hell's the matter with you? Get out of here, you big idiot!" I couldn't believe what was happening. Johnny had no more eyes for me than he would for a fat lizard. But he kept coming after me like a madman. I kept throwing things at him, shouting at him all the time to get out. Suddenly Howard was in the room.

"What's going on? Get out, Johnny," he said sharply. And Johnny went.

"Come on, Jane," he said. "I think you'll be better off in my room. He won't bother you there." Howard took me down the corridor to the master bedroom, which was large and beautiful with a pair of wide beds in it. "Now, you can have that one," he pointed, "and I'll sleep in the other. That way I'll be here in case anyone else gets any ideas."

Well, I decided, what the hell. I was safe with Howard. I sure didn't feel like a replay of that scene with Johnny, nor did I feel like getting dressed and driving home, so I climbed into the bed he'd chosen for me and switched off the lights.

As I was falling asleep, I heard a funny noise. I sat up. It was Howard standing by the bed. "What's the matter with you?" I asked.

"I'm freezing," he whined. "I must have caught a chill driving Ava home. Can I get in with you?" he asked in a small boy's voice. I reached out and touched his hand. It was like an ice cube. I was mad.

"Okay," I snapped. "Get in. But no funny business. Remember, Howard, I'm married, I'm sleepy, and I've already been disturbed twice."

I pulled the cover up to my chin and turned over. He curled up behind me. I was nearly asleep again when I felt his hand slide around my waist. I bolted upright.

"All right, Howard, that's it. Get out!"

He drew his arm away as though he had touched a hot stove.

"All right," he muttered, "I'll go. But let me get out when I decide. I don't like people telling me what to do. I won't touch you again. I promise."

I thought, "Wow, you've just given your whole act away." What a funny, stubborn man. That was Howard. He'd give in, but only on his terms. I knew he always kept his promises, so I turned over and went to sleep. The next thing I knew it was noon and he was gone. I never felt him leave the bed.

The next day it dawned on me that the whole act was set up with Johnny so Howard could come to my rescue, thereby getting me into his bedroom under proper pretenses. If I hadn't been so sleepy, I would have remembered Billy the Kid in *The Outlaw* and Rio climbing in the bed to warm him up. What a laugh! Oh, well, you can't hang a man for trying. As I said earlier, stand up to Howard and say, "Boo!" and he'd run—but at his speed.

I often hollered at Howard, and I think that in a funny kind of way I scared him. Jim Bacon, the columnist on the _Los Angeles Herald Examiner,_ told me Howard had once confided to him, "That woman terrified me. And I wasn't going to fool around with a married woman, especially with one married to Robert Waterfield. I knew that if I didn't run from her, she'd end up owning the studio." That's a laugh! Imagine, that poor, darling man afraid of me! Sorry, folks, another legend shot down.

T E N

The day finally came when Robert and I could move into the house. It was really a fabulous house, especially for two kids aged twenty-seven and twenty-eight. It cost $75,000 in 1948, and Robert was scared to death. He once had a car repossessed, and that broke him of over-reaching his grasp. But with my never-ending optimism I argued, "Look, if I was just a housewife, you would have to pay all the bills, so we'll pay for the house with my money and you pay the bills. My dream house is all I want." Actually, it was always "our" money, and Robert took charge of it all. Like mother, like daughter again. My mother used to brag that she didn't know how much money my father made. She had an allowance and that was that. So it was in our house too. Robert bought me the nicest clothes I had. I hated shopping. Usually I had no money in my purse, just a checkbook.

We couldn't furnish the house completely at first. That took years, but with borrowed furniture, it was time to move in. James Garner and his dad laid the undercarpeting, as he was cute enough to remind me some years later. We lived with that undercarpet for some time.

Robert got more moody as moving day arrived. He hated above all things to change. Here I was dragging him up to a strange house to sleep in a strange bed. Our friends arrived

to ease him into a housewarming. When he finally got used to it, he didn't ever want to leave.

A few weeks later was Grandma and Grandpa Jacobi's fiftieth wedding anniversary. We invited all the Jacobis and Stevensons who were living then, and they came from all over. There were the Henrys and Aunt Ruth Coe and the Russells and Waterfields all together. I could hardly believe it.

Night was my favorite time in that house. The lights below had an almost holy effect and gave one a marvelous sense of perspective. It put everything trivial away. Every night for nineteen years, after everyone was asleep I spent some time sitting there talking to the Lord and listening.

The meetings in Mom's kitchen were getting too crowded for words. I decided we had to have a place of our own. I still remembered the prayer benches from Chicago, and I envisioned a very informal building with trees around it. We started looking all over the Valley but found nothing we could afford. Land prices were skyrocketing. Finally we pulled into the property, feeling depressed. Mom came out and asked us what was the matter.

"We want our own chapel, but there's no land we can afford," we growled at her.

"Oh, maybe that's what the Lord is saving it for," she said.

"What?"

"That piece of land that you and Robert didn't want. I've tried to build a place for missionaries, but the building department won't allow a septic tank down in the wash."

"Show me the boundary line," I said, and we all piled out.

It was perfect, with eucalyptus trees all around. We would put the kitchen and baths on the high ground and the chapel proper down below. Garden steps would tie it all together.

The boys started building and the girls helped. Portia and I put all the tarpaper on the roof. It was "rustic modern" and the benches formed a large U around the wooden cross pulpit. We sat on the benches during Bible study and then turned around to pray. We had our own chapel, built out of tithe money. Nobody dressed up—it was shorts in the summer and jeans in the winter. Everybody got their baptism and hundreds of prayers were answered. Chapel was on Friday night so people could go to their own church or synagogue on Saturday or Sunday.

We always had Passover every year and followed it with Holy Communion. We were an oddball bunch, but the Lord was there, and I know most of the people who came had never been to church, or at least not since they were children. But they could handle this informality, and the Lord became their best buddy.

One very cute thing the Lord told us was that He was making a tapestry. We all represent threads of different colors and each of us attract people of the same color. Now it may look like a mess to us, all knots and twists, but we see only the wrong side of the tapestry. When He turns it around, we'll see that it is glorious.

My thread must be equal parts of shocking pink and orange, but I sure know I draw my own kind and, after all, that's all I'm supposed to do.

Before Howard bought RKO I was loaned to that studio to team up with Frank Sinatra and Groucho Marx in a thing called *Double Dynamite*. Having proven to Howard that I could sing, I was allowed to do so, but this script, too, was a big nothing. Frank played a sweet young guy and I played a sweeter young girl and Groucho played Groucho. All in all, it was sickening. Everyone was carefully polite to everyone else, and no one got to know anyone. Not many laughs on that set. One reason could have been that Sinatra was going through a bad spell in his career (this was prior to *From Here to Eternity*). He and Ava Gardner had just started going together, and it was pretty difficult for them. Frank and I sang together though, and to balance our voices he stood two feet away from the mike and I had to crawl in it. What a voice that man has!

It was just another picture done besides my being a wife, and it was over soon and forgotten. Eventually, Howard held up the release of both *Montana Belle* and *Double Dynamite* until much later. He didn't like them either. Then it was back to my beautiful dream house, where I was perfectly content to sleep late.

Robert and I had a perfect arrangement: He did the cooking and I did the dishes. I sat on the sink while he prepared the food and we'd talk over what went on with the Rams and at the studio over cocktails.

Louis Hayward introduced Portia and me to Nick Arden, who always wanted a small club with a piano bar. There were none at the time that any of us had ever seen. Portia and I always wanted a place, too, so Nick said if I would decorate it and Portia would sing and play for herself, he'd open one. We found a small place on Ventura Boulevard in Sherman Oaks with a patio in the front and a fireplace. Nick lived in the back and ran it.

The gang all came and we invited everyone we knew who liked music. The place took off like a rocket and its regulars were Johnny Mercer, Blake Edwards, Richard Quine, David Rose, Margaret Whiting, and Carmen Dragon. Everyone in the music business dropped in, because there was nothing like it. Different people sang or played, like the Mary Kaye Trio, Bobby Troup, and the King Sisters. Walter Gross played "Tenderly" so often Nick finally asked him to work there. Walter made Portia stand up and sing. She was fabulous. Even Robert enjoyed it, so you know it had to be good. But Portia wouldn't sing her own songs, which was maddening. She felt that would be pushy. She's one of the best songwriters I've ever known—both music and lyrics. This went on for two years, during 1948 and 1949. In 1950, she went back to New York to perform at the Blue Angel, and I got to tell Mr. Jacoby, "I told you so," once a year for nine years. She broke the record there for repeat appearances.

She also appeared at the Upstairs at the Downstairs for Julius Monk and many other chic clubs. Finally she came back to sing at John Walsh's club on the Sunset Strip. We could all see her now and not have to try to get to New York. It was heaven.

Eventually she played Sister Bertha in *The Sound of Music*. She's also written musical skits for singers such as Lena Horne, Julie Andrews, Debbie Reynolds, and Carol Burnett. My friend Portia is a most talented girl.

I don't remember when I first met Adrian Booth, who was married to David Brian. She had done gobs of pictures and, of course, David was a star. He was Joan Crawford's leading man in *Flamingo Road*.

I remember one night Adrian and I went to hear Portia at John Walsh's club. Robert was off on a football trip, so I had invited them for dinner. Somehow the subject turned to religion. They were adamant that religion was total hogwash, but I couldn't get them off the subject. I really never, and I mean never, preached to people, but this night I just tried to answer some of their arguments and then change the subject. It was impossible.

A few afternoons later, when Adrian was at the house, I told her I had to leave about seven. She wanted to know where I was going and she kept insisting until I finally told her it was chapel and that I didn't think she would be interested. But nothing could stop her; she was going with me.

Adrian was enthralled with Mother and the informality of the whole thing. It seems that when she was a kid their minister called up all the young people who were graduating to ask them what they wanted to do with their lives. Some wanted to be ministers, doctors, lawyers, and housewives, but Adrian said she wanted to be an actress. Well that did it. She was put out of the church in front of the whole congregation.

The humiliation and disapproval she experienced even with her mother could only have one of two outcomes: utter defeat or utter defiance. Adrian was a very strong girl, which is the only kind I attract, and she said to hell with them all and proceeded with her career.

When she heard about the love of God and how He uses you wherever you are if you let Him, she thought it was too good to be true. She started reading her Bible and wanted

her baptism immediately. I warned her to go softly with David, but she'd only nod her head and go right ahead talking to everyone about Jesus.

When she got home, on the night of her baptism, she washed her hair and was sitting under the hair dryer babbling away out loud in tongues. David came in and thought she'd gone around the bend. Well, instead of getting angry, he got curious, and the upshot of it was that they both came to chapel and became Geraldine Russell's sixth and seventh children. Adrian had become a preacher lady, if you please, and David gives the lessons once a month.

The boys were building spec houses that I decorated. Then, suddenly, Tom and Ken were asked to go back to Denver and Albuquerque to build a tract of houses. Tom was desolate at the thought of leaving home. When we prayed about it, the Lord said something we've never forgotten. It's oh so true. He said,

What is separation?

If a man goes to the corner for a loaf of bread—do you sit down to weep?

Is he, nevertheless, out of sight or gone, as you put it?

If one of you is in another state or another country, are you not closer to each other than you are to your next door neighbor whom you see every day?

Know you not that My children are bound together by My love?

Indeed, if one of you is in heaven and the other on earth, are you still not My children—under My roof?

What is separation?

One thing we had at chapel was a blackboard. On it were written prayer requests, and as they were answered, they were erased. The board was constantly changing, believe me. Most were personal requests from the gang in the chapel, but sometimes it would be for a disaster area or for a famous person who was in trouble.

Well, when Judy Garland tried to do herself in and was released from MGM, her name went on the blackboard. When we prayed, the Lord said I was to go and give her a message but that there would be a man who would interfere with my seeing her. I was stunned and felt like a jackass. I'd met Judy only once, and then very casually, but I didn't dare not go.

I knew her manager, Carlton Alsop, whom I adored, so, without telling him why, I dropped by and wheedled Judy's address from him. Then, with great trepidation, I went to her house and rang the bell. Vincente Minnelli, the talented director she was married to at the time, came to the door and informed me Judy was not to see anyone. I thought, "Lord, You're too much. You said a man would stop me." I gave him my phone number and said if she could call me, I had a message for her, figuring that would be the end of that.

But that afternoon the phone rang and it was Judy. I told her about the blackboard and chapel and that the Lord had told me to say this to her:

> The Lord is my shepherd; I shall not want.
> He MAKETH me to lie down in green pastures.
> *HE* RESTORETH my soul.

She gave a little gasp, mumbled thank you, and hung up.

It's well known now that Judy went east into a clinic for many months and that later she made a triumphant comeback. I never knew what effect my call had on her until several years later. She called me about a young friend of hers who was in trouble. She had asked for help and if we could pray. So, I guess Judy didn't think we were altogether nuts.

The Rams were permanently on the blackboard. I remember one football season Robert became ill and was running a fever of 101 just before a championship game. We prayed really hard for him to get well. Robert always let me go my own way as far as my beliefs were concerned. He wasn't interested for himself, and I never insisted he come to

chapel or even discussed it with him. But this time we felt that something stronger and closer to home was called for. The Lord had the answer.

On the morning of the game, Robert insisted on playing. "Deacon" Dan Towler, who was studying for the ministry, asked the team to pray for the first time right down there on the field. Well, they did. In the pregame huddle, just before the whistle Dan gave a prayer, and Robert, raging fever and all, turned in one of his best games and they won the championship in the final seconds. They continued the pregame prayer from then on.

And so, the Lord finally broke into pro football.

E L E V E N

My stand-in, Carmen, had told me a lot about Robert Mitchum and his escapades with her off-and-on-again husband Boyd. I was somewhat prepared for his shocking side, but I wasn't prepared for his intellectual, gentle, caring side.

Ever since Howard had bought RKO, both Mitch and I knew it was just a matter of time until we would be working together. His secretary, or I should say "right arm," Reva Fredricks, called me so that we could talk about scripts and so on. Mitch wanted very much to do something good, and he was afraid we weren't going to get the chance because there really wasn't anyone very talented running the studio. They were businessmen, not men of vision. Howard was busy with airplanes and I never saw him at RKO. We'd get phone calls about clothes and things, but he wasn't really running the studio like Jack Warner or L. B. Mayer of MGM.

But Edith Lynch, a good-looking lady who was in publicity at RKO, sort of saw him:

> When Howard moved his operations to RKO, he was given something that resembled an office instead of that converted storeroom he'd been using. The lock on the door was the kind with a button on the knob that had

to be pushed if you didn't want to be locked out after closing it. Of course, Howard being Howard, rarely remembered to do this, and was constantly locking himself out of his office. Luckily, however, there was a connecting door from my office to his. Well, not exactly a door, it was more like an over-sized mouse hole that once might have been for a safe.

The routine was this: Howard would lock himself out. He would then enter my office as casually as possible, hope I didn't notice him, crouch as low as his over six-foot frame would allow and slip through that mouse hole to his own inner sanctum. All during this, I would keep my eyes glued to whatever paper was lying on my desk so that I would appear so totally absorbed in my work that I had no idea that this tall figure had walked into my office and disappeared through a tiny doorway in a peculiar frog-like crouch. I wouldn't dream of looking up and thereby embarrass him. If he wanted to be invisible, then he was invisible.

Mitch was right. When we got the script for _His Kind of Woman_, it was just another man meets woman story with a little intrigue thrown in. It was a shame, because that man was a good actor and deserved better. He could memorize pages in just minutes. John Farrow, the director, a bright man who had an evil sense of humor, and Vincent Price, a brighter man, with a delicious sense of humor, made up the group.

An entire house and swimming pool were built on one of the big sound stages. I don't remember too much about the picture, but the people are with me yet. I fell in love with both Vinnie and Mitch. I learned to love several other people too. Up to that time I had a different makeup man, hairdresser, wardrobe girl, and cameraman on each picture. Only Carmen had gone from picture to picture with me. By this time, I had enough experience to know excellent from ordinary, and within one or two pictures I gathered the best crew one could have. They were all under contract and were always available for me. When I wasn't working, they worked at RKO.

Stephanie McGraw, hair stylist.

Stephie was an artist with brush and oils. She knew what was right for my face and dreamed up new things for each picture. She was a darling blonde with a disposition for the angels.

Mary Tate, wardrobe

Mare didn't pick and poke. She grabbed a zipper and zipped it. She knew her business and took guff from no one. A warm, great gal.

Shotgun Britton, makeup

I don't know how to describe Shot in less than ten pages. He was a mad Texan who got his name, no doubt, from his rapid unintelligible double talk. He dressed wildly in purple pants, a yellow shirt, a checked golf hat, and any color of shoes. He was a golfer and knew all the pros. People stood, stared, and gaped when he passed by. Everyone needed an interpretation to understand what he said. "Madam, he's had some o' them 'don't look now' pills and he's goofier than a pregnant Jenny in a traffic jam" meant that someone was very nervous. He had already worked for Mitch, so Mitch and Reva understood him.

Harry Wild, cameraman

Harry was a sweet little man who'd had many a call from "the boss" as to how to photograph yours truly. I never worried about a single angle—he was superb. Shot called him "the hat," for he was never without one.

I had a star dressing room on the lot that consisted of a sitting room, a kitchen, plus a dressing room and bath. I decorated it in mauve, silver, and pink. I also remembered the large square dressing room I'd seen Howard in at Goldwyn's and asked for it. The usual dressing rooms on the set were small and rather drab. When it arrived, it was taken to the art department and painted pale pink. The couch was covered in white and white carpet was

laid. I hung up pictures of my brothers and their families, got a coffee table and pretty ash trays, and had a very nice place in which to spend all the hours one spends between takes. Today, set dressing rooms have hi-fis, televisions, and private johns, but in those days, I was livin'.

I had a system worked out that saved me an hour and a half each morning. Most gals had to be in makeup between 6:30 and 7:00 A.M. I got up at 7:30 and arrived at 8:00 in jeans and a scarf. Stephie rolled my hair barely damp in my own dressing room. Shot brought tea and yogurt and set out the makeup while I made myself up under his watchful eye. Mary took wardrobe to the set, and I was in and out in one hour. I was always on the set at nine. I usually did a rehearsal in my robe, got dressed while they lit, and shot it. I'd had plenty of experience with those "too early" hours, where it was hurry up and wait. I'm extremely impatient! I went to bed at 10:30 P.M. and got my nine hours' sleep. If I didn't, everybody suffered.

Publicity was the same. I was getting wise. After I had frightened off a dozen or more publicity men, Perry Lieber, a Gemini, assigned Edith Lynch to me for all publicity. She said, "Perry, you're throwing me to the wolves." But she was a Gemini too, as quick as I, and became the last member of the group. Lots of stars want to know all about a publicity story or picture assignment at least the week before; I didn't give a damn. "Just don't bug me."

Edith:

> Howard Hughes demanded perfection from all who worked for him. We were required to send all of Jane's photo prints from un-retouched negatives to him for approval; guidelines were set for the type of interviews that could be done and written later; all publicity and advertising—all personal appearances—had to be first approved by him. Hughes had discovered Jane and guided her career. He had engineered the extraordinary publicity campaign for her famous first film, *The Outlaw*, made in 1940. The campaign was provocative and continuous and when Jane arrived at RKO ten years later

after Hughes bought the studio, we had a bonanza of international fame who seemed to loathe the very publicity that helped boost her there. She didn't like the label they'd given her.

The fun began. She was wary, but our staff managed to corral this new addition to the stable of stars—and bless us all, we became fast friends. She flexed her muscles once in a while, but was smart enough to realize the need for publicity to sell the motion pictures.

She's right. For instance, I'd like a classy portrait on the jacket of this book, but my publishers convinced me that this thing in the haystack is the J.R. people want to read about. Hope they're right. How disgusting!

Edith used to have her still photographer set up on the set and would grab me on my way to or from the camera. I stood in place, smiled, and walked. Later, if there was a story, she got it while I was in my robe and they were lighting for the next take. I didn't like lunch interviews because that was my time to relax, goof off, or learn the dialogue for the afternoon shot. With a crew like that, I was left free to think, feel, and remember lines.

The assistant director took a nod from Harry Wild five minutes before they were ready. I got into my costume and walked out the door on the button. I can't stand to keep anyone waiting and don't like to wait myself.

Fittings were another time-consuming effort. Another Gemini, Michael Woulfe, was an extremely talented designer who was on everything at RKO. I had learned what looked best on me, and he went from there. No belts, narrow skirts, etc. I'm short waisted, with legs to my armpits, so in a normal dress with gathers at the waist I look like a sack of potatoes tied in the middle.

I asked for the same fitter and always wanted a very rough first fitting. They usually had to have everything looking finished, but to me that was a horrible waste of time. I had imagination enough to see the finished product, so baste and pin on me the first time. It took a bit of doing, but they finally realized I meant it and they did it. They had a dummy figure, too, that got borrowed when I went to other studios and which saved hours of fitting time.

I absolutely adored my crew.

Mitch and I had barely finished *His Kind of Woman* when we started shooting *Macao*. Mitch said on the set the first day, "Honey, if it wasn't for you. . . ." The script was anything but good. Josef von Sternberg began as the director. He had guided Marlene Dietrich's career in the early years, but for 1950 he was definitely dated. He also was not very nice to the crew and didn't care for our happy family atmosphere. He used to pull Mitch aside and say, "Now we have to bolster this beautiful girl with no talent." Mitch would stop him cold. Von Sternberg insisted that there was to be no eating on the set, so Mitch brought a picnic basket and spread it out. Reva always appeared around four o'clock with his pitcher of lemonade made with vodka. It was all fairly unpleasant for von Sternberg, but he didn't have a chance.

Nick Ray was finally put on the picture as director. With some added scenes in the beginning and a new ending, which he and Mitch wrote, it came together. I was sick of being, as Mitch said, "the girl in the piece," and by now I really knew what he meant by doing something good.

Carmen's sister, Meg, worked in the publicity department, which Perry Lieber headed. He probably was one of the few people who was in constant touch with Howard, probably at 3 A.M., but Perry never complained. He loved "the boss" dearly and would do anything for him, as would all the old guard who had been with him for years.

Perry, a pixie type of guy, was Mr. Amiable himself. He was a fanny pincher who loved his booze in those days, but he never got mean, even after all the writers and newsmen had gone home. Meg used to take him home to his ever-loving wife now and then, and several times, when "the boss" called during the day, she knew the number of a famous madam's where he might be found playing cards. But for public relations, you couldn't touch Perry Lieber. Everyone adored him.

In the beginning, when he wanted me to go out of town on personal appearances, I'd bargain with him, saying that I would go if he would pick up the tab on some weird costume jewelry I'd pick out. I probably could have gotten the real thing, but I never believed diamonds were a girl's best friend. I was afraid of losing it or having someone steal it. Personally, I treasure land a good deal more.

Mitch's dressing room was down the street, and Reva had it stocked with food and booze at all times. That became the meeting place for actors and the latest goings-on around our little studio. Vic Mature, Janet Leigh, Jean Simmons, and Vincent Price all had several pictures on the lot, and they came and went, but for Mitch, Robert Ryan, and myself this was home.

I didn't stay after work often, but I remember one Saturday we quit early and called Vinnie to come back to the studio. We got him loaded and he was late for dinner. His wife Mary was mad as hell at us, but we had laughed ourselves silly.

Often I had no money on me, so I'd borrow five dollars from "the hat." About three days later he'd say, "Okay, kid, where's my dough?" I was delighted, because I hated owing money. I could never remember who owed me or how much.

One smartass broad came out from New York to make a name for herself as a gossip columnist writing for the fan magazines. She would talk to one star about their co-star and totally fabricate a lot of rotten things that were then printed. Then she'd go to the co-star, who was furious, to get quotes. It started some lifelong hates around town. She tried this on Mitch and me. First me. When his friends started saying, "About that Jane Russell, I thought she was your friend," he knew it was garbage and that I loved him dearly. So when she took him to lunch, he let go with such awful dialogue on every subject in the world that it was unprintable. She went away with glazed eyes, never to be heard from in Hollywood again. That man's command of the English language on any level is astounding. He used to say I was the most

inarticulate girl he'd ever known, and he was right. But he always understood me.

When visitors were around the set, he'd do things deliberately to shock them, like running his tongue up my bare back (I invariably had on a strapless dress) or shout something naughty. But when he saw someone being abused or mistreated, he very quickly put a stop to it.

There was a scandal sheet out at this time called *Rave Magazine*, and everyone in the industry was fair game. Someone eventually had to pick on old Jane, her crew, and her friends. It was really foul and some folks thought I ought to sue. At chapel we prayed about it, and Jerry Peters' mother had a vision while we were praying that was followed by a message.

Vision
There was a lake full of fish, and lots of fishermen. One man who had no license saw a great big fish, speared it, and dragged it up on shore. When it didn't die, for it was filled with living water, he was amazed. He looked for the wound he had inflicted, but there was none. Not a sign of a wound. Then the lake rose up and the waves swept him into it.

Message
Pray for the man who wrote it, for he stands on the brink of oblivion. You are in Me and can draw on My love and strength and faith, but he has nothing but his hate. Remember, hate and love are very close, and only fear, loneliness, and frustration cause hate to exist instead of love. I care not what the world thinks of you. I care only what you think of Me. Worry not for your reputation. "Vengeance is Mine," said the Lord. "I will repay."

Shortly after, the magazine was closed down by the courts. If I could only remember at all times that vengeance is His. Great-aunt Jane used to say, "I hate them with a hatred that's refreshing." But forgiving and letting the Lord handle it is so much better for one's health.

With five pictures in release or in production, this was my busiest year, with hardly a minute free to do anything other than work. Robert wasn't doing so badly either. In 1950 he'd won another Most Valuable Player award and continued being the leading Ram and the nation's number one quarterback. His spectacular playing was one of the reasons the Rams won the National Championship. Because he spent so much of the time on the road, our time together was very precious. I was always at the studio, and he was always off somewhere playing football.

I missed him terribly. Any chance I could get to see him I grabbed. So when I was in New York on a publicity junket, I stopped off in Chicago, where the Rams were playing, to surprise him.

Well . . . the surprise was on me. I was about to knock on the door of his hotel room when I heard female laughter. My hand froze. A second later I heard Robert's voice. I stood there motionless as a statue. I said, "Dear Lord, what do I do?" What should I do? What would be the smart thing?

Then all at once I remembered my great-aunt Bella, darling Aunt Bella who, when her husband was a naval officer, had once taken a cruise ship halfway around the world to surprise him at his station. When she arrived at the port, she spotted him on the dock in the waiting crowd. She couldn't believe her eyes when she saw a blonde woman dash down the gangplank and run straight into the arms of her husband. Well, my funny great-aunt just turned around, marched right back to her stateroom, and returned home. But she did stop writing, and he panicked. He finally got special leave to come home to be sure she was there. She never did tell him what she'd seen, not in all the years that remained in their happy marriage.

So, I turned around and did an "Aunt Bella." All the way home I kept praying that I was doing the right thing. I wonder if it would have worked out differently if I had kicked the door down. I probably would have today, but then I guess I had more sense. I just kept on praying, and when Robert came home I said I had missed him, and all was forgotten. The Lord says, "He will throw our sins in the sea of God's forgetfulness to be remembered no more." Mother used to say, "If you've truly forgiven, you've forgotten." I had totally forgotten this incident until a friend reminded me, I guess, just so I could tell the story. There are a lot of things I haven't forgotten, however, that I still pray about and really must forgive.

I started work on yet another of those forgettable epics. Vincent played my husband in *The Las Vegas Story* and Vic Mature was my old love. Hoagy Carmichael was the piano man who always played "our song." Vic was another "Peck's bad boy" who was really a softie inside. Females were either ladies or tramps to him, and I guess with good reason. I got to sing a couple of numbers in this picture, so I was satisfied.

I managed to get Vinnie and Robert together one day during the shooting and I said we were going to have a party. Vinnie said, "You mean he's going to be the host," and roared with laughter. Robert was always so quiet and stone faced that Vinnie couldn't resist. That's all Robert needed. Out came his nasty humor, and they were friends from then on. Vincent and Mary, Dorothy and Mitch, and later Pat and Richard Egan were about the only people in the business whom Robert and I saw, and then usually in each others' homes.

Mitch and Dorothy had a comfortable, sprawling home in Mandville Canyon. Vincent and Mary had a museum in Benedict Canyon. When that wouldn't hold everything they collected, they had to buy a huge old Spanish house in Beverly Glen Canyon. There were shelves everywhere to hold pre-Colombian art and gold leaf church artifacts from Mexico. And, of course, paintings everywhere. They were both marvelous cooks and it was a joy to visit them and see what had been done since I had been there last.

I'm afraid I am a born romantic. I never had any doubt that I could fulfill any man's dream if I chose to. My mother had given me the key: tender, loving care. And if she could make my grumpy, nervous father happy, then I could do the same. I've been in love only a few times in my life, but I've had crushes galore.

Vincent Price was never a crush. He was my Gemini brother. I loved his nasty humor and his wit and intelligence. Sometimes when I was in a wistful mood, listening to a symphony by a melancholy Russian or Pole, I'd write Vincent a letter. He knew me pretty well and, concerning my crushes, he wrote,

> Little sister, little sister! loves, like
> the unpinched envy buds
> Wither and dry; best for the big bud,
> murder the others,
> Then when the late sun wrenches it
> open, death is forgotten,
> There is the monster eager and dull,
> but the big bud, glorious!
> And they bottle the stench and write
> initials in hearts
> And drop they the anchor of living
> in a semi-safe bay.
> Semi-safe say I, for the flirt that's
> within you suffers but says:
>
> "Big and independent
> resplendent in love,
> I would not wager a dime
> on the time I've wasted
> Pretending and mending
> my heart for a nickel."

Isn't that wonderful! And he was so right.

When *The Las Vegas Story* came out, it was to open in Vegas, naturally. A parade and personal appearances were planned at the theater. The night before, Robert, Bob Kelly (sports announcer), Hamp Pool (Ram coach), Ozzie Lang (Schlitz beer representative), John Sanders (Ram coach), Don Paul (Ram center), and their wives, all drove up. I'd been working a lot and really missed Robert, but he wasn't content to just be with me. He kept looking for Kelly. I was feeling sorry for myself. We were all drinking a lot, and at dinner he said something nasty and I ran my fork down his face, leaving four little red lines. He didn't do anything, but tears of humiliation formed in his eyes. Everyone watched in silence. When we got home he went to the mirror and looked at his face. I came up behind him and said, "Honey, I'm so sorry." He just turned and slapped me. I fell back, but stupid me, I didn't stay there. I was mad as hell. He had never slapped me before. I said, "Oh, I'm sure you can hit harder than that," so he did. I got up as many times as I could, and finally, when the room was spinning, I said, "You poor fool, you don't have any idea what you've just done." He left without a word.

In the morning the left side of my face looked like a purple cantaloupe. I called Kelly's room and when Robert answered, I said he'd better come over. He just stood in the door, looked at me, then said, "Well, you'd better stay here. You can get a divorce in ten weeks in this state," and left.

I called Edith, who called Perry and a doctor. There was never a thought in their minds of canceling. I rode in the parade and stood on stage with a melon face. A story was given out about my getting hit by a car door from the terrible windstorm the night before. Vinnie was very sweet during the parade, but on the plane on the way home with all the newsmen, he hollered, "Come on with that wind story, we all know Waterfield hit you." Big laugh.

I called Robert to meet the plane and he did. We both had dark glasses on. When we got home he took my face in his hands and stared. He couldn't believe what he'd done. He said, "Honey, I'm so sorry I could die. I'll never hit you again as long as I live." He felt terrible. I had decided it was because we were drinking. If we hadn't both been loaded, it would never have happened. The Lord was trying to tell me something, so I quit for two and a half years. But it got very boring being the only sober person in the crowd, so eventually I went off the wagon.

T W E L V E

Robert and I had been married almost eight years and still had no children. This was unthinkable as far as I was concerned. Robert and I went to a doctor and the prognosis was no children for the two of us together. I was disappointed, but not daunted. I'd come from a large family; Ken and Lois already had three kids, Pamela and Jamie were on their second, and Wally and Mary Lou and Tom and Nola were on their first. Pregnant Nola would have to go to Denver or to Albuquerque to have her baby. We'd adopt, I decided. But there was a waiting list of no less than two years at any agency, and I didn't want to wait. I would be thirty years old the following June and that was plenty old to start a family.

I went to the Lord in earnest and prayed night and day. "Lord, You said You'd give us the desires of our heart, and if You've placed this strong desire in my heart, You surely must have an answer." As I was wailing at the altar one night, Brother Lennon walked up to me, placed his hand on my shoulder, and got a message in tongues and the interpretation. The Lord said He had a gift for me as surely as I would pull the ribbon and lift the lid of a box to see what was inside. I drove home at peace for the first time in weeks. The Lord had a baby for me. I didn't know how, but I knew He did.

The red carpet came to the fore again. When I did an interview with a woman from New York, I happened to mention that we wanted to adopt. Next month I received a letter from a grandmother to be saying her daughter would have a baby up for adoption some time in June and if I was interested, I was to call a Dr. Small out of state. I was afraid Robert wouldn't want to adopt, so I prayed again. "Lord, You made Gideon's fleece stay wet when the ground all around was dry and vice versa, so if this baby is ours, You make Robert say okay." When I read Robert the letter, he mumbled a bit but finally said, "Do whatever you want." That's all I needed. I said, "Praise the Lord," and went to the phone. When a baby is on the way, the natural parents always wonder what he or she will be like. But adopting parents are even more anxious. The waiting is awful.

I got the bedroom next to ours all ready. Mom had given me the white wicker cradle my father and my brothers and I had been in. I lined it in pink and got a white wicker rocker and a pink string rug to match. The walls in that room were already dark blue and the floor was dark blue rubber. I had known it was to be a child's room all along.

Keeping busy is the best possible way to take up time while waiting, and luckily I was kept busy. Frank Tashlin, who had written *The Paleface,* came up with a sequel called *Son of Paleface,* which he was going to direct. Frank was a big, fuzzy bear of a man with a delicious sense of humor, but underneath he was a serious, moody guy. Carmen and I became very close to him and even got him to come with us to chapel. Eventually he brought our musical director, Lyn Murray, along, who ended up writing a gospel chorus called "I'm Really Livin' Since I Met My Lord" for us.

Once again Bob Hope and I were teamed up along with Roy Rogers and Trigger. It was reunion time. I'd known Roy and Dale Evans for some time, and they are both as sweet as they appear to be, and he's a lamb to work with as well.

Son of Paleface was another happy picture, and I loved being Hope's straight gal. Working with him made me feel confident and at ease and it showed. The reviews on my Bob

Hope pictures were always good, and I was happy because I enjoyed doing comedy. Again I played a dance hall owner by night and a gang leader by day, and I not only got to sing but also had a choreographer. And, of course, my entire crew came with me to Paramount.

Bob was his usual funny self, and I would crack up looking into those twinkling chocolate drop eyes of his. I sang "Buttons and Bows" again, as well as a couple of other numbers, some with Bob. I even took a bubble bath in the very same tub Paulette Goddard had once used! It was a wild spoof of a film and did great at the box office.

A short time after that was finished I did a quickie guest shot in *The Road to Bali*, where I walked off into the sunset with Bing Crosby and Dorothy Lamour, leaving poor Bob Hope alone.

It was a fairly busy time for Robert as well, and before we were aware of it, it was June and my birthday. I was thirty. When I got home Robert gave me a lovely white knit dress and we had a marvelous dinner with friends at the Sportsmen's Lodge. It was a wonderful day, but there was more to come. I was called to the telephone. It was the doctor announcing that I had a baby daughter, seven pounds six and a half ounces, who had been born at 8:46 that same evening. Imagine, my daughter born on my birthday! I remembered the message that Brother Lennon had for me: The Lord "had a gift for me as surely as I would pull the ribbon and lift the lid of a box." Well, if this wasn't a gift, what was?

Robert and the others had piled money on the table, betting on the sex of our baby. Robert said it would be a girl, and the others all bet against him. When I came back to the table, I said, "It's a girl!" He pulled the money over toward himself, gloating, "See, I told you so."

Robert would have preferred a boy, but was delighted nonetheless. I assured him that we'd get a boy next time. I arranged for Frances to pick up the baby for us, since I was winding up work on the picture and couldn't leave town. Personally, I was delighted it was a girl, because my sisters-in-law and friends were having girls around that same time,

so my little girl would have a whole pack of kids her own age to play with, just as I had had when I was growing up. I named her Tracy Waterfield.

Our daughter arrived on a Wednesday evening and Robert, under pressure, and I went to meet Frances. She got off the plane and as she came up to us, she said in her most authoritative tone, "Well, you have a little doll here, let me tell you." It was windy, and I couldn't see her and Robert wouldn't. But as we dashed through the airport, I got a peek at her eyes. They were almond shaped.

When we got to the car, Frances got in the back with the baby. Robert started home and just overheard the conversation; he wouldn't turn his head in his mother's direction.

"Look at her, Jane, she really is a beautiful baby, and so good. She didn't move all the way here."

"Yeah, but her head . . . her face is darling, but what about her head? Will she have a forehead? Will it come forward?" I asked.

Before she could answer me that it would, Robert roared, "What the hell is wrong with her head?" But he couldn't see. Then, "Well, I guess I'm lucky she only has one. She does have only one, doesn't she?" We screamed with laughter.

At home Robert looked her over from head to toe. Then, while he was out watering after dinner, Robert said to Johnny Sanders, "I thought you said all new babies were ugly. Not mine. She's pretty cute." But around me, Robert seemingly couldn't care less.

My favorite time was sitting in the wicker rocker giving Tracy her bottle. I praised the Lord for this perfect little creature He'd given me for a birthday present. Tracy was definitely a beautiful little girl, with long slender fingers and small, perfectly flat ears. Best of all was her cheerful temperament. She slept most of the time, gurgled the rest, and never cried unless it was chow time and I was late in getting it to her. And then it was more like a whimper of complaint than crying. How like the Lord to choose a pretty little girl who was good on top of it to win my old man over.

A few nights later I was tired from working on *Son of*

Paleface, and when I fed her at 10 P.M. I whimpered to Robert, "You have to feed her at two."

To my utter surprise he said, "Okay, I'll feed her, but I won't change her—I don't know how."

At two he said, "I'll get up if you want, honey," but I went ahead, and then I thought, "Maybe he wants to do it and I'm not letting him." At 6 A.M. I didn't even hear Tracy, but Robert sprang out of bed to answer her first peep. Well, needless to say, I lay there wide awake, wondering like mad what was going on. Once I heard, "Shit," then silence. Ten minutes later, when I couldn't stand it any longer, I got up to go to the john. Robert was brushing his teeth and Tracy was sleeping like a little angel. I asked if she drank all her milk, and he grumbled, "No and I told you I didn't know how to change the diaper." I saw her plastic bottle nearly empty in the sink and said, "Oh, she did very well, honey," and went back to bed. At eleven o'clock, when I went to change her and bathe her, you should have seen that diaper. It was pinned around her sideways—one pin on her left hip like a sarong and one under her crotch and her nightgown up under her arms. It wouldn't hold anything. But Robert did it!

We had two Dobermans named Blitz and Katrinka, and everyone said, "Well, you can't have those dogs around children." I took all of Tracy's clothes off and laid her down on a pink blanket in the middle of the living room. Then Robert let the dogs in. They rushed over to her, sniffing up and down while I talked to them. It was love at first sight. From then on, every time they came in they tore through the house until they found her and checked that she was all right.

Having a baby in the house was probably the most exciting thing that happened to me. It was something to wake up for and something to hurry home to after work.

During the months that followed I made all kinds of inquiries about a boy one or two years old. I was told there were none available. Then I received an invitation to a Command Performance to be held

in London for King George and the royal family. I was thrilled. It promised to be a marvelous experience, plus it would be a great chance for me to look for a baby boy.

I wanted very much for Tracy to have an older brother, as I'd always felt somewhat cheated that I hadn't, and since I was aware of the long waiting period necessary in the States, this looked like just the occasion to look for him. I asked Mother if she'd like to come along, and she was thrilled. Robert couldn't come, since football season was with us once more. Michael Woulfe started designing two dresses. The first dress was to be worn when we were presented to the royal family. I said, "Everyone wears white, not I." I wanted ruby red velvet à la *Wuthering Heights* or *Rebecca* with a low bodice trimmed in mink.

Edith Lynch remembers the second dress for the stage show like this:

> When Jane was invited to London in 1951 to attend the Command Performance, Hughes told Michael Woulfe, head costume designer, to "see that she is properly dressed" for the occasion. There was a flurry of fittings and fits.
>
> It was hilarious to come across them in the wardrobe department. Michael was apoplectic. Jane was frozen. He was yelling, "But you can't use satin, Jane. Crepe is softer, more appropriate."
>
> "I want satin!" said the witch.
>
> Now all stops out, Michael shouts, "All right. You want to look like a galloping whore, I'll use green satin, and I'll get a pot of philodendron and hang it on your ass! That ought to look good to you!"
>
> Solemnly, with the beginning of a grin, she said, "But I don't like philodendron, Michael." Then the laughter begins. The fitting goes on and the gown is satin. A normal discussion between friends. . . .

All the gang was thrilled I was going to do a Command Performance, now called the Royal Film Performance. As we were all sitting by the pool one Sunday afternoon, I was full of myself telling them about the gowns Michael was having whipped up for when I met their majesties. Robert quietly said, "Honey, please don't say 'shit' to the queen." We broke up.

I took Mother and we left a month early for France. Bayeux Baker, a friend from Santa Barbara, was in Paris working in the embassy. He escorted us all over town, to shops and fashion shows, making sure that Mother would remember her first trip to Paris. Then he helped me get into an orphanage to see children. At the first place, the nuns brought the two-year-olds in to lunch in a long room with long benches and tables, where the children sat and stared at their tin plates. No talking or laughing or crying—nothing but apathy. I thought of our kids at home, my nieces and nephews of two. They'd be throwing cereal all over each other and themselves, babbling a blue streak. These children had no personality and I suddenly realized it was because no one had ever loved them. They didn't know how to love or even to hate back. I thought of how God loves us first so we can return it. But someone has to start the ball rolling. I was terribly upset when we left that room. The nuns said that none of these children were available for adoption. They had been put there by some member of their family who never saw them. But they wouldn't think of adopting them out. How depressing.

Next we went to Eze Village where Pat Dawson lived with her husband John Lodi. A friend of John's was living with them, and after several days I talked him into going down to Italy with me to see the orphanages there. In Genoa we met a *marquesa* who did charity work. She got us in to see one child only—although the building was full of children. There I found you had to be Catholic and the child had to have a first and last name. This little guy didn't, but a year and a half later they made one up for him and he was adopted by a Catholic American family of Italian descent, whom I knew.

After spending a week with Pat, Mother and I left for London. When the plane stopped in Paris, who got on but Bayeux. His mother had sent him some money to buy suits in London, so he was going with us.

When we got to London, the first thing Mother did was send a cable to my brother Tom that read, "Have arrived

safely in London. God save the King!" Tom's return message to her was typical of him. It read, "God HELP the King, YOU will save him."

Rehearsals for the Royal Film Performance were starting soon, but I wanted to go to Germany to look some more. We roared down the *autobahn* and cut through miles of pine trees. In the orphanage six tiny boys were lined up, all available for adoption. Most of the children were adopted by service personnel in Germany and it took a special act of Congress to get a child into America now. The special immigration act had just run out a few months before. The woman in charge tapped her head, indicating that most of them were retarded already, but one little blonde named Klaus was still holding his own. It was sickening. I knew nothing about getting a special act of Congress, but I said I'd try.

Back to London, Mother, and rehearsals. The previous day England had held her national elections and Winston Churchill had become prime minister again. On the front pages of the newspapers two large photos appeared side by side: Churchill and me. Over mine were the words "MISS RUSSELL IN LONDON TO ADOPT BABY BOY."

One afternoon, after rehearsal, Mother told me an Irish woman had called the hotel. She had read in the paper that I was looking for a boy to adopt. We knew that no one other than a British subject could adopt a British subject, but this couple was from Ireland. I didn't want to know the parents of a child of mine, and I felt a lot of trepidation when the mother arrived. She was a sweet little woman, and she put the fifteen-month-old baby on the bed. He had blue eyes that looked straight through you and a mass of golden curls. He looked exactly like the pictures I'd seen of my brother Billie who had died at sixteen months. The mother explained that they had other children and knew they could never provide him with an education. She wanted him to go to America with a Christian family. I think she thought she was sending him to heaven. Mother did all the talking. I was numb. Now it was my turn to be afraid. I finally said we'd let her know.

When they left, I went to the bedroom and prayed. Hard. I prayed in tongues and, though I'd never gotten any English before, it came out loud and clear: "Take him. Take My babies. I hear their cries. I will break down every barrier. They do not give him, I give him. Take My baby."

I called the parents and told them I'd take him. The next day we found it would take weeks to get him cleared to go. He would have to follow later.

That night we stood in the long line at the theater, all dressed up, to meet the king and queen. I wore a ruby-red dress and Mother was in black velvet with crystal and turquoise beading on the jacket. She looked stunning! King George was ill and couldn't come. The queen was truly dear, though, sweet and unassuming. She had something to say to each one of us. She told me she had enjoyed my pictures with Bob Hope. The princesses seemed shy and were very pretty.

The show was successful and there was a grand party afterward, but my throat was sore. The next morning I awoke with strep throat. The phone rang. Gordon White, a British publicist, and Bayeux had miraculously gotten all the papers cleared and if I came down to sign them, the baby could go with us. I left Mother packing and staggered to the car where Gordon and Bayeux were waiting. I couldn't believe what was happening, but I was too sick to worry. As I signed the paper, I saw the baby's birth date, July 29, 1950. Robert's birthday was July 26, 1920—thirty years and three days earlier.

When we got to the airport to check in, I went ahead and got on the plane. Mother finally came and she and the baby sat across the aisle. I didn't dare let him catch what I had. Next thing we knew, there was Florrie Kavanaugh, his natural mother, and a photographer. She had wanted to say goodbye again and the photographer had followed her on. I started crying, the baby cried, and she cried. She said, "His name is Thomas. Take good care of him." I promised. Talk about being emotional!

When we arrived in New York RKO personnel were there to meet us, as well as a horde of photographers and television camera crews. The news had preceded us by about eight hours. They fought, hollered, and climbed on boxes and

each other to get pictures and a story. The lights were blind-
ing.

Mother was going to Albuquerque to see Tom and Nola
and her new granddaughter, and I sent the baby with her. I
went straight home to try and explain to Robert. I knew he
had heard the news. He had and was quite annoyed by all
the publicity. The Los Angeles newsmen were following us
everywhere to get pictures and a story. You'd have thought
there was nothing else happening in the world other than my
adopting a baby. One bright guy tracked down my brother
Tom in Albuquerque and got a couple of shots of baby
Thomas. When I found that out, I wired Mother and told her
to change her flight and her name. I didn't want a repeat of
what had gone on in New York. To make doubly sure, I asked
Jamie to go to the airport to meet the plane instead of Robert
or myself. It was really paranoia time.

When the whole gang was at our house, Jamie drove up
the driveway with our son. I took him in and sat him on the
floor while everybody stood and viewed him. He looked all
around the room, and then at Robert, and raised his arms.
As he picked Thomas up, Robert said, "Well, I guess he knows
how to get on my good side." Everybody laughed and I knew
my worries were over.

Tracy, who was now four months old, and Blitz and Trinka
all adored Thomas. I finally taught him to walk. He was
breaking my back. He followed me everywhere like a shadow.
One mother had disappeared and, by George, this one wasn't
going to if he could help it.

Tracy walked at nine months and was into everything and
always out of sight. She was utterly independent. But Thomas
stuck right by my leg, hanging on most of the time. He was
jealous of Tracy at first, and if I wanted to play with her, I
had to go in another room, but she only wanted to hang by
her heels or play roughhouse. There was no cuddling for her
anymore.

It wasn't long before a mem-
ber of Parliament stood up and demanded that American
movie stars stop stealing British children. Thomas had come
in on an Irish passport, so what was he talking about? Well,

it seems he'd been born in London and therefore had dual citizenship and there was this law.

The papers had another field day and I was called to the studio front office, where all the RKO attorneys and the studio manager said I should return Thomas to London. Otherwise this might cause an international incident and everyone, including Howard, was against that. When they were all through, I said, "No. The Lord gave me this baby, and I intend to keep him. We'll see what happens."

Robert panicked and said, "My God, send him back." He was really crazy about Thomas, but he didn't want to be hurt more later. Then I was called to the Immigration Department, where I told them all the legal details. They said if England didn't push, they certainly wouldn't. We had to hire a barrister in England to defend the Kavanaughs, who were being charged with breaking British law. This lasted for nine months. The Kavanaughs stood by their guns and never wavered, although neighbors were blasting them from all sides. Finally the judge reprimanded them but said he was sure the best had been done for the child. The hearing was to clarify the law that no one other than a British subject could adopt a British subject. That law has since been changed, but it was a hairy nine months. Only after that were we free to complete Thomas' adoption and request citizenship for him. I certainly had learned the meaning of "I will break down every barrier." If the Lord hadn't forced it out of my own mouth, I might have wavered.

Nineteen fifty-one was a year to remember. Besides our beautiful children, that was the year the Rams won the championship and Robert was the NFL leading passer.

I had my own children, yes, but I couldn't forget the children I had seen in the orphanages. There were too many people waiting, longing for children here. It just wasn't right; the laws were made to help people, not hinder justice. I called my friend Adrian Brian and asked her to help. I didn't know what or how, but I wanted to do something to help these kids and the parents-to-be waiting for them.

Adrian and I prayed for guidance and asked others to join

us. She knew Adela Rogers St. John, who knew Congress-
man Pat Hillings. Perry Lieber wanted me to do personal appearances, so I said, "I'll go on one condition—I get an open
ticket from the junket on, and I go wherever I please." He
had heard rumors and said, "Please, don't tell me anything,
just go, but I know nothing." He was afraid of "the boss." I
went directly to Washington after my public appearances,
where Adela had set up meetings with congressmen.

On an earlier trip to Washington, I'd been to the State
Department to try to find out approximately how many children were available for adoption in foreign countries. The
answer from overseas was, "No children available." I knew
that was hogwash, for the Children's Bureau, which was across
the street, stated that they knew there were children but they
had no idea how many. At any rate, immigration laws had
to be changed before any child could come into the country
off the quota, so I was off to see the lawmakers, the Congress
and the Senate. At the moment there was a big uproar concerning immigration. The right wing wanted to close immigration as much as possible and the left wing was trying to
open the doors to more people. It was a heated situation. We
were asking that children be allowed in just as the bride of
an American soldier could come in. A child was a member
of the immediate family who had no politics or axes to grind,
just a great need to be wanted and loved. This was okay with
both wings and in a sense took some of the heat off while
senators and congressmen were considering a special immigration bill.

I still had to work. Darryl Zan-
uck, the head of Twentieth Century-Fox, had just bought
Gentlemen Prefer Blondes for Marilyn Monroe. This was to
be her first big picture, and he wanted Howard Hawks to direct it. Hawks wanted me to play Dorothy, Lorelei's best
friend, and he made sure both parts were equal. After all these
years Hawks and I were finally going to do a picture together. He had been so wonderful to me when I was still wet
behind the ears, so with him at the helm, I knew it would be
great. So my whole crew and I went to Fox for the first time.

Thanks to Howard Hughes, my crew went along on all "loan out" deals.

Everybody's jaw was hanging at Fox when this strange outfit converged on the lot—until they got used to us. I must say we put on quite a show for them. I screamed at Shot and he played the crazy, browbeaten Texan and we all laughed and giggled behind the closed doors of my dressing room. Every one of them later worked at Fox after I quit working.

Marilyn had Whitey for her makeup man, and she got her first big dressing room next to mine. We got along great together. Marilyn was very shy and very sweet and far more intelligent than people gave her credit for.

We started dance rehearsals with Jack Cole and Gwen Verdon, his assistant. Jack was every dancer's idea of a genius and many people were terrified of him, but I adored him madly. He had a slight, wiry build, practically a shaved head, a prominent, regal nose, a cast in one eye, and a positively evil sense of humor. Jack worked dancers to death, but with Marilyn and me he was patience itself. He knew we didn't know our left foot from our right, but he stayed tirelessly with us. I worked until I got fuzzy headed and said, "Ol' Jack, I'm not learning." He'd say, "Go baby. Tomorrow." Marilyn would stay for an hour or two after I left, and he'd stay with her. She was worried and determined. Jack said she wouldn't really learn anymore during that time, but he understood her insecurity. We all referred to her as "Baby Doll."

Hal Schaefer was Jack's rehearsal pianist, and we became the best of friends. He and Jack worked the entire arrangements out before they ever went to the music department to be orchestrated. He always used a drum and a piano at rehearsals.

When all the male dancers were there, Jack worked with them and Gwen with us. These rehearsals were hard, sweaty work. I never dressed up but always wore lips and lashes. Marilyn looked like she'd just crawled out of bed—no makeup, tangled hair, and blue jeans.

We had fittings and then a test for makeup and wardrobe. Zanuck had held out for his designer, Billy Travilla, and when we put the clothes on, Marilyn's were fine, but mine

were ridiculous. Billy knew it, and Zanuck knew it, and I had a new wardrobe after I'd had a session with Billy about what I could and couldn't wear. Any designer has to experiment with a new body.

I had a ball on that picture, but I don't think Marilyn did altogether, because she was torn between the front office, who was calling her a cheap, dumb blonde, and Natascha Lytess, her drama coach who worked with her every night. It started going wrong when Natascha began directing her on the set. Marilyn's eyes would turn immediately to her when a scene was finished. Howard Hawks, who was trying to direct the picture, wasn't pleased at all. He was a director that even producers didn't interfere with. He was lord of the set.

Finally, Hawks threw Natascha off the set, but things continued to be strained. Marilyn started coming to the set late and that didn't go over too well, so I talked to Whitey. He told me she came in long before I did and was really ready, but she'd stay in her dressing room and putter. "I think she's afraid to go out," he said. So from then on I'd stand in her doorway and say, "Come on, Blondl, let's go," and she'd say, "Oh, okay," in her whispery voice, and we'd go on together. She was never late again.

The press tried their best to work up a feud between us, but they were sniffing up the wrong tree. We were both Geminis and really complimented each other. She was dating Joe DiMaggio then. He came to visit on the set a couple of times, as did Robert. Marilyn had lots of questions to ask me about what it was like being married to an athlete. I told her, "Well, they're birds of a feather and you'll get to know lots of other athletes—otherwise, it's great."

One of the last things on the picture was my dance routine with the muscle men. Jack, who was terrified of heights, rode the camera on a giant crane. At the end of the number the guys were supposed to dive over me as I sat down by the pool. One poor cluck didn't clear me, and I went head first into the pool and came up like a drowned rat. The scene had to be reshot, but since this was Saturday noon, it would be done first thing on Monday. Thank God! Robert picked me up and took me to Palm Springs to rest. I was exhausted.

Monday we did shoot the scene over, but in the final cut the first take was used, including my impersonation of a drowned rat. It *was* better. When the movie is shown on television, many times the whole number is cut. Thanks a lot.

The reviews were great and so was the box office. Apparently everyone loved the Monroe–Russell combination. The *New York Herald Tribune* called it the "The Haystack Brunette versus the Blowtorch Blonde" and said how very well we worked together. They loved everything about the picture. They liked our singing, our dancing—even our acting—and especially the "Diamonds Are a Girl's Best Friend" number. We were delighted with the reaction the film got from both the press and the public. I was especially happy, because I had another chance at comedy and had brought it off.

Later, Marilyn and I were invited to add our footprints to those already cemented in at Grauman's Chinese Theater on Hollywood Boulevard. We were both wearing light, summery dresses and high heels as we posed, arms linked together, for the photographers. We were thrilled beyond words. While I was placing my feet in that square of soggy cement, I thought of all the times when Pat Alexander and I tried to fit our feet in the footprints of famous actresses and how we figured that they must have worn the tiniest shoes for the occasion. Our feet never fit in. Now my prints were in that cement and I couldn't believe it. I'm sure Marilyn felt the same. Always one for personal comfort, I was wearing my usual big shoes, so no aspiring actress will have any trouble whatsoever getting her feet into my footprints!

At just about this point I began living a split-level existence. I was wife–mother, I had a career, and now I had the adoption program. I was constantly occupied with one or the other or all three at once, while Robert had football, his first love. The previous year he had developed a duodenal ulcer and was plagued by such pain that he was afraid this might be his final year as a football player. When the season was over he went to a doctor, who advised him to give up football. He told Robert that he was

psychologically unsuited for the career he'd chosen, that he took the responsibility for the team's success too personally, and while it made him the great player he was, it could also kill him if he didn't get out.

This, of course, didn't go down too well with Robert. When I talked with the doctor, he told me in no uncertain terms that Robert would have to change his lifestyle or the ulcer would get worse. He went into depth about Robert's character. His overwhelming need to win placed him under constant tension and made football a tough business for him, rather than the game it should be. A professional athlete like Robert, the doctor said, is always competing, and his achievements measured against either his previous ones or those of his competitors. Whereas someone in the arts, such as a writer, painter, sculptor, or composer, has merely to be good, someone like Robert has always to be best. Robert was shocked and angry, but he knew the doctor was right.

On December 1, 1952, at the age of thirty-two, Robert Waterfield announced his retirement. He had played pro football for eight years. He led the NFL in passing for two of those years, kicked 315 extra points and sixty field goals, averaged 42.4 yards in punting, and, as a defensive back, intercepted twenty passes. He was some outstanding football player. Then he got an offer from the Rams to be their assistant coach. I hoped this would keep him busy but would take away the pressures he used to have as a player. So Robert went back to his football, and I started working on adoption again.

I got the bright idea of trying my luck with the United Nations. Off I went to see Eleanor Roosevelt. She reminded me instantly of Aunt Bella and Aunt Dovie. She received me very graciously and was most sympathetic with the problem. When I told her that it was an international organization we were putting together and I thought the United Nations with all its facilities in various countries could be of great help, she just shook her head.

"Oh, my dear," she said, smiling her wonderful smile, "you don't ever want to go to the UN with anything like that. They're so clogged up and overburdened and the paperwork is way out of control and you'll never get anything accomplished. If you can possibly do it on your own, you'll get it done much better and quicker. Stay on your own and just plough ahead." I did just that.

From our efforts and those of many other organizations, the Orphan Adoption Amendment of the Special Migration Act of 1953 was passed. Children could come into the country off the quota if they were to be adopted.

David Hempstead, a producer friend of mine, suggested that I visit the Ford Foundation to find out whether there was any organization already involved in intercountry adoption. The foundation knew of none, but the International Social Service (ISS) had just received a large grant to facilitate helping people separated by national boundaries. It was organized in 1921 and had an excellent reputation. I got a quick reply to a letter: "Could you come to New York for a meeting?" signed William T. Kirk, director.

Bill Kirk was like a father to me in many areas of my life. I liked this warm, calm, gray-haired Aries immediately and learned to love him a great deal. He had just returned from international headquarters in Switzerland. At a board meeting of their international branches *children* in all forty-five countries of the ISS network were the main topic. The ISS had the offices and some social workers, but if an intercountry adoption plan was to work, they would have to hire additional staff. Bill could find the staff if I could find the money. Well, I've never raised a penny in my life and didn't have the vaguest idea how to go about it, but I knew Adrian did. Sam Zagon and Bill agreed that WAIF, as we called our organization (a waif is a child without a home), would be the adoption division of ISS. We shook hands and left. All the way home I praised the Lord for opening the doors.

At home, Adrian was thrilled. She called two dynamite gals: Marilyn Hinton, a walking *Who's Who*, became the first president, and Vicky Rosenberg published an ad book that raised over $50,000. Marilyn arranged a party and we invited everyone we knew. It was packed. Adela spoke and so did Hedda Hopper. I told them what I'd seen in Europe and about Bill Kirk and ISS, and from that party the first chapter of WAIF ISS was formed.

Our first WAIF ball was finally held at the Moulin Rouge (the old Earl Carroll Theatre). It was a smash. Every name you can think of was there—Robert Mitchum, Fred MacMurray, Clark Gable, John Wayne, David Niven, Red Skelton, James Franciscus, Gregory Peck, Jimmy Stewart, David Brian. I don't know how Marilyn and Vicky got them all, but it looked like an evening at the Academy Awards.

The next WAIF chapter was started in Palm Springs, and then one in New York. Poor Edith was driven batty by my activities. Her boss, Perry Lieber, had given up on me long before. Then one day an edict came down from "the boss." Any show I did, especially if it was on orphans, had to first be cleared with the publicity department. This meant Edith would have to go everywhere with me in order to make sure, which was okay with me.

I went down to her office with a wide grin on my face. "All right, Edith," I told her, "you now have official sanction to help me with my WAIF work." Edith described RKO's side as follows:

> No matter that Hughes didn't want his big, sexy movie star tied to an intercountry adoption program. The publicity it generated at the beginning was so adverse to any campaign ever dreamed up by a studio that we really didn't know how to deal with it. Hughes gave explicit orders that the studio was not to get involved. Jane persisted—maneuvered in her usual style and we were eventually drawn in—our excuse being we could then control it. Actually, it was bigger than all of us!
>
> A publicity campaign at RKO in New York? Sure, she'd go. Too willing for someone who was constantly in demand and hated to leave town. But here was an opportunity for WAIF. She didn't shout her intentions, but subtly dragged her WAIF promotions alongside the studio campaigns. The New York chapter grew under such action. A call to friends; a catered cocktail party donated by Vincent Sardi; Joan Crawford accepting honorary chairmanship which she later passed to the beloved Helen Hayes who carried on. The Hawaii

chapter was formed when Jane was on location for a
20th Century-Fox film. In Chicago, she met with pro-
spective WAIF chapter members at the home of Martha
O'Driscoll Appleton, her roommate on a war bond tour
some years earlier. And so it went, opening doors for
WAIF and the adamant Hughes, unwittingly underwrit-
ing the project! Perhaps it was bigger than him, too?

Some time back a terrific gal
named Henrietta Mears had a college class of about 500 kids
from USC and UCLA at Hollywood Presbyterian Church. They
were really a gung ho group of kids. I went for a while and
my friend Colleen Townsend came out of this church group.
Miss Mears and Dick Halverson, who is now Senate Chap-
lain, suggested to Colleen, Connie Haines, Rhonda Fleming,
and myself that we start meetings in our homes for people
in show business who felt it was difficult going to a strange
church. We had different ministers speak and at first it was
great. Dale Evans and Roy Rogers, Donald O'Connor, Hugh
O'Brian, Beryl Davis, Peter Potter, and lots of others met with
us once a month. It was called the Hollywood Christian
Group. I even talked Marilyn Monroe into coming to a meeting at Connie Haines' house when we were doing *Gentlemen,* but she didn't think it was for her.

When Beryl and Pete were trying to help their Episcopal
church raise funds, Beryl, who is British, "lumbered" her
friends. Connie was going to sing, but Della Russell, who was
married to singer Andy Russell, and I had nothing to do. So
Baptist Connie and I, knowing all the old spirituals, taught
Catholic Della and Episcopal Beryl a chorus of "Do Lord"
in harmony backstage, which we then did on stage. An A&R
man happened to be in the audience and he asked us to record the spiritual for Coral Records. We thought that would
be a blast and did, Perry Botkins' banjo and all. Connie remembers the recording session well. We did many takes, and
each time it just wasn't right. In desperation I finally said,
"Let's pray. Come on, you guys, join hands." The bewildered musicians and the four of us asked the Lord to help us
get it right. We all held our breath as we listened to the next

playback. A familiar voice came over the loudspeaker: "That's a million seller if ever I heard one." It was Bing Crosby, who was an owner of Coral Records. From then on we always prayed before recording dates.

Peter Potter, Beryl's husband, put "Do Lord" on his television show "Juke Box Jury," and we were all in the audience. When the panel finished listening to it, panelist Tennessee Ernie Ford said, "I don't know who that is, but it's absolutely great. A hit for sure." But another radio panel, which was made up of singers and music critics in New York, also listened to it without knowing who was singing, and Dinah Washington said, "That's the most sacriligious thing I ever heard. They ought to be tarred and feathered." That's how far ahead of our time we were. Spirituals belonged on religious labels. No pop label had ever recorded anything like it. Well, the darn thing sold over a million. We each gave ten percent of our royalties to WAIF and our churches.

We then recorded an album of spirituals called "Make a Joyful Noise unto the Lord." Rhonda Fleming took Della's part on top when Della divorced and moved to Mexico. We did a lot of television guest spots on the "Ed Sullivan Show" and "The Red Skelton Show," among others, but it was tough getting the four of us together to rehearse. Rhonda and I were still busy making pictures, so when Capitol Records wanted us to record an album, "The Magic of Believing," it was just the three of us: Connie Haines, the girl singer with Harry James and Tommy Dorsey; Beryl Davis, who sang with George Shearing and on "Your Hit Parade" with Frank Sinatra; and me.

Lyn Murray, my friend from Paramount, did some arranging for us and Connie knew all the musicians in town since she had worked with the big bands. Beryl hadn't sung since the "Hit Parade." She had married Peter Potter and retired except for guest spots on his show, but now she wanted to work again.

People were confused with me singing spirituals and reading the Bible. They had the image of the Hughes publicity and his arguments with the censors firmly planted in their minds, and, not really knowing me at all, couldn't put the two pictures together.

I just merrily went on my way doing what I liked and let the confusion lie where Jesus flung it.

When Howard saw *Gentlemen Prefer Blondes,* he decided to make a musical of his own, and I was back at work. *The French Line* was about a Texan millionairess who felt everyone was just after her money, so she trades places with a young bride on a trip to Europe on, what else, the *French Line.* I read the script and decided the role was like a Texan Pat Henry. I could do that easily.

I meet a dashing Frenchman, played by Gilbert Roland, who is Mexican. We couldn't find a dashing Frenchman for some reason. I'd seen Gilbert earlier in Palm Springs at the racquet club and thought he was one of the best-looking men alive. He claimed I started his career all over again. This lady does a lot of musical numbers aboard ship with a designer buddy, played by Mary McCarty. Arthur Hunnicutt played her guardian who was in hot pursuit. Howard also used the film as a screen test for a lot of girls—some under contract—so Mary McCarty had a fashion show where these girls paraded down a long curved stairway. Kim Novak was one of them.

Suddenly there was an order to find another song. A torrid number called "Lookin' for Trouble" was written. Billy Daniel was the choreographer and Hal Schaefer laid out the music. I'd been taking singing lessons with Hal ever since *Gentlemen* and we were best friends. Howard wanted a test of the costume he had chosen for me, a silver-beaded bikini. At that time bikinis were only worn by a few naughty girls in the south of France; no one in America ever wore them. I stood before my horrified camera crew, feeling very naked. I went back to the designer Michael Woulfe and said forget it. The arguments between Howard and me all went through Michael. I honestly think he was afraid to talk to me. Meanwhile, I was rehearsing the number and shooting other scenes. Finally, when the fight was at an impasse, I took a friend and went to the Beach Club, which had once been Marion Davies' home. No shooting, no rehearsal, nothing, till they found a decent one-piece costume.

Poor Michael was forced to please both Howard and me and he came up with the famous *French Line* costume. There were holes below and above the waist, but it was one piece.

The only problem, as I saw it, was that it was never made clear in the story that the millionairess did the naughty number to get even with her fellah, to make him mad. I begged them to put in one short scene to show some motive for it. They all looked at me like I was bananas. I'd already held up shooting for two weeks. Finally a scene was shot. No film was in the camera, I'm sure, for I never saw it, nor did anyone else.

Well, the shit hit the fan again. Censors screamed. Howard couldn't get a seal of approval. Even my old friend Dr. Evans of Hollywood Presbyterian Chuch said, "That girl's no Christian." I was sick. I had done everything in my power to make it work. Since the motivation scene was never used, this perfectly nice Texan girl suddenly turns into a raving maneater for no reason, which audiences couldn't accept. I did the whole number very tongue in cheek, and I saw nothing wrong with it whatever, if only there'd been a motive. Gilbert grabs me at the end of the number, throws me over his shoulder, carries me out, and the characters live happily ever after. Television cuts out this number, too.

Afterward Howard and I had a good long talk about censorship, and this was one of the things I loved most about him. He promised me I'd never be involved with another censorship problem again, but I had to promise never to tell anyone he said so. And I never did as long as he was alive. But now, with so much garbage being written about him, I think it's time people knew his real side. We may have fought and disagreed about some things, but we were both very loyal and respected each other a great deal. Ours was truly a platonic love affair.

Underwater! This turkey was handed to my friend Harry Tatelman, who was then head of the story department at RKO. He had been promised a producership, and I think it was thought this was the way to finish him off.

He came to me saying that if I would do this for him, I could work with the writer, and we would put it all together. I felt for him, and I thought it would be fun to try and do it from the beginning, so I said okay.

We wove a story out of the worst B picture we'd ever read. John Sturges was set to direct. In the story, my husband was the partner of my Mexican brother. Gilbert Roland would be perfect for the brother, but who would play my husband? We had a tight budget, so we started looking for a fairly unknown actor. We looked at films and tests until we were blue. Finally, we saw him. He was strong, very good looking, and I said, "If he had some blonde streaks in his hair, the guy would look like an underwater seaman." We called him in and on top of all his other good looks he had light, penetrating blue eyes and a marvelous sense of humor. His name was Richard Egan. I fell in love again. I took him up to Larry Germaine in makeup and told him what I wanted. Actually, it's what they call streaking or frosting today. But Larry proceeded to bleach this Leo ego blonde to the roots. Richard howled. When they put the toner on he screamed, and I mean screamed! His eyes were bulging out of his head and he flew out of that chair and lunged at me. I ran like hell.

Still not right, Richard looked more like an albino, so I told Larry, "It should be dark at the crown and light on the tips, like anyone who spends a lot of time near the beach."

Richard shouted, "Oh, fine! I'm blistered all over my head with running sores and you're still not happy."

The madder he got, the more I had to laugh. It was dynamite!

When the real skin diver, Jack Ackerman, who was to double for Richard, arrived from Hawaii, he had exactly the look I wanted. So when the blisters healed, back Richard went to get dark roots and blonde ends.

Richard and I spent hours on the roof getting black tans, learning our scripts, and getting to know each other. Richard, a Catholic, was a bachelor. He knew that when he got married, it would be forever, so he was in no hurry. His

brother was a Jesuit priest named Father Willis. They both had the same marvelous deep voice. I started working on Richard to get married from then on. As I've said, since I was "born married," I thought everyone else should be too.

When we got to the shooting, you'd have thought *we* were married. We fought and laughed and had quiet times as any happy married couple does. It was a joy working with him. Gilbert felt like my brother too, since we'd done *The French Line* together. He was a love to work with.

Jack Ackerman taught us to use the diving tanks and underwater gear in the tank built on the set. Richard and I felt at home in the water, so it was learning to breathe through a hose that was our lesson, but poor Gilbert, who was great on a tennis court or on a dance floor, hated swimming. The whole routine of going under with all that paraphernalia strapped on was miserable for him, but he finally managed. Our swimming doubles were sent to locations in the Bahamas and Hawaii to film all the big underwater scenes while we worked in the studio.

All in all, it was a very happy picture and made pots of money, which surprised the clowns who'd set it up.

One of the things I very much wanted was a beach house. Robert and I always loved the beach, and I wanted our kids to have the same enjoyment. One Sunday on the drive back from the beach I spotted a sign that read Open House. We stopped to investigate. "Just to have a look," I told Robert, but he was skeptical. It was a two-story pink stucco house with a large deck in the back that had two bedrooms and a bath separated from the main house that would be great for the kids. They could use the deck as an outdoor living room, play in the backyard, and run to the beach without messing up the main house. The rest of the house consisted of a living room/dining room, guest bath downstairs, and two bedrooms and two bathrooms upstairs. And best of all, the price was only $32,500 for a double lot on Malibu Beach. Those were the days.

"Okay," he said at last. "But," he added, "no money to decorate It!" Agreed. I worked like crazy over that house, deciding that since it was to be a beach house inhabited by a bunch of kids, I would be practical. My brothers built low beds of plywood, which I painted black and covered with gray denim for couches. I managed with bric-a-brac rescued from a fire sale, a white Mexican fur rug trimmed in black tossed casually in front of the fireplace, gray walls, two black and white striped slip-covered rockers, and bright pink denim café curtains for the living foom.

Four sets of bunk beds and an extra cot (which could sleep a total of nine kids) furnished the children's bedrooms. Redwood furniture on a huge deck made an outdoor living room. A swing and teeter-totter were set up in the sandy part of the fenced-in backyard. We were ready.

We moved there the day after school let out and didn't return to the Valley until the day before school started. The kids and I enjoyed it tremendously, but unless Robert's friends were visiting us, he would drive back to the Valley every day to see them, only returning for dinner and to sleep. He couldn't stand being too far from his familiar hangouts. When his gang and their kids visited, he was always there, but when they were off hunting or at training camp, he was nowhere to be seen and that's when my friends and their kids would come.

THIRTEEN

At the end of *Underwater!* Howard sold RKO. We were out of our home away from home, and it was rather sad.

My second seven-year contract was soon to be up and new negotiations were started. Lew Wasserman and MCA again wanted me to leave Howard. They had plans for me at MGM or Warners or some big studio, but I still felt it would be disloyal. One day, Lew called me out in the hall at an MCA meeting and said, "Look, are you sleeping with this guy, or what?"

He and Edie and I had been friends for a long time and he knew I would answer him. I must have looked shocked, because when I said, "No, Lew, my God! He's my friend," he said, "Okay, baby, I just couldn't understand."

Howard put a stop to the entire squabble by proposing a contract so unique I didn't even understand it. I would make six pictures that he could loan me out for in five years, but my payments would be spread out over twenty years. He had already okayed it with the Internal Revenue. I could also make pictures on my own or anything else I wanted to do, such as clubs, television, records—anything! I was speechless!

My only concern was about loan-outs. I wanted some assurance it would be for A pictures. Howard said, "Just go

back to Wasserman and those sharks at MCA and repeat what I've said."

I did, and they were flabbergasted. Lew said, "If he'll put that on paper, you'd be a fool not to do it. I've never heard of a contract like that." It was for 1 million dollars; the year was 1955.

Afterward, MCA helped Jimmy Stewart and many stars set up the same format, but mine was the first of its kind.

I got director approval on the loan-outs to take care of my worry, and that was that. I felt very proud of Howard for outthinking everyone again. He lived up to my ideal picture of our relationship, even though he wasn't in the picture business anymore.

MCA and Sam Zagon, our attorney for WAIF and the motion picture business, immediately started forming our own company, Russ-Field, with Robert as executive producer and president and me as vice-president or something. Mainly I was an asset. We had to produce pictures with me in only half of them. Robert wasn't too enthusiastic at first. He felt he was entirely out of his field.

Sam made a deal with United Artists for six pictures, but they insisted that we make *Gentlemen Marry Brunettes* first. They thought it was a natural. Mary Anita Loos Sale and Richard Sale, who had written *French Line* for RKO, would co-produce and Richard would direct. Anita Loos, Mary's aunt, had written the book, but a new story was written and only her title was used. Jeanne Crain had been signed on as one of the leads.

I didn't like the property, but Max Youngstein, one of UA's vice-presidents who dealt with stars and properties, was convincing. I felt that a big expensive production was being hung on my shoulders, and they just weren't broad enough. Jeanne is a darling girl and had proven herself as an actress, but at the box office she wasn't a Marilyn Monroe. Richard and Mary said the script would be written after the stars were set. That made sense, so I went along. Jack Cole was to do the choreography, which picked up my spirits no end, and Bill Travilla the clothes. It seemed there were hundreds of outfits.

Rudy Vallee was to play our older friend who introduces us to Paris. We were to go to Europe, Paris, and Monte Carlo on location and then finish up at the Shepperton studio outside London. Shooting time was to be three and a half months. It all sounded so glamorous, especially after my days inside a studio. I was excited in spite of myself. Mary and Richard started writing.

In the meantime, we set up our offices on the old Goldwyn lot. I felt I had come home. But we needed other properties fast. An old friend, Margaret Obegi, had written a book called *The Way of an Eagle* with me in mind. I'd always adored it and now talked Robert into buying it. We could make it.

Then to find my co-star. Margaret and I went to movies, looking, looking, and finally saw him playing an Indian. It was Jeff Chandler as Cochise. But how could we get him? He was under contract to Universal. They agreed to loan him to us if I did a picture for Universal first, so I ended up doing *Foxfire* for Universal with Jeff and Dan Duryea. Joe Pevney directed and Ketti Frings wrote the screenplay. I adored Jeff and was in love again.

Each day after shooting on *Foxfire* I had fittings for *Gentlemen Marry Brunettes*. I didn't get home until half past eight or nine. It was rough. They were still looking for the two leading men and came up with Scott Brady and Alan Young. I was frantic. Both guys are dear and I had loved Scott like a brother since we worked together in *Montana Belle*, but how were we going to sell enough tickets to cover that very expensive budget? Practical I have always been.

I was excited but concerned about this trip. I hated leaving the children. I'd never been gone for three and a half months from my family. When I prayed about it, the Lord said,

A word of admonition I would speak unto thee: Linger long before the Throne of Grace. Linger long in thy bedchamber and seek wisdom, for I am wisdom . . . then thou shalt know how to choose when thou dost go across the sea. Thou shalt know to choose sturdy oaks

to go with thee across the sea. Choose thou sturdy oaks
to hedge thee in and build thee up. Be thou therefore
admonished, My little girl.

I took Carmen, my sturdy oak. Since the rest of the crew
weren't allowed to work in Europe, we had to find a British
crew. Thank God for Carmen; we could stay together, pray
together, and get through the three months away from our
children and husbands. Robert was coming over in about a
month, and Boyd left before we did. He was with Carmen
off and on, but he couldn't stand the idea of her going to
Europe and not him.

I was so homesick a month later that when Robert arrived, I knocked him to the floor and raped him. Then I threw
my arms around him and cried like a baby. He couldn't believe it. I had deliberately left Thomas and Tracy home because of the British press, I didn't want the children driven
mad with photographers. I wanted them to be as normal as
possible, but if I had it to do over again, I would probably
have taken them. It's better to all suffer together than be miserable apart, and we were miserable. Robert planned to stay
for only one month but ended up staying three.

Carmen and I had a beautiful white Daimler convertible
(with a French driver) that was used in the picture in both
Paris and Monte Carlo. We shot all the beautiful spots of
Paris—the Arc de Triomphe, the Rodin Gallery, the ques-
tionably beautiful Eiffel Tower. In Monte Carlo we were at
the Hotel de Paris and visited the grand old stuffy Casino de
Monte Carlo across the square. Again, it was location shooting, with the best locations one could imagine.

Our French driver was a true Parisian. I had only Sunday
off and was anxious to go sightseeing a bit, but he left us
sitting on the hotel porch all day. We finally got a cab. Later
Robert had a stern talk with him and tried to appeal to his
sense of honor. Richard wanted to fire him, but stupid me
thought that there must have been some misunderstanding.
He really seemed so nice.

When we were leaving for Paris, the driver took Scott,
Robert, Boyd, and me to the airport and promised to go back

for Carmen and the bags. We had bought him a beautiful cashmere sweater, which was with Carmen, but he never returned for her or the sweater. Too bad for him.

Robert had been invited by the U.S. military to visit our boys in Germany. A football hero would give them quite a kick. He took Boyd with him, and they would meet us in London. Carmen and I had to return to Paris with the company to pack everything up. We would be shooting in a studio outside London from now on.

Carmen and I lived in a beautifully furnished flat in Belgrave Square in London. An Italian couple came with the flat to cook, clean, shop, serve, and keep a fire going in the fireplace whenever we were there. It was lovely. Across the street was the park with black trees etched against the gray winter sky.

Florrie and Michael Kavanaugh came to visit, and we had a long talk about Thomas. They were still pleased that I had him.

The British film studios are all more than an hour's drive from London. Our driver picked us up at 6:30 A.M., packed lap robes around us, and drove off through the dark. Carmen and I had bought huge, hairy black coats and boots in France and they were our uniforms for the English cold. Shooting was very pleasant, on the whole, and everyone got along very well.

Carmen and I found out we were spending our monthly allowances long before the month was up. Nothing was cheap in either Paris or London, so when we got to London, we told our Italian cook we were going on a diet—no more fancy desserts and stay on the budget.

I had started the picture fat and was slowly losing pounds and inches. It was impossible to diet before I got there, because I was too busy. But now, with only one picture to work on, dieting was easier. Richard wanted to kill me. He wanted me to look the same all through the picture. Oh, well.

Robert and Boyd came back from Germany and life became routine. Robert didn't have anything to do and was bored to death, but he stayed on because he knew it helped me. Both Boyd and Carmen couldn't believe that he had no

interest in anything outside his own environment. Robert and Boyd finally left for home to spend Christmas with the children.

We moved to the MGM studio outside London, where Jack Cole was choreographing the last big number, "Ain't Misbehavin'," in which Jeanne and I were dressed like quail and put in a huge cauldron by a bunch of African dancers. The yellow dunes and the shields, headdresses, and spears of the savages were so artistic that they inspired me to paint a mural in our dressing room—anything for diversion.

The music was done at another studio, with Bob Farnum conducting. Anita Ellis sang for Jeanne; Alan Young, Scott, and I did our own. There were fabulous songs in the picture, such as "My Funny Valentine," "Ain't Misbehavin'," "Have You Met Miss Jones?" "I Wanna Be Loved by You," "Daddy," and "I've Got Five Dollars."

Finally, we could go home. Carmen and I had reservations out of London right after the final day's shooting. Richard didn't know if we'd make it or not, but we were all packed and ready to tear to the airport. We made it.

Perry Lieber had called: I was wanted in Florida for the opening of *Underwater!* I screamed no, but to no avail. I wanted to see my children. Perry said, "We'll fly your mother-in-law to New York with the children; you go to Florida, overnight, then back to New York and home." Frances, or Nana, as the children called her, had been raised in New York, as had her friend Kate, so I knew the two Irish gals would like to visit the city and see some plays, the park, and Brooklyn, since they hadn't been there for some forty years. So I agreed.

Carmen went straight home. The RKO boys in New York took me to meet the kids' plane from Los Angeles. Thomas and Tracy remembered me! We cried and laughed. When Thomas saw a photographer, he buried his head on my shoulder as we dashed for the car. That night, we had dinner in our rooms. Thomas slept with me and Tracy with Nana. I couldn't pry Thomas loose. The next day we met Vincent Price at the Plaza for brunch. He was doing a play in New York. After brunch we took a horse and buggy through the park in the snow, all bundled up in furry robes. The kids loved it. It was exhilarating and so good to see Vinnie, too.

The next day I snuck out of bed, leaving Thomas sleeping, and went to Florida.

Edith said this about the premiere:

> Hughes said, "No Jane—no premiere!" Incredible as it now seems, we flew her kids and her mother-in-law to her in New York, after she arrived from Europe, for a day's visit before she traveled to Florida, a day late for the festivities.
>
> We always believed that Jayne Mansfield, then a newcomer at Fox, was first boosted by RKO. She had brought a bathing suit that Jane R. would never have dared wear.
>
> One look around after her arrival, Jane asked, "Who's the blonde tomato?" Never one to articulate, she gets it all said in one sentence.

A publicity man wanted me to get into a bikini, not to be outdone. I said, "No way. I wear my one-piece suit, do my job, and get the hell home. This isn't a cheese cake competition for you guys."

It's hard to believe, but RKO decided to stage the world premiere of *Underwater!* underwater! A specially constructed theater was set up at the bottom of a small lake, where Richard Egan and I, outfitted with Aqua-lungs, flippers, and goggles, were to sit on iron benches, along with other daring souls similarly equipped, to view the film on a special screen. It was ridiculous. Amazingly enough, *Underwater!* had the distinction of racking up more bookings than any other RKO picture in the preceding decade.

Back I flew to New York. When I landed, I was rushed from one plane to another, where the children were waiting. I settled back with Tracy, but Thomas was mad that I'd disappeared on him, and he wouldn't have anything to do with me. Finally, he gave up and crawled into my lap and we all slept. It was so good to be home. Robert wouldn't let go of me; he thought I didn't respond as usual. I did, but it just

didn't show. I was too exhausted. I didn't know it then, but my husband was embroiled in an affair.

Thomas had started stuttering while I was gone, and even though our housekeeper, Mrs. West, took him to a child psychologist, he continued stuttering. A few months after I was home, he stopped. His mother had left him again, that's all.

Gentlemen Marry Brunettes was entertaining, but it ran way over shooting time and overbudget and lost money. I was right to worry. Although Robert was supposed to be a co-producer, he had nothing to say about this one, but he kept his eyes open and learned an important lesson: Watch where the dollars are going!

But no sooner was I back home than I was off again—this time to Durango, Mexico, for *The Tall Men.* Clark Gable was the lead. Cameron Mitchell played his brother, Robert Ryan was his competition, and Raoul Walsh directed. Gable called me "Grandma" in the script, and from then on all the time. We called Raoul "Father," and I have ever since. I fell in love with Raoul. I'd heard what a tough director he was to work with and found him instead to be a marshmallow with my kind of humor. Raoul had had an accident years before and wore a patch over his right eye. He rolled his own cigarettes, and would snap, "Take it before they forget it," after a single rehearsal. Who wouldn't love him?

I had a phone call from Robert asking me if I wanted a divorce. Carmen and I had done a lot of praying and the Lord had said, as we had prayed for Boyd and Robert, that *they* were no mistake, but divorce was in the mind of one, that in the midst of the feast he stood starving. We didn't know which one then, but now I knew. I wrote him and listed all the good things we had and said, "No, I do not want a divorce." In a few days, he was there. He was quite distant at first and then I finally knew everything was all right. I wasn't the least bit worried, I guess, because the Lord had told me.

Robert liked Raoul, Gable, and Joe Boehn, our unit man. My friend David Hempstead had a script called "A King and Four Queens," which I'd given to Robert. He thought Gable would be perfect for it, and when he showed it to him, Clark agreed to do it. Russ-Field's second picture was set.

Clark was a doll to work with and a terrible tease. He kept bringing up John Payne, just out of Robert's hearing, since I was dating John when I first met Clark. He was now engaged to Kay Spreckles and obviously was very much in love.

The Tall Men came back to finish at the Fox studios, and that was my first experience with fake snow. It's ridiculous to be hot with warm, cotton-like plastic snow blowing all over you.

Raoul made me redo one scene. He said I was bitter rather than sad when I talked of my mother's hard life, and he was right. A dear man. I kept in touch with him until he died; he was eighty-one and blind, but still funny and bright as a tack. I always sent him Father's Day wires if I was away and called him when I was home.

Having been to Europe on Marry Brunettes, then going immediately into The Tall Men, and still trying to figure out why Robert "stood starving in the middle of the feast," I was exhausted. When Nick Ray came up with his gypsy story, Hot Blood, to be made at Columbia, I was apathetic to say the least. It's too bad, because Nick and I had wanted to work together ever since we met on the retakes of Macao. He was, as Mitch said, "a very talented sophomore." But he wasn't like a lot of the people at RKO, who didn't care and just ground pictures out. He had innovative ideas and had already done Rebel Without a Cause, among others—fine films.

When I first came on the Columbia lot, I met Harry Cohn, the tyrannical head of the studio. His office was just like in the movies—enormous and equipped with his own barber chair. He was a very attractive man and quick with words.

"Well, I'm glad to meet you. You're the only girl around Howard Hughes who doesn't sleep with him, I hear."

"Oh, there are quite a few of us," I answered, "but it's nice to know the word's out."

The rest of the lot was old and musty. I felt sorry that Rita Hayworth had such a rickety home away from home.

During the shooting of *Hot Blood* I was just as tired when I woke up as I was when I'd gone to bed. Instead of going to lunch, I would get into a steam cabinet, because I ached all over, and then have hot soup and lay down until it was time to patch my makeup. Poor Nick wanted a buddy to get excited with, but I was a dead loss.

The only good thing about the picture, as far as I was concerned, was that Nick gave my brothers Jamie and Wally parts in the picture. Jamie played my brother, a slothful lug who lived off me, and Wally was the right-hand man of the gypsy king, played by Luther Adler. Wally was supposed to sing, but Nick finally felt it would seem too operetta-ish, and he was probably right. I really couldn't care less at the time, I'm sorry to say. I was just too tired. Cornel Wilde, my co-star, got nothing from me.

I know this, however: Producers are really wasting everything when they force performers to work when they're tired. They cheat the public. And that's exactly where drugs take hold of performers. If they were rested, most wouldn't even think of drugs in the first place. But many take uppers just to keep going. I never got caught in that trap, thank God, but I can certainly understand how it happens.

One day when I got home from the studio, my brothers called and said they wanted to have a meeting. I had been too tired to go to chapel or do anything but sleep on my one day off. Robert said, "What the hell for, you're beat." But I went anyway.

They were sitting in chapel and wanted to know why I was always tired. Was I sick? Why didn't someone do something about it? I tried to explain that everything I was doing had to be done, and no one else could do it.

The next morning these four six-foot brothers of mine walked into Lew Wasserman's office and demanded that he do something. I don't know what Lew told them, but I was touched at their concern.

F O U R T E E N

Early in 1956, I got a call from Dr. John Sibley, who had found children for friends of ours. He knew of a baby who was to be born in April. Were we interested?

I was. I wanted two more. So out came the fleece again. "Lord if You want us to have this baby, make Robert say okay." Robert said no, emphatically. Disappointed, I said, "Amen, Lord," and called the doctor and told him no.

Eight weeks later, Robert was out late, which was unusual, and I had gone to sleep. But at three in the morning I awoke with my husband teetering over me saying, "Honey, call that doctor. We've got to get that baby. You were right. Call him now."

Being like a bear with a sore tail when I'm awakened, I snapped, "That baby's been given to someone else weeks ago, you ass. Go to bed."

"Honey, call Dr. John, please," he continued.

"I'm not calling anyone at 3 A.M. I'll call tomorrow, but I know that baby's gone."

The next morning when I called, Dr. John said, "Well, I just thought you might change your mind, so I held off calling anyone else on my waiting list. The baby's due very soon and you can have it."

About a week later, Jack Benny had Connie, Beryl, and me on "A Shower of Stars." During rehearsals, Beryl and I carried Connie to a stool in front of a mike: Connie was five months pregnant and crippled due to a hormone imbalance in her body, which prematurely separated her hip area. Back in our dressing room, while we were having a pray about the show, I got a phone call. I had a baby boy. "Bucky," or Robert John Waterfield, was born. Connie's Robert was born a few months later.

Bucky's godfather, Bobby Jackson, went into the hospital and brought him out to the car where Mary, our house-keeper, and I waited. Bucky was a fine, healthy baby with red hair. I couldn't get over the fact that the Lord changed that stubborn man's mind at the last minute. He wasn't kid-ding when He said, "I'll open doors no man can close and close doors no man can open."

Buck had more fun as a baby than our other two kids for several reasons. For one, his father was now used to the fact that babies didn't break if you played with them. When Mary wasn't there, I put him on a blanket on the floor in the dress-ing room under my vanity table with a comforter over him so I could hear him when he got hungry. At first this was at 6 A.M., but pretty soon he slept as long as I did and every-body was happy. Thomas and Tracy were old enough to adore him. They were not jealous of him and were a big help in the "watch the baby" department.

This spoiling turned Buck into a very bright, happy char-acter who kept the whole family in stitches. Robert would try his best to discipline him with a stern face, but invariably Buck's actions would make his father turn away so that Buck couldn't see him laugh. He seemed to be without fear, even of his father. People called him Huck Finn, and it fit because of his freckles and dancing brown eyes. Occasionally he ran into trouble with Thomas or Tracy because he was too ram-bunctious and they'd flatten him. There were several baby boys born to our gang around that time, and they were all named Robert John, but each one had a different nickname: Robbie, Robey, Rob, Bobbie. I had wanted Buck on his birth certificate. Robert was nicknamed Water Buckets—Buckets then Buck by the Rams—so we decided that Buck would be the baby's name. But with all the Robert Johns, I acquiesced and let Robert John go on the birth certificate. But his name was Buck!

It was beach time again, and the days were long and wonderful. When the guys were hunting or at training camp, my girlfriends and sisters-in-law and their kids were there. We all helped, so there was loads of leisure time. We philosophized, laughed at our problems, and giggled, and the kids had a ball because they had their friends.

At night we showered, put on caftans, had wine, music, and more talk by the fire. If the others went to bed, I often sat and stared at the water "night dreaming." One lone boat was all lit up way out on the horizon and spots of light from the house lit the waves as they endlessly rolled in. A time alone at night was always necessary to me during those people-filled years.

On one such night I thought of Marilyn Monroe. I wished I had had her phone number, because I knew she belonged there, where we were all laughing about our problems.

The next day Robert arrived from a hunting trip and said, "Marilyn Monroe's dead, I heard it on the radio." We were stunned. If only, if only. . . .

Even today, my children seem to think that I was gone all the time, and I'll admit it does sound like it. But I was home a good deal more than they realize, or I'd have gone mad, and they wouldn't be the responsible citizens they are today.

Let's see: ten pictures since they were born that took up eight weeks apiece. Even if it took ten weeks to make a picture, which it hardly ever did—eight is more like an average number—these pictures were done over a ten-year span. This leaves 440 weeks I was home day and night. I was always home at night, except for those awful five and a half months on location on *Gentlemen Marry Brunettes,* and the few weeks on *The Tall Men.*

For club dates and plays, which followed the picture years, I would only sign for four weeks; and at the most there might be three of these dates in a year. That's twelve weeks out of fifty-two. Too bad, kids, you only remember the rough times, the lonely times. The rest of our lives were spent at home, and ninety percent of the time happily.

When I wasn't working I was usually the last one up, at about nine. Robert had his coffee at the corner coffee shop at seven and the kids had breakfast and left for school. I would have many cups of tea and go about telephoning at my desk. I always had something in the fire, something to talk to someone about—either WAIF or scripts or an idea I had for the kids' bunk beds or a commercial house plan for families with children.

I often went to lunch with one of my gal friends and Robert did the same with the guys. Afternoons were the times to see friends and talk. I might pick the kids up at school, or not, but always everybody was home by half past five. The phone was unplugged by six so we could have dinner in peace followed by a quiet evening. Many of the WAIF gals were always in hot water with their husbands because the phone went until eleven at night. Not us. Dinner was always at half past six. On the housekeeper's days off, Robert cooked venison, deer liver, pepper steak, or stew. He would tie a dish towel around himself and make our drinks, I would sit on the kitchen counter, and we'd talk about what went on with the Rams or the latest gossip with our buddies. He and the kids were always looking out for deer across the canyon from our large kitchen windows, which was a big thrill for them. The dogs, Blintz and Katrinka, were let in as soon as the kids were home. It was always a warm, happy time.

After dinner there was homework to be done and television. We all piled on our kingsize bed for television. Then there were goodnight kisses and prayers. Often after Robert fell asleep I'd go to the living room to watch the diamonds in the valley below. It was my private time to contemplate the day and my navel.

Weekends were barbecues with the gang down by the pool or at the beach. Frances always came up. On anniversaries or birthdays we went to dinner with the gang and on to nightclubs to see whomever was in town on the Strip. On those occasions I usually got two dozen red roses from Robert, knit dresses, always something beautiful and expensive. We had marvelous times.

New Year's was always a ball. Our gang (Bob Kelly, Hamp Pool, John Sanders, Ozzie Lang, Don Paul, and their wives) got sitters for the kids and took off for one house to spend a two- or three-day holiday. We played jokes on each other right and left, everyone had an acerbic sense of humor, and no holds were barred. Hamp got drunk early one night and had to be helped to bed. John tucked him in and placed a large raw sirloin steak in his armpit under his T-shirt. The next morning, with his huge hangover, Hamp looked down at that warm, bloody steak and almost died!

My job was to fix breakfast on New Year's Day. Since the only thing I could cook were eggs, I made *huevos rancheros* and eggs Benedict. The guys made Bloody Marys and screamed, "You said you couldn't cook! You're just too damn lazy!" I said, "Why should I cook when my darling husband is so great? Besides, I clean up everywhere I go." And I do. I'm constantly emptying ashtrays, even in total strangers' homes—anywhere.

These times were always sensational and Robert felt perfectly at home, all his reserves were dropped. He could say all the nasty things he thought and would get it back in spades. It was needling humor—husbands to wives or guys to guys. Hamp would holler at Olive and swear he was going to replace her. She would answer him in her slow way and then stick a zinger in. I called her "acid mouth," because she looked so sweet and motherly but knew just where to cut you off. Peg always acted like she was mad at John, giving him the silent treatment. When he would give her a hug or a pat on the fanny, she'd give out with, "Have another drink, fatso." It was all a game.

One year when we were in Palm Springs, Kelly had to get back to Hollywood to do his sports broadcast. The guys put Limburger cheese all over his motor. The temperature was 102 degrees and he had to keep stopping all the way home to throw up. He called from town, laughing, "You bastards. My car is ruined and I damn near died."

One Christmas morning Robert woke up and looked out

to see fifty Christmas trees standing around the pool. How in hell was that accomplished? He quickly went down and threw them over the side of the hill. We had open house on Christmas, and he didn't want the jokester to see them there. He waited, never letting on that anything had happened. Nobody mentioned anything all day. When Bob Kelly came home from his house in the mountains and found trees all around his pool, too, Robert knew it hadn't been him. They agreed to keep mum and keep their eyes and ears open. Finally it was narrowed down to Hamp and his teenaged son Johnny. At the Ram office Hamp never let on. Robert and Bob tried to think of a good way to get him. Hamp's dog, Yeller, was the light of his eye, so they called the Valley paper and put an ad in for a month that read, "Magnificent golden labrador free to anyone with good home," with Hamp's phone number. Well, it started. The phone rang and rang. Slow Olive tried to tell the callers she just couldn't imagine why that ad was in the paper and that the dog certainly wasn't going to be given away; her husband liked the dog better than he did her or the children. This went on for weeks—calls night and day. Finally, in desperation, Olive called the paper to try and cancel the ad, only to be told that only the person who placed the ad could take it out. She then went down to the paper, talked to the editor, and explained our gang—I'd love to have heard how! This was one of their practical jokes and if the ad wasn't taken out, she'd have to change their phone number. Those guys really deserved each other and us, and we them.

In deer season, Robert, Garcin, Jackson, and their sons usually went hunting somewhere up in the Cuyama Valley. Bob and Merilyn Garcin raised their four kids and cattle there. Bob and Peg Jackson had three kids, lived at the other side of the Valley, and raised hay. Our kids were always with us.

We spent part of every summer up there on the Garcin's ranch and then Merilyn brought her kids down to Malibu until the fellows got through hunting. At the beach I taught my own and all the visiting children to ride waves. The little ones could only wade until they could swim, and they got their butts beat by me if they broke the rules. I often thought some of the neighbors might call the cops on that mean Jane Russell for abusing her and her friends' children. But in a group of gossiping mothers with nine kids, I was top sergeant. It was a tough life, playing all summer at the beach.

Fox was making *The Revolt of Mamie Stover* with Raoul Walsh, my dear "father," and Richard Egan. I was loaned out for it and was happy to be with my buddies. The book was wild and I was delighted the Hays office was in control—I wouldn't have done it if it had been today. Fox watered down the story so much that it was slush. The scriptwriter thought that being a whore was a lovely occupation and gave my character no stress at all. Raoul wanted to put some guts into it, but Buddy Adler, who was running the studio by then and not Darryl Zanuck, thought the writer was the living end, and all decisions were slanted his way. Raoul was very unhappy. He wanted, at least, to show some of the rough times that a lady of the night had.

As usual, I just learned the lines and had fun. There was no point in trying to fight studios. Who could understand their thinking? I did open my mouth about a very simple thing and got nowhere.

As you know, Agnes Moorehead was a strong redhead, and Mamie was supposed to be a platinum blonde. I knew a lot about myself—what I could and couldn't wear, what colors looked good on me—and I definitely knew very dark or very white hair goes best with my skin tones. But Buddy was afraid that such a big departure from my usual hair color would throw the audiences. So I was to have red hair and Agnes, who played the madam, was to wear a blonde wig. I called Buddy and suggested that Agnes keep her own great hair and I go platinum. He sounded annoyed that I'd gotten him so early in the morning and told me to forget it. "Just do as you're told," he said.

It was things like that, and listening to Raoul and others I worked with, that made me want to be on the decision-making end. I was to learn the precariousness of that end of the business, too. I already had, somewhat, during *Gentlemen Marry Brunettes*. So screw it. It was Fox's picture, so I played Little Bo-Peep who had a swell time being a whore and who bought up half of Waikiki. But the film wasn't like the book and it wasn't like Raoul would have done either with "dramer" as he used to say. I did manage to make Mamie someone believable who was from the wrong side of the tracks.

Richard Egan had a suite across the hall from mine in the hotel where we were staying during the picture. He and I were together the first night and I was still needling him about getting married. He said, "Oh no, you're a long time married, and a long time dead." We fought our way back and forth all through the picture. It was our joke and we understood perfectly, but obviously some other people didn't. One New York actor went back home and told Portia he'd never heard people so nasty to each other. "They hated each other," he said.

One night, Doug, the hotel manager, and his girl, who were old friends of Rich's, were going to dinner and Richard asked me to go. "What, no date?" I queried. "Oh, shut up, Blackie," which is what he'd often call me. I'd dyed my short hair penny red and wore a long wig over it in the picture. He hated it. So we all went to dinner. A large table of servicemen were sitting next to us. We never stopped deviling each other, and finally one of the soldiers came over and bent close to my ear and said something. I said, "No thanks. Later maybe." Richard was staring at me when I turned back to the table and he wanted to know what the guy had said.

"Well, he said that if you were bothering me they'd be happy to beat the shit out of you."

Well, Richard was apoplectic. I'd never seen anyone so mad. It was truly marvelous to watch his face turn to rage. He glared at the table of guys, who seemed oblivious to him. Finally he couldn't stand it and went over to the soldier while I'd gone to the ladies' room. I came back and saw him talking to several of them and he smiled and said, "All of you have a drink on me," and returned to the table.

"What did you do?"

"I went over to ask that guy to step outside and then he

told me he just asked you to dance. I never felt so humiliated in my life. I just paid for twenty drinks, you bitch."

Well, we left and I laughed all the way home. It was things like that the poor New York actor didn't understand.

During the picture I won the Golden Apple Award and was asked if I'd shoot some film of my acceptance to send to the Women's Press Club. William Holden had won the man's award. So I was put in a black bathing suit and I sat on the sand and talked to my friends at the Press Club and congratulated Bill and reminded him of our meeting at Arrowhead when we were teenagers.

When Mrs. Alex Budge, a school chum of Mother's, gave a lovely luncheon for me, I got a chance to say a few words about WAIF. I thought a chapter in Hawaii might not be a bad idea at all. It took two years for it to come about, but it finally did.

The picture was nearly over, but Christmas was just a few days away and I was promised that I could be home for Christmas. The last Christmas in London was more than too much and I was determined to get home. But when a terrible storm came up and we couldn't get our last day's shoot on the golf course, I learned we'd have to stay over. I went bananas. I had felt so confident that we'd go, I simply started bawling. We were in the hotel and Raoul and Richard were in Rich's room with six or eight tall rum drinks lined up in front of each of them. Raoul had his wife, Mary, with him and Richard couldn't have cared less where he was on Christmas. I seemed to be the only one upset. I stayed in my room as long as I could, then stormed over to those two boozing lugs.

"Grandma, the planes aren't going. Come on, have a rum," Raoul said.

"No, you bastards, I don't want a drink, I want to go home."

They tried everything for me. Then Richard said, "There's two feet of water in the lobby, be reasonable."

Finally, when I'd given up, Raoul, with his sweet Pisces heart, said that if one plane left that island, we were to be on it. There was a possibility that one would leave the next morning, so Raoul took Mary, Richard, and me to a motel near the airport where we spent the night. We did get on a plane. I was thrilled and "Father" kept saying, "I'm taking my baby home." Down in the bar, Richard and another actor were drinking, and I joined them. Rich never stopped:

"Well, here comes the spoiled brat. You don't care about the picture, that they can't make the last shot. You're just thinking about yourself."

"You aren't married," I said. "Wait till you have a wife and a bunch of little kids waiting for you. You'll find out what it's like. I missed one Christmas, that's enough."

He came back with, "We could all be killed, you know. They've never had such a storm over here." The water had covered the end of the runway.

I stormed topside and lay down on two seats with a blanket over me. Richard finally followed, and as he passed me he was laughing. He leaned over and rocked me in the seat saying, "Is it mad? Is her going to pout?"

I threw the blanket back and snapped, "Go shit in your hat," and covered my head again. He roared and wandered back to his seat.

Pretty soon, someone tapped me and handed me a card. It was from a clergyman and said, "If there's anything I can do to help, please feel free to ask." I thought, "Oh Lord, they think we're serious. How could they ever understand?"

Christmas at home was sensational. I've often goaded Rich about it since. He now has a wife and five kids and will *not* be separated from his family over Christmas.

F I F T E E N

We now had six chapters of WAIF in Los Angeles, New York, Palm Springs, Hawaii, San Francisco, and Chicago. We had brought thousands of children from Europe and the Far East for adoption to American couples. International Social Services hired extra social workers for their offices overseas to process children. One gal, Susan Petiss, had contacted agencies in every state to process parents. The plan worked beautifully.

I've often been asked if I'm not proud of what I've done in WAIF. The answer is no—grateful and amazed is more like it. The Lord gave me the idea and asked me to obey. I simply put one foot in front of the other and started knocking on doors. That's really all I did. Other people did all the rest. I feel humble about WAIF. It's as though I am watching a wonderful parade pass by and my only part in it is that I've told it where to line up. Each chapter has decorated its own float in this parade. Each chapter president has been behind the wheel. The agencies did a wonderful job and learned a lot in the process about our own "hard to place" children. But it's the Lord's parade, not any one individual's, and nobody knows that better than I.

I got to see a planeload of the first children arriving from Greece that I'll never forget. There were eleven children, from babies up to nine-year-olds. The girls were in dresses, but their heads had been shaved about a month before, for lice, I suppose.

At that time all the parents waited in one room, and the children were delivered in a bunch after they cleared customs and immigration. As we stood waiting, someone came to tell us there was a hubbub going on at the other end. One of the older children had started crying and now all the others were crying too. A tall, well-dressed woman standing next to me said, "That's probably mine."

"Why do you say that?" I asked.

"Because she's very bright, she's been in seven different foster homes, is eight years old, and she's a hellion."

With that, the children started through the door, the older girl crying hysterically. A short Greek–American woman said, "That's my baby," and tried to throw her arms around the hysterical girl, who lunged away from her, right into the arms of the woman I'd been talking to. She immediately sat down with the girl on her lap and said to the little Greek woman, who was still after the child, "Please, let's let her calm down, and then we'll figure it out." The Greek woman then went to grab someone in authority to insist in a loud voice that that was her child. You see, every parent had a picture of their child.

The other parents and children seemed to have found each other in the pandemonium, but I noticed one little girl with blonde stubs sitting on the floor in the corner by herself.

Then I looked back at the sitting lady holding the girl. The girl had a small purse. Each child had been given one before they had departed. She was fingering the lady's bracelet and looking at a picture the woman was holding. "Is that you?" the woman asked. The child then opened her purse and took out a picture. Well, it was a picture of the woman whose lap she was sitting on and her husband, who was standing quietly beside her. I couldn't hold back the tears.

The little thing alone in the corner turned out to be the Greek lady's child. The woman hadn't recognized her, because in her picture the child had dark hair. "Well," the social worker escort explained, "this is summer and her hair lightens in the sun."

They told the woman that she didn't have to take the child; they'd find another home immediately. She should think it over. By afternoon you couldn't have pried the child away from her.

After that, of course, they had the children meet their new parents in separate rooms. That mixup would never be repeated. But for raw emotions being displayed, you can't beat adoptive parents meeting their new children. I don't think there was a dry eye in the place.

Eventually even the Hughes office joined WAIF, openly took a table at every fund-raising event, and gave us ads for the books, signed only with "From a friend."

And so, in the end, Howard Hughes and RKO were involved in the business of finding homes for orphans. Edith, on the other hand, was extremely aware and in no time at all was indoctrinated in our work and became very involved indeed. When new bylaws were needed, it was Edith who helped Everett Laybourne, our new attorney, draw them up. She also came up with a wonderful idea.

WAIF had been in existence long enough to have quite a number of ex-chapter presidents, so Edith suggested we have a board consisting of only past presidents, since they, she reasoned, would be totally WAIF oriented. Everett Laybourne was the only person with an outside job who was on the board, all others were past presidents of WAIF chapters. It worked out beautifully. Edith eventually wound up on the board herself, which just delighted me.

Robert started in earnest with Russ-Field now that he had Clark Gable and Raoul Walsh set for *A King and Four Queens.* Joe Boehn, the unit man from *The Tall Men,* was with them, and we moved into a larger office at the Goldwyn studio. Gable wanted me to play one of the gals, but I declined, since I knew we were going to have trouble getting pictures I wasn't in. For tax purposes I could only be in half the pictures we produced.

That picture went very well. The next was a story Robert found called *Run for the Sun.* Reading scripts became our daily and nightly chore. It was fun being involved in something together for a change. Before this we'd been going in opposite directions all day and sharing things that happened at night, but now it was a united effort. Robert caught onto the picture business very quickly, but he still felt he needed a co-producer. Harry Tatelman was on this one with him, and they signed Richard Widmark to star and then Jane Greer and Trevor Howard. Mexico was the natural location, so we went to Acapulco and had a lovely time. I did, anyway, because I wasn't working. I slept as long as I wanted and lay by the pool until the poor actors came out of the jungle where they'd been shooting all day. We all went out to a different restaurant every night. I didn't have to worry about learning lines or getting to bed at all. It was really a great vacation for me.

Margaret's story, *The Way of an Eagle,* was lost, and she tried telling the story to another writer who'd done scripts before, but he turned out nothing at all. Our time to use Jeff Chandler had run out, so that was the end of that. I've always been sorry about it—I loved that story. But both Robert and I liked the book *The Fuzzy Pink Nightgown* (dreamed up after Marie McDonald was "kidnapped"), so we had a script written for that, and this was to be my next picture.

Finding a story, writer, director, and leading man was no easy job in those days. People were still under contract to studios for the most part, and the independent actor–producers were all working on their own projects. I wanted to find a stage actor for the lead, but I didn't know that many stage actors. Our lack of actor, writer, and director friends began to tell on us for the first time. We really only knew football players.

Norman Taurog was hired as the director. He wanted Dean Martin, who had worked only with Jerry Lewis up until then, to play the leading man. Norman saw the picture as strictly a Technicolor camp, while I had the mystery and romance of it in mind, in black and white.

It should have been one way or the other, but as it turned out it was neither. That was one time the star should have had nothing to say, I guess, because Norman would have made a comedy in color with Dean in his first semiserious role—which he's done fabulously since—and the publicity alone would have pulled it off. Or we should have had another director.

Unfortunately, Norman told Dean that he wanted him, so when Ralph Meeker, whom I'd seen in *Picnic* on Broadway, got the role, Dean was very unhappy with me. He's never said anything, but every time I was offered to his television show, I was turned down. Oh, well, such is life.

I also turned down *Love Me or Leave Me* opposite Jimmy Cagney (which set Doris Day up for years at MGM), because I was dying to do *I'll Cry Tomorrow*, which was being made at the same time. The author, I was told, wanted me. As a result, I did neither. Lew Wasserman should have strapped me in a chair with a gag in my mouth, but he was much too nice to do so. He didn't even try to convince me. Levis was long gone to Seattle, Washington. Too bad, he'd have yelled at me and said, "Do *Love Me or Leave Me!*"

At any rate, *The Fuzzy Pink Nightgown* was made with Ralph Meeker and Keenan Wynn, whom I adore, in black and white. Norman still got his slapstick ending, but it just seemed old-fashioned without color. That picture was neither fish nor fowl, but I still liked it. We did start one trend. We got Billy May to score the picture, and since then many pop arrangers have scored movies.

Near the end of the picture, we had sort of a party in my dressing room with just the cast and my crew. Robert had gone to play handball and then was going home. It was a Saturday night, so there was no work the next day. One of my old loves, whom I'll call Lance, telephoned, and I invited him over. He was separated from his wife and feeling blue. One by one the kids from the picture left and pretty soon the two of us were sitting there alone, quite loaded, and talking about old times, swearing our undying love. Neither of us wanted or needed the whole physical act. We'd sidestepped that for years. I'd written to him a long time before:

> I love you.
> For no immediate reason at all
> I feel compelled to tell you

That I love you with a love which is wonderful to see,
It seems to want nothing
But stands and wonders at itself with wide trusting eyes
Too peaceful to cry
Content to leap and dance at joy of knowing that it is,
And indestructible.

It had been a truly beautiful relationship. Yet, because we were drunk, I'm sure, we did the one thing I'd sworn I would never do. We went to bed.

Robert awoke at 3 A.M. to find me not home yet and became very worried. It wasn't like me. By the time he drove to the studio, he was angry. When he walked in and found us, clothed but still talking in the sitting room, he was livid. He said nothing but stood over my old friend with his jaw muscles working and his hands clenched into fists. I left the room scared as hell. My friend said quietly, "Sit down, Bob." With that Robert turned on his heel and left.

I said nothing, but just walked out after him to my car. I had no business driving and I don't know how I got home. I was stoned. Once going over the canyon, I slammed on the brakes just in time to see the great black abyss of the canyon right ahead of my wheels. Backing up, I continued somehow until I finally got home. I was numb as I entered our dressing room. Robert grabbed the front of my shirt, pushed me up against the wardrobe doors, and said, "Did you go to bed with him? Did you?" When he raised his other hand, I said, "Go ahead, hit me. It'll cost you thousands of dollars if we can't shoot." I was scared but calm. He simply dropped both hands and left the room. I crawled into my nightgown and into the bed, my head swimming.

When I woke up, I was so hung over I couldn't move. Robert came in and sat on the side of the bed. I said, "Robert, I'm so terribly sorry." I was destroyed that I'd broken my word. Sitting me up, he put his arms around me and said, "Honey, we're just going to forget this ever happened, okay?" I couldn't believe it. I was so grateful I could have died. Huge tears welled up in my eyes, and we clung to each other.

I went to Chapel to pray with Carmen. The Lord said,

When thou seest thyself thou sayest, "I am a sinner," but I say ye have truly made thyself humble before Me and thy spirit has been exonerated of all which would blemish or mar. Foolish have ye been, yes, but I have renewed thy faith and you will be freed and you will find that you are to maintain . . .

For the next two years everything remained the same to an outsider. But Robert, in spite of his decision to forget everything, never forgot. Nor did I. I wasn't allowed to. The atmosphere was perpetually chilly. We still made love, but no words were spoken, and it was usually in the middle of the night after we'd both been asleep, rather out of a subconscious urge.

Once at the beach house he got on the subject of infidelity. I was in bed and he was pacing back and forth. "Oh, come on, Robert, do you mean to tell me that in fourteen years of marriage you've never had anything to do with another woman?" I asked.

He walked over to my bedside, picked up my Bible, and put his hand on it. "I swear on this that I've never had anything to do with another woman since we got married."

I was stunned, but had to believe him. He wouldn't dare do that. So I backed down, feeling guilty for the hundredth time and hoped he'd leave it alone. He did for a while, but he never really forgave.

However, my direction was clear. I hoped I could outlast him. Meanwhile whenever the chance came, I ran.

One of the places I ran to was Korea. Now I was to see another part of our WAIF operation. Johnny Grant was taking a show to Korea and wanted me to help entertain the boys. Terrific! WAIF had a connection with the Choong Hyun Orphanage in Seoul. I would go to entertain our boys and see how they prepared our little kids at the other end while I was there. Edith would go with me. She had been under contract to both Hughes and Russ-Field to handle my public relations since RKO closed down.

First we flew to Hawaii and then to Tokyo, where we were greeted by a throng of Japanese and U.S. Army personnel.

One army daddy met the plane with his little girl, who'd been adopted through WAIF. She was darling, and he obviously adored her.

We were whisked off to the Imperial Hotel, which had been designed by Frank Lloyd Wright. It was old, Japanese in feeling, and I loved it. I've always like staying in hotels that have the feel or flavor of the country. There's nothing more boring than the new Americanized hotels; they're the same the world over. I want to be in foreign surroundings in a foreign land. It's the difference that makes it interesting.

Tokyo was much bigger than I expected. It's miles and miles across, like Los Angeles, all solid city, with paper cherry blossoms on the trees in the center of the city.

Then we started the tour, which was why we had come—to see our boys so far away from home, much like M*A*S*H. There were a lot of girls in the show, naturally: singers, dancers, comedians—anyone Johnny Grant could dig up for this tour. He had made countless trips and was the buddy of every man over there, from the top general to the bottom private. He called himself "the poor man's Bob Hope," though I'm sure he made more trips than Bob.

Kay Brown, Virginia Hall, and I rehearsed a trio number on the plane. It was so darn cold, I wore my fur coat over a heavy hooded sweater and furry boots all the time except for the show. Then I froze in beaded gowns. I always took them on junkets, because they never wrinkle.

We'd arrive at a base, have lunch, do an afternoon show, rush to another base for dinner, and do a night show. Never have there been such audiences. They went wild. After the night shows, we were entertained by the officers a bit and then we crawled into bed with our sweaters on and our coats on top of the covers. The next morning it was breakfast and a bus ride and a repeat of the previous day. This lasted about sixteen days.

One night after a show, we were billeted in the WAC barracks. There was a phone in my room, although it was an utterly barren, impersonal room off a long hall. We were beat and desperately needed sleep. I'd just fallen off when the phone rang. I picked it up and someone said, "Is this Jane

Russell?" and then giggled. I didn't need a fan or a heckler—
I needed sleep. This happened three more times just as I'd
doze off. Now, I've warned you I'm a bear when I need sleep,
so I grabbed my fur coat and boots and stomped down to
Edith's room and ordered her out of bed.

"You go in that room, I can't stand it."

She laughed and grumbled, "What the hell am I supposed to do about it?" but she went. It only happened to her
once. Then she got hold of an MP and said, "Can you do
something about this damn phone? We've got hecklers on
it."

"Yes, Ma'am," he said, and yanked the phone right off
the wall. Now that's service!

Each outfit tried to outdo the last. Those men were so
glad to have females around, they did everything but carry
us around on satin pillows. We've never felt so treasured and
feminine before or since. It really spoiled us. Edith said, "We'll
probably kick our old men when we get home."

When we got to Seoul I went to the Choong Hyun Orphanage. There they had these gorgeous children, fathered
by servicemen of the various countries who participated in
the Korean War. Because they weren't full-blooded Koreans,
they would have been ostracized by the community. At the
orphanage they slept in beds instead of on pads on the floor;
they ate with knives and forks instead of chopsticks; and the
social workers tried to teach them a little English so that it
wouldn't be so totally strange to them when they got to
America.

The children in Korea were the first ones I had ever seen
in an institution who were happy, outgoing in affection, and
laughing. Maybe it was because the young women tending
them were sweet and affectionate, but it made me think.

Some children were already spoken for, and some were
simply waiting for adoptive parents. They'd all been found
in the street, eating garbage out of cans or, if they were babies, bundled up and left in doorways.

One ten-year-old boy was so dear and helpful to the other
little kids, Edith fell in love with him. That's when the Lord
hooked Edith on WAIF. She didn't gain a son, but she never

stopped working for WAIF from then on. The Lord's really cute, and He knows just how to hook the fish He wants. My mother always said, "If the Lord wants you to go to work on something, He rubs your nose in it to get your attention."

All in all, it was a very soul-satisfying trip, between the kids in the show, our men in uniform who were so home-sick, and the children who were lost and had been since they were born.

Back at home things were still rocky, though smooth on the surface. One way or another, Robert punished me. Everything seemed normal on the out-side, but essentially it was far from that. It was then that I started in with Mrs. Browning.

Mrs. Browning, a psychologist, was a bit younger than my mother, gray haired, and terribly bright, the sort of woman who could operate on only three hours of sleep and still be bursting with energy. I learned a great deal from that lady.

Since my sister-in-law Pamela was having problems with Jamie at that time, she and I would drive all the way to Pas-adena together, each have our hour with Mrs. Browning, then get in the car and cry all the way home. "Well, that's an-other perfectly good day ruined!" Pamela would say. One by one, Mrs. Browning helped most of my family, including Mother. "There's one thing I've learned from all you Rus-sells," she once told me. "Although each one of you is dif-ferent, there's one main thing you all have in common. You can be led anywhere, but you can be driven absolutely no-where." How true.

I took my problems and my guilt to Mrs. B., and she understood. For months we went over how to get along with Robert and how to deal with the whole mess. As for Lance, that had been a mistake really. It had nothing to do with our relationship.

Then an interesting thing happened. I received an offer from the Sands Hotel in Las Vegas to do an act there. It was for a good chunk of money and the first time in years that I'd gotten such an offer. Because of the bad press I'd gotten years before when I did that appearance in Florida, I was sort of "off limits" for nightclubs. I was delighted when that Vegas offer came from out of the blue. It could prove to be a breakthrough at last.

For the act at the Sands, my choreographer came up with the idea of having me make an entrance carried on a litter, playing the movie star bit to the hilt, and singing "Be Happy with the Yacht You've Got." It didn't quite work. People weren't quite sure whether I was kidding or not. We had also planted my youngest brother, Wally, who has a beautiful singing voice, in the audience. I would say that there was someone I wanted them to meet, drag a visibly reluctant Wally up on the stage, and he'd sing a duet with me followed by a solo. It was a good gimmick and the audiences loved it. So did Wally.

I was in Las Vegas for four weeks, doing two shows a night with no day off. It was totally different from the pictures. You worked at night, went to bed at dawn, and slept until three in the afternoon. I got tired, especially with no days off, but the hours seemed to come more naturally to me. I was never a morning person.

All my friends and family took turns coming over to see Wally and me—Pat, Alberta, my brothers and sisters-in-law, Mom, my children, and Robert. For them it was a wild vacation.

My brother Ken had a system he taught us, and though I hadn't gambled since the funny money in grammar school, I took $500 just to "blow," and we all played roulette with Ken's system for the four weeks we were there. Next to the last night Wally and I were alone, and we lackadasically sat down to play. We had about $2,500 in our bag of chips that we were going to divvy up with the other boys, and don't you know we lost the whole thing! In minutes it was gone! We were in shock. I've never been tempted to go near a table again. I'm much too tight.

At the opening, Robert was there when Lance called to wish me good luck. Robert found out and immediately went home. The siege was still on.

Being so cut off from Robert, I started becoming obsessed with Lance. It was an impossible situation, I knew. That bothered me considerably, and when I prayed about it with Carmen, the Lord said,

> Leave him where the message is—deep in the inner chamber—for I say, "Who can understand the deep yearnings of the soul? Who can fulfill the desire that springeth up from the innermost parts of thy being? Who hath time to listen even if he understood?" It is I who hath time, little one. Incline that longing, that unfulfilled portion of thyself, into the inner courts of the Father. Keep thyself free from the harmful rays of the enemy who cometh in the still of night when you have put the cares of the day far behind thee and fills thee with hidden traps, unseen hungers. The sun warms him who uses it wisely, but he who has no wisdom and thus no protection can be destroyed by the same rays from the same sun. Warm thyself or be destroyed.

Soon after that I had a vivid dream that I can still see to this day. I told it to Mrs. Browning. Since I'd been seeing her rather steadily, I was learning to interpret dreams a good deal by myself.

In my dream, I was walking down brown stone steps as though to a small medieval basement (my subconscious). There was a large barrel in one corner and from behind it came a large, beady-eyed rat, slowly crawling toward me. It was a loathsome thing (the part of myself I loathed). I grabbed a piece of cardboard and whipped it back into the corner, but it simply turned and started for me again. I repeated this a couple more times and the results were the same. When I realized the rat wasn't going to give up, I took a large safety pin from my skirt and opened it up like a spear. This time as the rat came close to me and I stabbed it in the eye. I felt panic. Then, slowly, dark red blood ran down the pin, and with great relief I knew the rat was dead. With that I picked it up on the end of the pin, threw it in the barrel, and walked up some other stairs to a garden (my conscious mind).

Mrs. B. said, "Well, your interpretations so far are correct, but you missed something very important. You used a safety pin, a female emotional symbol, and turned it into a

"Russell's Raiders."
Joe E. Brown, Jr. (in cockpit) and cadets greet their pin-up.

Mr. and Mrs. Robert Waterfield.

Tracy, Thomas…and Buck

Richard Egan and I get serious in *Mamie Stover*.

Mitch and I as onlookers in *Macao*.

Cornel Wilde and director Nick Ray on the set of *Hot Blood*.

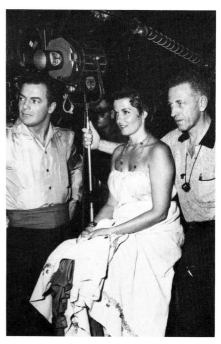

Dottie Mitchum, Jean Simmons, Robert and I join Shotgun's wedding party.

I'm asking Noel Neill, "Ain't There Anyone Here for Love"
prior to the muscle man number in *Blondes*.
The hunk on the right is my brother Jamie!

Jeanne Crain and I with cannibals in *Brunettes*.

Blondl and I plant 'em at Grauman's.

"I've been to London to see the Queen."

Beryl, Leslie Uggams, myself and Connie meet LBJ at the White House.

masculine, intellectual phallic symbol. That's what killed the rat. One of your main problems is that you're always following your emotions instead of your head. Since you also threw the rat in the barrel and walked away, this problem will never bother you again. You've already solved it in your subconscious." She was absolutely correct. Everything was in its proper perspective. I was warmed by the friendship, and not destroyed.

A public relations man from the Holland American Line called me several months later and said they were looking for stars to entertain the last night out on a trip to Hawaii. Would I be interested? They'd take my family too. Those were the magic words.

Esther Williams was interested in taking her three kids and her Mom and Dad, too. She was separated from Ben Gage and had been dating Jeff Chandler, but she thought it would be good to get away from men in general to think for a while. I felt pretty much the same way.

I asked the public relations man if WAIF could have a cocktail party aboard in Honolulu to give the chapter there an excuse to raise some funds. He agreed, and we were off.

I took my mother, Thomas, and Tracy. Buck was too small. My mom and Esther's mom got along great talking about the Lord, and the kids were all around the same age and had a ball roaring around the ship. On the *Statendam* Esther and I became well acquainted and talked about husbands and marriage and divorce a lot.

The last day out she entertained in the swimming pool and gave prizes for pool games to the children on board. I sang in the salon with the band.

After the WAIF cocktail party, Esther and I stayed in a hotel with our entourage of kids and "old folks," as Esther called them. We swam several times a day, and when we went out at night, Esther would say, "Let's go swimming again." So between dinner and dancing, she'd drag whomever was with us into the pool. I found out one can stay up quite a bit longer without getting tired or totally sozzled that way.

Jack Ackerman, who'd doubled for Richard Egan in *Underwater*, lived on Maui, and I wanted to see him again, so we all flew over to Lahaina. He and his partner, Larry, met us and took us to the old hotel there. When we arrived a bunch of the Hawaiian beach boys had come to see Jack and they were all smashed and playing ukuleles and singing. Between our kids and the drunken Hawaiians, it was chaos.

The next day we were to drive to Hana Maui, several hours away. Esther said, "Larry doesn't drink, so he's to drive the 'old folks.' I'll take the kids with me, and, Jane, you go with Jack and the Hawaiians. We'll all meet halfway for a picnic lunch." When we finally got to the beautiful, quiet Hana Maui Hotel, the Hawaiians were still singing and a bit drunker. The kids jumped into the gorgeous fish pond by the entrance and threw pebbles. The "old folks" just stood and stared. I thought the proprietor was going to have apoplexy. Esther and I attacked the kids. That night there was more revelry. The hotel was mighty glad to see us leave the next day.

When it came time to go home, Esther decided she wasn't going back on the ship to entertain again. She was going to fly. I stood there with the president of the line as we pulled out, and he felt like he'd been had. I would have loved to have flown home too, but a deal is a deal. I spent several days with my kids and my mom and several nights alone. I'm glad I stayed on board, however, because eight years later the *Statendam* became very important to WAIF.

When I got home Robert was still giving me the silent treatment, and I thought, "How long, O Lord, how long?" Richard Egan was getting married in San Francisco. I couldn't miss that, since I'd been nagging him about getting married all those years. So after I delivered the kids and Mom home, I flew up to the peninsula.

Richard's brother, a Jesuit priest who had Richard's exact voice, married the couple in a formal wedding at a large church in San Francisco. It was odd: It sounded like Richard was marrying himself. Pat, his bride, looked beautiful and he was very handsome in his tails. When he knelt down you could see that even the bottoms of his shoes were blackened. After the ceremony, while we waited for the car to pull up to the side door so we wouldn't get entangled with the fans outside the front of the church, I went up to the altar to pray. The church was empty, and I thought, "Lord, if I were standing up here with Robert Waterfield today, when the priest would say, 'Will you take this man to be your lawfully wedded husband?' I would run out of this church, screaming NO! at the top of my lungs."

But when I got home, and don't ask me why, everything was as it had been before my two and a half years of punishment began. Robert was genuinely glad to see me and greeted me with open arms. The banishment was over. Everything was back to normal and it was wonderful! All I could do was thank God.

S I X T E E N

In 1960 Robert replaced Sid Gillman as head coach of the Rams. Russ-Field, it seemed, wasn't going to make any more pictures for United Artists. They hadn't okayed any other scripts.

Of the four films we did, two lost money (the ones I'd been in) and two made money. We had one more script that we wanted to do, but United Artists kept dragging their feet and never did give their approval. When it finally dawned on us they weren't going to play ball, we closed up shop.

My feelings? Well . . . *Gentlemen Marry Brunettes* was their fault, and *The Fuzzy Pink Nightgown* was mine, so it was a draw. Robert kept himself busy coaching, and I went back to staying home for a while—my very favorite occupation.

Robert was delighted to get back to football with all his buddies. Not that he hadn't seen them all along, but now they would be working together again. He had been anxious making pictures and he'd rather be anxious about football, which was his first love.

So once again football became the keystone of our life. As far as I was concerned, my appreciation of the game depended on who was playing: If Robert or the Rams were involved, I loved football, but otherwise I couldn't have cared less about the game.

At home games, I sat with other faithful wives in the stands at the Coliseum and cheered our guys to victory. Once when "Ye Olde Rams" threw themselves a banquet, I supervised the skits put on by the wives and got Giselle MacKenzie to sing a few songs. We lived, ate, and talked football in the Waterfield house—whether we liked it or not. That's the way it was. Yet these were our happiest times, the ones I can look back upon with some bit of pleasure—times when we were more or less involved in the same things.

Every day at five o'clock, Robert and I would have a quiet drink together and catch up on conversation and family talk. I looked forward to that hour all day. He would be at home, I'd be finished with the usual chores and errands, and we'd sip our drinks and just be "together." I don't mind being alone so long as I know someone's coming home, but I don't like being lonely. So that lovely peaceful hour with Robert before dinner with the kids was very important to me; it was a sort of an oasis of calm shared by us both.

Life was good, our marriage seemed okay, and all was going along well.

Then I was invited to the opening of a couple of Hilton Hotels in Cairo and Athens. It was a fun idea, because Bayeux Baker was now with the U.S. Embassy in Cairo, and it had been much too long since I'd seen his laughing face.

There were a lot of celebrities on that junket: Hugh O'Brian, Anne Jeffreys, Robert Sterling, Lauritz Melchior, Hedda Hopper, Linda Cristal, Leo Carillo, Van Johnson, and Robert Cummings. A cablegram was sent ahead to the embassy in Cairo requesting that Bayeux Baker be seated next to me at all official functions. I didn't know it then, but no one at the embassy had ever heard of him. He held some insignificant job, and since he was a bachelor with a penchant for Egyptian belly dancers, he did little or no socializing with the other members of the diplomatic corps. They hardly knew he was there until my cable arrived. He was thereupon excused from his duties, whatever they were, and assigned not only to be my official escort but also to meet me at the airport.

The scene that greeted us when we landed was one I shall never forget, and neither will any of the others, I'm sure.

Bayeux said it was a good example of an Arab mob running amok. Good example or not, I was scared to death. I was told that I was very big in Cairo, their favorite movie star, and they looked on me as a sort of Mother Earth figure. I could have done without that!

We managed to battle our way through the crush and get into the bus that was to take us into Cairo. We were surrounded by the fans and were really frightened that we would be run off the road. Hedda just couldn't stand it any longer, and called out in a shrill voice, "Throw Jane Russell to those wolves so that the rest of us can get to the hotel." For a minute there I wasn't sure she was kidding.

But we weren't out of the woods by any means. We had to fight our way through an even bigger mob at the hotel. The crowds never seemed to leave the entrance, so we had to fight our way through each time we went out or came in.

All sorts of things were planned for our entertainment, firsts for most of us, like riding on a camel in the Sahara Desert, viewing the pyramids and the Sphinx by moonlight, and dinner parties in great big tents. We had an official dinner at the embassy and went to the Grand Ball at the Nile Hilton.

Bayeux, of course, was always at my side and sat next to me at all dinners, at the table of honor no less, and would look around at all the important embassy people seated at lesser tables. They were no doubt wondering who the hell he was.

As a result of my visit to Cairo, Bayeux was elevated to a more important position at the embassy. He was given his own office, still doing nobody's sure what. Someone high up must have figured he had powerful connections in Washington, and so Bayeux was treated accordingly. It could have proved a big boost to his career, he told me later, had he remained in the diplomatic corps.

When it was all over, I said goodbye to Bayeux and flew off to Greece to preside over the laying of the cornerstone of the projected Athens Hilton. There we went through more or less the same routine, but in Greek: official receptions, dinners, and visits to the local sights and taverns, where we stomped on wine glasses and sampled the local firewater, ouzo. Then, tired but happy, we came back to the States.

During this time, I found that since there wasn't much film work, many stars were either breaking into television, going to Europe to work, or doing summer theater. Those little theaters operated on the system of having their own resident group of actors who would do all the parts except the lead, and for that a "name" would be brought in.

For actors with no stage training, this was very difficult, because they were working with people who had done the play before. Added to that, the Hollywood actor was working under totally unfamiliar conditions. Acting in the round, with an audience surrounding you, is nothing like acting in a studio, where if you make a mistake, you can do it over.

I was offered a great many plays, but I didn't find one I was interested in doing until I read *Janus*. I signed to do the play and was immediately beset with doubts. How the hell was I going to retain all those lines for the entire run? In films I would learn my lines for each day on the night before. If I were asked to repeat them one day later, I couldn't. So naturally, I was scared to death at what I was facing.

I had almost two months in which to prepare myself. I read the play over and over, memorized one page at a time, then went back to it the following day to see how well I remembered it. Then I went on to the next one, always going back to the preceding pages as I went ahead. Slowly and methodically I learned the whole damn play.

Janus was to be performed in three New England cities in three different tent theaters. Ella Gerber, our tough but talented director, knew exactly what she wanted from us. I had to get used to acting with the audience around me, and Ella kept saying, "I want to be able to sit anywhere in the house and still see your face. I don't mind your turning your back to me once in a while, but this mustn't last more than a couple of seconds."

We had to keep moving all the time. Ella helped by working out all the moves at home before she even came to rehearsals. On opening night I was terrified, wondering what I was doing here so far away from the safety and security of a movie set. But I got through it all right and was well received by the audience. I even enjoyed the experience. We played a week in each town, and it got better and better as I became more and more at ease on stage. That was my first stage play, and from then on I did a lot of plays and even went to London to do Val Parnell's variety show *Sunday Night at the Palladium*.

But after *Janus* I came home and fell back into a routine of restful pleasure with my old man and children.

The success of my Las Vegas engagement led to another offer from the Latin Quarter in New York and one from Rancho Vegas. Lou Walters had since died, so I okayed the Latin Quarter as a break-in for Vegas. Jack Cole staged the act. He had a hot ten days to put it together, too, because the Morris office (I had left MCA and was now with the William Morris Agency) had hired one of their choreographers, who had suddenly walked out, leaving Joe Rotondi, my piano conductor, and I staring at each other in disbelief. The choreographer had said we were impossible, but I swear we had been lambs for two weeks waiting for him to come up with an idea. I called Jack, frantic. He said, "Oh, that idiot. Come up to the house right now." He helped me pick out songs, including a spiritual medley from the records Connie, Beryl, and I had done. He also rehearsed four boys, including Ronnie Field, a noted choreographer today. This was a damn good act and one I could be proud of. Jack came back to New York with me to open the show.

On opening night E. M. Lowe, the owner of the club, sent two dozen long-stemmed roses to my dressing room. A few minutes later he knocked on the door and greeted me with a broad smile.

"I thought you were never going to work for me again because I sued you in Miami," he said. I stared at him, stunned.

"You mean it was you who sued me?" I managed to get out.

His smile widened, "Who'd you think it was?"

"I . . . . I thought it was Lou Walters."

"Lou managed my clubs and put the shows together. I did the suing."

"Damn you," I spluttered. "If I had known it was you, I wouldn't be here today."

"That's my good luck," he said, that big grin splitting his face. I felt awful. Poor Lou, I had blamed him all those years and it wasn't his fault at all. From then on, whenever I would bump into E. M. Lowe, he would grin that wide grin of his, and after a while I began grinning back.

While I was in New York, I stayed with my East Coast arranger–conductor, Hal Schaefer—the same Hal who was on *Blondes*—and his psychologist wife, Dr. Leah Schaefer. They had an apartment on Riverside Drive, and I had my own room until their daughter Katie was born. Then it was "our" room. At any rate, I adored them and it was my New York home.

After Rancho Vegas, where the kids and Frances and my friends and family could all get to, I subsequently sang in Mexico, South America, Italy, Spain, Australia, and other places in the States. Either Hal or Joe Rotondi went with me and, of course, Edie Lynch. We saw the world together.

SEVENTEEN

In the fall of 1961, Robert and the Rams were scheduled to play the Forty-Niners in San Francisco, so I decided to go up a few days early and stay with my friends Christobel and Jake Erlich. They fought with each other as hard as they partied. As usual, when I arrived, they were in the midst of a donnybrook, and Jake was beside himself. He had two men up from Los Angeles on an important business deal, and now Christobel refused to join them for dinner unless I agreed to go along. Jake begged and pleaded. I went.

His business associates turned out to be two brothers, Phillip and Dan Darby. The moment we were introduced, I realized I'd met Dan before and had felt at the time that we would meet again. And here we were in San Francisco about to have dinner together. Dan had sandy-brown hair, a medium stocky build, and devilish blue eyes. He was somewhat shy, had a low, sexy voice, and dressed immaculately. I started needling him the moment we sat down. He laughed, and within minutes we were all laughing. Phillip and Jake tried to talk business, but it was hopeless. When we finished the meal, Phillip excused himself. "See you tomorrow, Jake." Then he turned to me, shook his head, and said, "Now Jane, take good care of Dan." I replied with great sarcasm, "Oh, I certainly will!"

Dan was obviously embarrassed, but laughed. I glanced from one face to another. Everyone had a kind of "knowing" look about them, the kind of expression people have when they expect something special is about to happen. I smiled to myself. They thought that the way we had gone on Dan and I might be an item. Too bad, dear friends, you don't know me as well as you think you do. I'd had dinner with hundreds of single men, had gone on trips with them—nothing happened then and nothing was going to happen now. Robert had never given my men friends a second thought, and this would be no exception.

Phillip had concluded his business and already returned to Los Angeles so it was just Dan, the Erlichs, and I the next evening. Once again we drank, dined, laughed, and had a marvelous time. Dan explained that he had to return to Los Angeles the next morning. No problem. Robert and the team would be arriving in San Francisco the next afternoon. We had a wonderful time. After Christobel and Jake went to bed, Dan and I talked a while and exchanged telephone numbers. He gave me a gentle kiss goodnight and that was that— the end of a pleasant but not too important interlude. Or so I thought.

After the game Robert and I returned to Los Angeles and life resumed its normal course. By "normal" now, I mean Robert did his daily coaching job and met with the gang at the Pump Room every afternoon at five, and I was alone wishing there was someone I could have a drink with as well. Life at home was fine, but I couldn't understand *why* Robert couldn't be with me instead of the boys at cocktail time. It was one of the few times we could be alone and relax. The kids were doing their homework or outside playing with their friends, the housekeeper was cooking dinner, and I was alone. Once or twice, out of sheer desperation, I dropped in on the boys. Robert would assume a hangdog expression, leave his seat at the bar, and steer me over to a corner away from the other guys and their football or girl talk. Our conversation, or lack of it, together with his stony stare let me know in no uncertain terms that I was trespassing. I stopped going to the Pump Room. Then I tried dropping in on married friends during the cocktail hour. Through no fault of theirs, I felt like a fifth wheel. I stopped doing that too.

Back to reality. Those two hours, between five and seven, were the loneliest hours of the day. Finally, one drizzly afternoon when I was particularly bored, I searched through my phone book and found Dan's number. I dialed.

"That's funny," he informed me after we'd said our hellos, "I've been thinking of calling you every evening, but I didn't think I should. Would you like to come over and have a drink?"

He lived in a pretty little "bachelor pad" in the hills, beigy brown, cozy, and lushly furnished. No need to decorate here. Soft music was playing, he had a chilled bottle of wine in the fridge, and a fire was burning in the fireplace. The hour was spent talking, laughing, and appreciating each other. We were able to discuss everything about life, ours in particular. Dan never knew what to expect from me, but I knew he enjoyed my company as much as I enjoyed his.

That's how it started. I'd drop by his place every afternoon about five or so, have a drink, talk, relax, and be home in time for dinner. This went on for months. He was very special; but in spite of the fact I knew Dan was very attracted to me, I was determined to keep him just as a friend. In the eighteen years Robert and I had been married, I had been unfaithful only once. I would never, under any circumstances, put myself in that position again. Dan was safe. He had a girlfriend and he knew just how married I was. Yet I needed that time with Dan. He spoiled me rotten and I loved it. Never in my wildest dreams did I suspect that this contented feeling would turn into love.

Our meetings were interrupted when I accepted an offer to do a play at Chicago's Drury Lane Theatre. Edith Lynch went with me. Each night during my stay there either Dan called me or I called him. One weekend he flew out for a visit, and the three of us together with a friend of Dan's went to dinner. Edith said very little, but it was obvious she sensed there was something between Dan and me, and she didn't like it one bit.

Dan's friend took his leave, and we went back to the

theater apartments, where Edith excused herself and went straight to bed. Dan and I sat up talking, but something was different. We weren't smiling anymore. We searched each other's face, then looked away; the attraction between us was so strong you could cut it with a knife. Still, I would not, could not, have an affair. It was enough just to be together in the same room—even conversation seemed unnecessary. I had a show to do the next day, so reluctantly, around four in the morning, we said goodbye. Dan and I clung to each other in the doorway and he looked up and said, "I'll always see you in this crazy lavender room. . . ." The next day a dozen silver roses, which are really lavender, arrived after he'd gone back to Los Angeles. That was the first of dozens of lavender roses I received from him everywhere I traveled for the rest of the year.

When the play was over and I returned home, I felt more confused than ever about my relationship with Dan. I must have acted perfectly normal, for no one said a word about my behavior being any different, but I felt different. I thought about Dan twenty-five hours a day. Robert seemed oblivious to any change in me.

I had had a crush on almost every leading man I'd ever worked with, but it had never gone beyond the "crush" stage. My feeling for Dan was different. I was in a turmoil. The devil was having a ball.

The situation came to a head one weekend while the Rams were playing out of town. Whenever I went out, I always left a telephone number where I could be reached in case of an emergency. On this particular night, while I was at Dan's home having dinner, Christobel called, hysterical. She and Jake had had a drunken fight involving a knife, and Jake was in the hospital; she was at her mother's. Dan and I assured her we would be there on the first available plane. It was impossible to get a reservation till morning, so I agreed to spend the night there at Dan's. Christobel's tragedy left me unnerved, and staying with Dan, although it was the first time, seemed perfectly all right. I was wrong. The inevitable happened, and it changed my darling, needling friend into my darling, passionate lover. From then on I was sunk.

When we arrived in San Francisco, Dan went right to the hospital to see Jake and I went right to Christobel's to hold her and pray. She couldn't stop crying or worrying about Jake. She still loved him and had no idea how it had all happened. Christobel was finally notified that Jake was off the critical list and would live. She seemed calmer, and I was able to leave her for a while. Dan and I headed immediately for the Mark Hopkins Hotel. It was my first experience at playing that deceptive game of using separate elevators, not registering, dashing out side doors instead of the front entrance, and checking to see if the coast was clear. In the middle of this madness I would suddenly think, "What am I doing? Dear Lord, what am I doing?" Yet, even as I asked the question, I knew the answer. I had to be with Dan! It was as simple as that. It was insanity.

There was a second offer from Chicago to do my nightclub act at the Living Room. I took it. Dan came for another visit, but this time he stayed with me for two nights. Hal Schaefer was with me, and he, like Edith, instinctively disliked Dan. That didn't disturb me one bit. What did disturb me was what was the Lord thinking. I called Carmen and asked her to pray. The Lord said,

> The devastation of the soul brings on the mortification of the body—and but for Me the lusts of the flesh would consume them. Receive Me as I revealed Myself to the Holy Prophets of old, and ye will know that ye have been no place that I have not been with you—and there is no place that you can go that I am not there also.

As David said in Psalms, "Though I make my bed in hell, Thou art there."

My next out-of-town date was in Houston, at the Cork Club. Edith went this time, and every time Dan called she managed to be in the room. We finally had a screamfest. She thought I should make a clean break with Robert, *then* go with Dan, if I had to, but, she insisted, it would be a hell of a lot better if I dropped Dan completely. She couldn't understand that it was impossible for me to make the break with

Dan or Robert. Eighteen years of marriage and three children still had a powerful hold on me. And I still loved Robert. I wasn't sure of what I was doing with Dan; I only knew I couldn't give him up. Edith packed her bags and went home.

Between club dates I always rushed home, wild to see the children, glad to see Robert, and mad to see Dan.

The William Morris Agency had booked me into Checkers, a famous club in Australia. Edith and I patched things up and she went with me. It seemed as if it took weeks instead of days before the plane finally landed at the Sydney airport. We were both exhausted, and my back felt as if it had been broken from trying to sleep in the cramped seat. And of course, when we deplaned, we walked right into a mass of reporters gathered together for a press conference! Both Edith and I were wrecks from jet lag and felt like zombies as we tried to be pleasant to the newsmen. I smiled through clenched teeth as I told them how thrilled we were to be there.

Almost twenty-four hours later, I felt human again and went to Checkers for rehearsal. My conductor, Arnold Ross, whom Peggy Lee had found for me, was rehearsing a tune with lyrics that Peggy had written especially for me. The tune was "Big Bad John" with the lyrics "Big Bad Jane!" It tickled me because the song had become popular already both in Australia and in the States. It would have been a perfect engagement, fun and exciting, except that all the time I was starring at Checkers, I was trying to play checkers with the men in my life.

It was Easter—my wedding anniversary. I tried most of the day to call Robert and felt alternately relieved and sad that I couldn't reach him. Finally I sat down to write him a letter. I struggled with the words.

> Robert,
> Three or four times today I tried to phone you to say Happy Easter but simply couldn't. My heart wasn't in it. It was instead very sad and heavy. I truly feel, as I'm sure you do too, that this is our last Easter together.
> I've thought and prayed for two or three years now

and never come up with the answer. I go my way lonely and you go your way lonely, and we're both too nice to do that.

I realize many people live together and beat this, but our problem is I stifle my life and you live yours. So one of us lives and the other dies. Consequently, we both die, because one must have communication to live.

God knows I've always loved you, but I can't bend or bury ME any longer. I've done it now for over twenty years and it's catching up. Now I walk around like some zombie, I care very little about anything. I don't blame you for one thing . . . you've been a good, dear, kind husband and the most wonderful father I've ever seen. But . . . and this distresses me more than anything, I haven't been a good mother these days. I'm so unhappy with me that I can't be the friend, buddy, disciplinarian mother they need and miss so much.

You always say, "Hell, do what you want to do," but I'm such a weak sister when it comes to doing anything alone. I simply must share. And we have shared so much. Our funny sense of humor. Our children. Our house. But in all honesty I think that without our children and our house, what would we have had to discuss at the dinner table? And when we do have a discussion, we get into such chaotic battles that we both try to stay away from that subject from then on.

Now our only worry and responsibility are those three young things I forced on you and you nurtured. *Very, very* important. But surely if they can get the best from you and the best from me, it's better than halfhearted attempts from both of us. If I could say whatever I want to, whether you liked it or not, it would be different, but I always try to fit in and all my natural desires I shove to the bottom until I can get together with my kookie oddball friends. And if I can't, they stay buried. This isn't your problem. You are you, and while it may be selfish, it's at least healthy. I wish I could be that way. I'm trying, but I'm forty now and haven't learned yet.

I guess what's scaring me really is that this is the halfway point and I can't bury "me" any longer. Not

for anyone. And more important I don't want to go it alone anymore. Won't in fact. I'm so tired and worn out from doing things alone that I could die.

So I in this late, but not too late hour, am flipping out. And I beg of you to let me go. Let us both go. Let us both be ourselves, whomever they may be. Please, darling, wish me well. I wish you well and will always love you. . . .

Jane

I didn't even have the guts to tell him there was someone else. When the letter was finished, I flung myself across the bed and lay there, too numb to cry and completely exhausted, until it was time to dress and go to the club for the show. I slipped into my glittering gown and piled makeup on my face, feeling more like Pagliacci than Jane Russell. I was a clown trying to make a sad face into a happy one. On stage the bright spotlights couldn't blind out the pain I felt, but it was hidden from the audience.

It was not until after I arrived home that I learned Mother had called Robert before my letter reached him. She informed him, "If you care about your wife, you'd better start paying more attention to her." The conversation had shaken him, because Mother rarely said anything at all to Robert. Naturally he assumed I'd met someone in Australia, and by the time I arrived home he was a wreck.

As I walked down the ramp I immediately spotted the ashen faces of my kids, staring at me through huge frightened eyes. Robert was as pale as the children and his green eyes were filled with questions.

Very little was said on the way home, but when I put the children to bed, they asked me if I was going to leave them. When I asked what they meant, they told me that Daddy had said that I might not ever come home again. I was horrified, and tried to reassure them, "I looked all over the world for you kids, and I will never, never leave you! I love you!"

I held them and rocked them until they were convinced, then we all kissed, said our prayers, and for the first time in days they were able to go to sleep peacefully. Satisfied that the children were okay, I went to the kitchen to face Robert and ask him why he had told the children what he had before we had a chance to talk about it. He looked directly at me, squared his shoulders, and folded his hands on the table.

"Who's the guy?" Silence. "There is another guy, isn't there?"

I nodded. It was like a dam bursting. I admitted everything and told him I'd been seeing another man for nearly a year.

Robert was stunned. He sat quietly for a moment, allowing my confession to sink in. "Look, you're *my* wife, and those three kids out there are *our* kids. I don't want you to ever see him again. I want you to call him now, *now,* and tell him so. Call him!"

"I can't. I can't tell him over the phone. I'll have to see him to tell him face to face." I knew now, after seeing the children and from Robert's tone of voice, that he was right.

"Do it now," he replied, his voice a monotone.

I picked up the car keys and walked slowly to the door. My shoulders weren't sagging from the strain of the flight but, rather, from the tons of guilt and misery I was carrying. I cried all the way to Dan's, wishing I could become two women, one that could go home and be a faithful wife and mother and another who could rush to my lover's arms and stay there forever.

The moment Dan opened the door he knew there was a problem. When I explained what had happened and what I knew I must do, he turned away.

"I thought this was going to be such a happy homecoming. I suppose you have to do what you think is right," he said.

"Dan, this has been wrong from the start. I don't know how I'll stand it, but I know I can't see you again. I belong with my family and I can't leave them."

God must have finally given me the strength to leave, for I went home and stayed there. I was filled with a sadness inside I just couldn't shake. It was as if half of me had died, but I held fast. Robert understood. He was as loving and tender

as a man could be, but I'm sure he watched me with butter-flies in his stomach most of the time.

Several nights later, we drove to the Sunset Strip to hear my friend Beryl Davis. It seemed that every song she sang dealt with the misery of love and I couldn't control the tears. Robert watched me quietly. Patient. Kind. He would wait out the pain.

For weeks our days continued as usual, but I was itching to reach for the phone. I finally did and Dan was as relieved as I was. Other phone calls followed, but finally that wasn't enought and we met. Nothing had changed, except the abandon we'd felt before. I started parking my car in his ga-rage with the doors closed. His swimming pool was totally private; we swam, lay in the sun, and touched. We both knew something had to be done, but what? In the meantime our guilty lovemaking and furtive meetings continued.

I prayed, "Lord I can't make a decision. Please help me. Make this turn out the way You would have it."

The next step, I believe, was the start of His direct an-swer. Dan got a call from Robert asking to meet him for lunch. How did Robert know Dan's name, phone number, or that we were meeting again? I'd been so careful to make sure I wasn't followed or anything. I got the gist of the conversa-tion from Dan afterward.

Robert, with his most formidable stone face, had said to Dan, "I want you to stay away from my wife."

"Well, that's up to her I believe. If she wants to see me, I certainly will see her. She's a very honest person. Ask her how she feels."

"I know my wife is honest, don't tell me about my wife; just you stay away from her. We'll work out our own prob-lems if we have any. You leave her alone."

At least that's what I heard from Dan.

When Robert got home, I told him I knew about lunch, that I had tried to stay away but I simply couldn't. I loved Dan and wanted to see him; perhaps we could have a trial separation until I could sort things out without sneaking around. Well, that was where his patience and understand-ing snapped. His temper came out in full swing. It wasn't

2 0 2

unusual for him to lose his temper at home; however, he never hit us. But this time I'd gone too far. He grabbed me by my shirt front and systematically banged my back into the full-length cupboards in the breakfast room and finally flung me into the wrought iron chair of the breakfast table, shouting, "All you want to do is fuck around!" The sculptured iron rose from the back of the chair flew across the room. He was through, and with that walked out of the room.

I sat there, stunned. I understood his anger but I was a limp rag and my back hurt like hell. I thought to myself, "Well, that's that. I can leave now." I grabbed my overnight kit, which was always packed for trips, got the kids up and in the car, and drove to the beach house in Malibu. School was out and I'd stay there all summer. I was exhausted and angry but relieved. I'd made the break and the worst was over.

The next day I went to a doctor to see if there was something broken in my back. It hurt like crazy, but the X-rays showed nothing. Lots of friends came down with their children so I was never alone and the children had their buddies. They seemed oblivious to the trouble. Robert never called and I didn't call him. I called Dan. He came down several times, but furtively. He didn't feel comfortable at the house, so we'd leave there and drive around, go to his house, Santa Barbara, wherever. My back kept me flat most of the time.

On Robert's birthday, July 26, I drove the children back to the Valley for the day. I couldn't keep his children away on his birthday. Robert and I said nothing, but the kids were glad to see him and he played with them all day. Then we went back to the beach.

A few days later Pat Dawson grabbed me and said, "Listen, stupid, have you never head of a chiropractor? That's what you need. No back can break a wrought iron chair and not be out. You're coming with me." Dan was there and drove us to a chiropractor who adjusted my spine, and that was the end of that. I was perfect. I was so damn mad that I'd spent all those weeks in pain when one adjustment could cure it all. I now love chiropractors.

When school started I felt I had to go back to the Valley. Mrs. Browning, my psychologist, lived miles past the Valley and I had been able to speak to her only on the phone. I wanted to see her. I wanted Dan to see her, too. I got the kids in school. Robert and I were totally ignoring each other.

I ran to Mrs. Browning and laid it all on her. I happened to mention that Robert had never been unfaithful to me as I had been to him.

"How sure are you of that?" she said. Her eyes seemed to bore into me.

"Quite sure. He swore on the Bible."

She paused, then, "Have you ever tried to find out for certain?"

I shook my head. "No. And even if I wanted to, I wouldn't know how to go about it."

Her manner became gentle and her voice soft. "Why don't you ask some of your friends."

I didn't have to look far. A girlfriend lived on my way home. I stopped and asked her directly, "Do you know positively of anyone Robert has had an affair with? I don't want rumors. It's very important to me."

She sighed, "Oh, dear."

I had my answer. "Who?"

"Your secretary. She thought he was going to get a divorce and marry her."

I was stunned. She had not only been my secretary, but she had also been my friend. "Where and when? Do you know?" I asked.

"At the beach house when he came home from Europe from *Gentlemen Marry Brunettes*. It lasted until he went to Mexico when you and Carmen were on *The Tall Men*."

Suddenly all the messages I had received there—his asking me if I wanted a divorce, his discontent with the feast—all came into focus. My shock turned to cold fury.

Robert was in bed when I arrived and I flew at him like I never had before. Like a wild woman standing over him, I shouted, "You rotten, lying bastard! No wonder you can't stand it if the children lie. You're the biggest liar and cheat that ever walked the face of the earth! The hell you put me through, mentally punishing me for two years when I'd made one mistake and two years before you'd been screwing someone for months who worked for us, paying her on top of it! Your holier-than-thou attitude, and swearing on the Bible—it's a wonder God didn't strike you dead! Now I *know* about this and *when* and *where* and I want you to tell the truth for the first time in your life. Tell me her name. Say it! SAY it, you son of a bitch!" He just laid there staring at me through my whole tirade, and when I screamed, "Say it!" he turned and put his head in the pillow and cried, sobbing her name.

As I stormed into the dressing room I said, "I don't want to hear another word about Dan and me and I want a trial separation." After that there was no more of his standing on a pedestal looking down at this terrible, rotten, fallen woman I was supposed to be.

All during that time my friends had known that there were circumstances that could have equalized the situation as far as I was concerned, yet none of them ever told me. Robert and I might have had a more honest relationship, might have reached some sort of understanding before I ever met Dan had they done so.

The next morning Robert packed some things and moved out as meek as a lamb.

I still saw Dan, mainly in the daytime, for I wasn't about to leave the children without a parent in the evenings. Football had started and Robert was trying to coach, which I'm sure wasn't easy.

Finally one day Robert called and said that the press was snooping around and it was rumored he wasn't living at home. Would it be all right if he moved back just until the end of the season? He told me that he would be gone on trips most of the time and wouldn't bother me. I reluctantly said okay. Neither of us was ready to let the whole world in on our problems.

One afternoon the Lord continued his answer to me. I was having a swim in Dan's pool, and when I finished I walked into the house just as the front doorbell sounded. Forgetting about the frosted glass panel alongside the door, I crossed the hallway to tell Dan that someone was at the door. I was usually more careful than that. Dan's girlfriend pushed her way past him and stormed in like a wild woman. "I saw her!" she screamed. "She walked past here as naked as a jaybird!"

For the record, I wasn't naked at all; I was wearing a bathing suit. Anyway, I went into the bedroom and got dressed, letting the storm play itself out in the living room. My going in there at that point wouldn't have done one bit of good, I was sure. But then I heard her say, "How long is she going to hide in there? Doesn't she have the guts to come out and face me?"

It was like a hideous soap opera. I walked into the room in time to be hit with a renewal of her tirade. Dan was trying to get her to calm down but was getting nowhere. I took as much of it as I could, then turned to him and said, "I think I had just better go. Get in touch when you have a free moment." As he took me to the door I said, "Be kind, she's had quite a blow." With that exit line I left.

Dan didn't phone until the following morning, explaining that he had been sitting in a bar by himself most of the night. He told me that his girlfriend had called him every name in the book and that he had broken up her marriage and two marriages before that. "I feel like a heel because I'm doing the same with yours. I'm beginning to wonder just what kind of bastard I am."

"I must see you," I replied.

We met. But it didn't work out, nothing was the same. Something had died for keeps. There had been too much pressure from every side for anything to last.

I asked Carmen to pray in the hopes she'd receive some message to help me. I was really floored when she got one and sent me its interpretation:

> That which is intended for temptation is made to restore that which is a proper relationship between one man and his wife. You must believe that for one who is blind there must be one to lead the way. Forsake not this one who cannot see for himself.

When the mailman arrived with the following letter, I knew the Lord was doing His thing:

Dear Wife,

I'm writing this on the loneliest night of my life. I can't quote the Bible and I really can't do a great many things, but I guess, like you, I know what lonely means. Wife, where are we that we can't find each other again? Maybe sanity is the only thing that's life for you, but what is sanity? Temporary or permanent?

Sanity to me is not being anything but with you and Thomas and Tracy and Buck. Without this there is no life or sanity. I know the Lord has kept us together for twenty years, and who am I to say now that it shall be destroyed? Someone gave us each other and three kids and moments of great happiness as well as stress. I surely can't say what will take it away without the Lord coming and telling me.

I love you. It's really very hard for me to even write what I feel. What I feel when I'm quiet and say nothing are the things that are most important. When I yell and shout it's my outlet. I do have tender feelings. Feelings so strong that I can't say what I want to say. So many times I've asked myself . . . "Why am I so stupid that I can't tell my wife I love her?" And this has been so for many, many years, not just the last few.

This life of ours has been to me one of you and the children. When I'm alone fishing the only thought I have is I'm alone. But when I'm with you . . . even if I'm yelling at you or loving you or just near you . . . I'm never alone. I'm so terribly sorry that this same feeling isn't with you; I'm sure it's not your fault or mine.

I've never at any time been in the position where I need to ask myself, "Do I love my wife?" That situation never existed. I have always loved my wife. The fear of losing you has said to me, "Come on, wake up." I can't live in fear. I want my family and I want them to want me, and I'll do everything possible to work toward that end. I need to know which way to turn my head, and I'll turn it any way in the world to save you and what we have. If this makes you unhappy, then I will be sorry

that you are unhappy. Like I'm unhappy now, because
I don't know when I'll hear from you.

I'm terrible with words, but what I'm asking is . . .
Is there love or is there no love?

Now I'm waiting for you. . . .

Robert

When the Rams came home I was waiting with all the
other wives as the team came off the plane. Robert looked
rather surprised to see me. I took his hand as we walked to
the car; there was no conversation until we got home.

I told him it was all over with Dan and that I was willing
to try again if he still wanted to. He said, "Are you sure?"

"I'm sure." He put his arm around me and led me to the
bedroom.

EIGHTEEN

That was the beginning of three of the closest years Robert and I ever had. The entire episode was never mentioned again. He truly tried in every way to make things perfect for me. We even started going to church on Sundays. Guess who was there? Perry Lieber—he had stopped drinking altogether and was in church every Sunday. And the Lord had told us "he was a kindred soul." Louis Evans was the new young minister of the Bel Air Presbyterian Church. Robert had coached him. Colleen Townsend Evans, his wife, better known as Coke, was a very dear old friend of mine. Lou was a sensational speaker and for one whole month gave a series of talks on marriage. Robert and I would both be teary eyed. After church we'd go to brunch at the Tail o' the Cock in the Valley and talk and talk. The communication lines were totally open for maybe the first time. He went to see Mrs. Browning a couple of times, but that was a bit too hairy for him. But he'd drive me over and wait for me till I was done! And we always had our cocktails together.

Robert had always bought and picked out my good clothes. He and Bob Kelly would go down to Saks at Christmastime, check out the pretty models over free drinks, and come home with beautiful knit dresses and coats. There was a new Cadillac every other year. I never wanted jewelry: I

was too afraid I'd lose it. But time together was what I cherished most, and we had just that for the next three years.

Robert still wanted me to work, saying, "Just a few more years, honey, and we'll have it made," meaning our insurance would be paid up and we could draw from it. I worked in plays, clubs, television, but I always hated the road, and I was always homesick.

In 1962 in New York State at a dinner theater where I was doing *Bells Are Ringing,* he called and said, "Honey, do you care if I quit?" He'd been having a terrible time coaching. There were five owners and only two would speak to each other. He had to get five okays to make any decision. It was killing him.

I answered, "Hell no. Come back here with Edith and me. We'll go to New York, the two of us, and have a blast seeing the shows on Broadway. He did, just like that. When the press asked him what kind of a coach he thought he'd been, he gave the typical Waterfield answer. "Losing," he said. He resigned in November . . ."for the good of the team" and came East the next night.

At home I tried to talk him into opening up a racquetball club. He adored handball and I liked tennis. We could have started a health club in the Valley, but he said no. He wanted his security right where it was. He was still afraid of taking chances. Changes of any kind still bothered him enormously.

I refused to go back to Malibu and sleep in the bed he'd had his affair in, so he agreed we could sell that beach house and buy one in Newport Beach next door to Richard and Mary Sale. They had a boat docked in front of their house, and we'd taken trips to Mexico and Catalina with them and had loads of fun. It would open up our social life a bit, and I loved nothing better than changing and decorating a house.

The house in Newport had three small bedrooms upstairs for the kids and a large master bedroom that I turned into a childrens' television and living room, adding an outside porch and stairway they could use to go down for a swim in the back bay without tracking up the house. I knew there'd be dozens of kids, and there were.

It was a wonderful party house for both kids and adults. As before, if his friends were there, Robert stayed, but if not, he often drove all the way back to the Valley in the morning and back at night for dinner, an hour each way. Forget about making new friends in a new community. It couldn't be done.

We were back home in the Valley celebrating Robert's birthday when suddenly Frances Waterfield got sick. She had been suffering from a chronic congestion of her lungs. Having been a nurse, she hated hospitals and refused to go to one, but she did agree to have a doctor come in. She was given medicines and told to stay in bed.

On July 25, 1963, the doctor said we had to convince Frances to go to the hospital, as he felt her condition had worsened. But she adamantly refused. The next day was Robert's birthday, and as we were having breakfast a friend who was taking care of Frances phoned to say that she had died.

We couldn't believe it. Frances was such a vital person. Even when she'd been sick before, she always bounced right back, so we really expected her to do the same thing this time. We were in shock. Robert was absolutely incapable of doing a thing. He just sat in his chair and stared at the floor. I made all the funeral arrangements. Whenever the subject of dying came up, Frances had always said, "I don't want any goddam undertakers or expensive boxes or any of that garbage when I go. They're a bunch of grave robbers." So, when I went to the mortuary, I said, "Show me the cheapest box in the place."

That man looked at me in shocked amazement. "But . . ." he started, and I cut him short. "I mean it," I told him emphatically. "She's going to be buried just the way she wanted to be. Simply and with no fuss."

Tracy, who was then close to nine, had insisted on coming with me. All those great big ornate caskets looked positively obscene. With that worried man dogging our footsteps, Tracy and I wandered among the caskets until over in the far corner we came upon a simple lavender box.

"What do you think, Tracy?" I asked.

"Oh yes," she replied, "that looks just like Nana."

"We'll take it," I told the man, enjoying the expression on his face as he realized what a small profit he'd be making.

The word spread fast and all our friends, who adored Frances, started arriving from everywhere: the Apples, the Jacksons, the Pools, the Sanderses, the Kellys, and the Langs—the whole gang. We had a real old-fashioned wake down by the pool. Robert went through the whole thing like a zombie, sitting at the bar staring into space.

At one point he wandered out toward the pool and stood there looking out over the Valley. I followed him and placed my arms around him and tried to get him back inside the house. Without saying a word or even looking at me, he shook his head. So I left him alone with his sorrow.

I wasn't able to attend the funeral; I had to catch a plane that morning for the East Coast. I had signed to do a play and rehearsals began the following day. I hated not being with Robert, but it just couldn't be helped. He's one of those people who has a real need to have people around him, especially when he's under stress. But, I knew all our friends were with him and they would see him through the bad time as well as anyone could.

When I got back to Los Angeles he seemed to be on a more or less even keel once again, although I doubt if he ever got over the impact of losing his mother. It clouded every one of his birthdays from then on. She had been such an enormous comfort to us all.

Connie Haines and I were both working on our own and tired of being on the road alone, so we got Beryl Davis, our English buddy, and decided to put on an act together. We already had all the music from our albums; all we had to do was find someone to book us. That was no easy job, because agents simply couldn't imagine three broads singing spirituals in night clubs. However, we persisted and finally talked Hershy Martin at William Morris to get us a couple of break-in dates, one in Bakersfield and one outside San Diego. After much prayer and grappling with clothes and musicians and lighting effects, we fell into our own groove and opened in Las Vegas at the Riviera Hotel with the great Louis Armstrong, helping him celebrate his fiftieth year in show business.

Richard Blackwell designed fabulous clothes for us, each cut differently to suit our figures but all coordinated in color and fabric.

We three broads came running on stage in white feather full-length coats that we threw off at the end of the first number, revealing gold lamé dresses, all different. We sang three songs in perfect harmony, and then Beryl and I, the two "thorns," faded and Connie, the "rose" of the trio, had her spot. For the end of her third number, we came back and harmonized on a bit ending and did two more as a trio. Then Connie and I left and Beryl did her spot, and so on. Each time the two thorns came back in different gowns, but always keeping the picture coordinated. Beryl took charge of the clothes, Connie the musicians, and I the lighting.

We dragged Andy Thomas the piano conductor and Sid Bulkin the drummer every place we went, and we went all over the bloody States: the Copa in New York, the Palmer House in Chicago, New Orleans, and always back to Vegas every six months to the Sahara, Riviera, and Tropicana.

We'd always grab our two boys and have a pray before we went out on stage. Once Connie's zipper got stuck, and we only had time to rush to our places as they announced us. Andy and Sid gave us hell when we came off. "Don't do that again! We didn't have time to pray!"

I don't think any of us ever laughed as hard or had such a good time before or since. If one was down, the other two were up, so it was impossible to stay down long. All five of us gathered in Connie's room, where we had a refrigerator full of 3 A.M. snacks, cheese, turkey, rye bread, etc. We drank wine and the guys drank beer and we joked and tormented each other unmercifully. The Lord simply kept pouring out joy, because we turned the whole act over to Him, and it worked in spite of all the people who said we were crazy.

Lots of people said I was nuts. Rhonda Fleming's agent

told her her price would go down if she joined a group, so she didn't. I was told the same thing, but I was much more interested in having fun and being happy while I worked than being miserable and lonely and making more money. We could have worked fifty-two weeks a year, but I wanted to go home a lot. Often we took all our children with us—Beryl's three, my three, and Connie's two. They had a marvelous time.

Of course the press were having a field day with their sarcastic, tongue-in-cheek wisecracks. They couldn't put Jane Russell of *The Outlaw* and God and spirituals together. Poor Connie tried to be straight with them and explain that we were all Christians and very serious. I didn't even try. They'd come out with headings like "Bosoms and Bibles," and I told the girls, "Leave it where Jesus flung it. Audiences feel good when they listen to us and the Spirit isn't something you can nail down or put in a box. Praise the Lord, kids! It's all His doing anyway!"

I know it sounds like we were gone a lot, but I refused to sign dates that lasted more than four weeks, and then I wanted two months off. I was the only one with a marriage intact, and I still wanted to get home. It was heaven to get back to my beautiful children and cute, funny old man. But maybe it would have been better if I hadn't come home for good.

Several things happened in 1966 that were entirely new to all of us. It started out difficult and finally became impossible.

The tension started mounting between Robert and Thomas. Thomas was fifteen and had gone out for football, but the coach seemed to be jealous of his father and wouldn't play him. He was marvelously coordinated, like Robert, but high school football was a big disappointment for them both. Thomas sat on the bench.

Thomas also was hoping to get a car when he turned sixteen, and so he and his best friend, Tim West (who had also been adopted by my high school friend Maxine and John West), wanted to get a job after school washing cars to earn some money. Robert was very saracastic with him and said,

"You couldn't keep a job, you spoiled-rotten kid. Who do you think you're kidding?" When I pointed out to Robert that he'd had a car with a hand-tooled dashboard when he was in high school, he just grumbled.

Robert kept up the "no job" bit and finally, on Thomas' sixteenth birthday, he walked in with keys to a sturdy second-hand car and threw them across the table at Thomas. It was ridiculous. Robert had done all the right things but with the wrong attitude, so what should have been a happy day turned into something ugly. It was so sad. Thomas didn't know whether to thank him or throw the keys back. He looked stricken and mumbled, "Gee, thanks, Dad." The entire year went that way for both of them.

It seemed to me that as long as Thomas kept Robert on a pedestal and let his dad make all the decisions, everything was fine. But should the boy get a thought of his own, his dad couldn't handle it. Poor Thomas was terribly unhappy, and there I was, caught in the middle and trying to be the mediator. It was simply a case of the son having to understand the father, not the other way around.

It took years, but eventually everything worked out and the kids learned to understand their father, know his shortcomings and his strengths, and they all loved him very much.

Not only was that year a bad one for Thomas, but sudden change was in the air for Robert and me. I don't know whether it was the lack of football and purpose in his life or the fact that we didn't go to church anymore (Coke and Louie Evans had left our area), but Robert did a 180 degree switch.

I can pinpoint the actual start of that change. In January 1966 he rediscovered pool. He had been dropping by that neighborhood bar for years and had never picked up a cue, but suddenly he started playing and everyone wanted to play him. It became his life. Every morning, from the minute he awoke until 2:00 A.M., he was at the Barrel, except for dinner. He'd come home then, eat, and ask me to go back with him. I did try a few times, but it was not for me. The guys were all decent enough, but the conversation never left football or pool.

Robert seemed totally incapable of understanding why I

didn't connect with his Barrel buddies or their wives. He was very much at home there. He breathed the air of the Barrel so easily that it was impossible for him to realize that I gasped like a fish stranded on the beach in its atmosphere. So I stayed home with the kids. This went on for a full year and I was miserable.

In the middle of that year Robert fired our housekeeper, and I had the kids and the housework on my own. My mind was left on the shelf.

Then I got an offer to do *Catch Me If You Can* in Chicago, again at the Drury Lane, and since the theater was a good distance from the center of town, the management arranged an apartment for me on the premises. Tracy and Buck went with me, since it was summer vacation, and a friend of Tracy's came along because she had a driver's license and could use the car that had been placed at my disposal while I was busy with rehearsals. Thomas preferred to remain in Los Angeles, so he stayed at the Eagle's Nest, (the coffee room that had been built for the chapel at Russellville) and ate his meals with Grandma. It all worked out fine.

During the week of rehearsals we stayed at a beach club hotel, and Robert was in town to coach the East–West game. On the weekend he came out for a visit. The fights we had were just unbelievable. I don't recall what triggered them, but there was always something. We were also doing a great deal of drinking. The kids would pull the covers over their heads and wish we would go away. I too wished we could just disappear somewhere.

Between the fights and the hangovers I wasn't much good at rehearsals. Our director told me that I absolutely had to do something about whipping myself into shape, since we were opening in a couple of days. So I stopped drinking and one of the actors, Ralph Foody, went over and over my lines with me at the beach until I had them down. Opening night I made it all right.

Once we opened we lived out at the theater's living quarters, and the kids really had a ball. Buck was only ten years old and adored Tony de Santos, the owner of the theater, and followed him around everywhere. Tony gave him little chores to do around the place like feeding the fish, for which he got a small salary. Buck just loved it.

During the run Buck decided to become my prop man, so he would be waiting in the wings whenever I came off stage to hand me whatever it was I needed for the scene—a pitcher, glasses, a cigarette. He was most dedicated to his job. I'm convinced that had he spent his growing years with me instead of Robert, he would have become an actor. He was so very likable and gregarious and made friends with everyone he met. As he grew older he changed a lot and became almost stone faced.

Our plan was to return home once the run was over, but for the first time in my life I didn't feel like going home. Instead, I decided to go to New York.

My new manager and friend, Kevin Pines, had flown in to see the play and caught my moans about not wanting to go back to Los Angeles. Kevin is a wild, zany, absolutely mad character with whom I fell in love immediately. He'd already sensed that things were awry in paradise.

"My friend Jerry Shaw is doing a film in New York," he told me "and there's a perfectly marvelous part in it for you. The lead. Jerry's done a lot of top shows on television and this is his first try at motion pictures. Why don't you come back and do it?"

"Why not?" I said. "But what about the kids?"

"Bring 'em along," he replied, and that's what I did.

Tracy's friend went back home and in New York Tracy and I stayed at Kevin's apartment while Bucky went with some friends who had kids his age. We started Jerry's picture but never finished it. The financial backer didn't have enough money to cover Jerry's cutting the picture and was at a loss to know what to do with the material that was shot. It was all one big waste, but as far as I was concerned it was just what the doctor ordered. Tensions were gone, I was relaxed, I'd worked, had fun, and was now ready to go back home and face whatever was there.

Nothing had changed. Absolutely nothing. I'd been hoping for miracles, but none happened. Robert was still keeping up the old routine at the pool table and there wasn't a thing I could do about it.

Christmas was approaching and I wanted it to be the way it used to be, something special. We had certain rituals, such as taking the kids to see Santa Claus and to dinner at the Valley Tail o' the Cock on Christmas Eve. Then we would open only one present each before bedtime and the rest would wait until morning. It was always an exciting time, but this year it was different.

Robert decided that the children were too old for the Santa bit and family dinner. Instead, he accepted an invitation for the two of us to a party given by one of the gang from the Barrel. To keep the peace I gave in, but I made him promise that we would come home early enough to open that one present before the kids went to sleep. He reluctantly agreed.

There wasn't a soul at that party that I knew or wanted to know. It was just an excuse for everyone to get crocked. "What a way to celebrate Christmas," I thought.

At last, after looking at my watch for the hundredth time, I said to Robert, "Let's go. The kids are waiting to open a present."

"I don't want to yet," he informed me.

"Well, I'm going," I told him, "and you don't have to bother driving me, I'll take a cab." With that I stormed out of the room in search of a phone.

"Oh, all right," he muttered as he followed me into the hall, "I'll come with you. But we're coming right back."

I said nothing.

On the drive home Robert took out his annoyance on the car, driving like lunatic. When we got there the children had gone to sleep, very disappointed.

I felt miserable. Robert simply said, "You see, they didn't give a damn. We could have stayed at the party."

"Then go back."

He glared at me. "It's too late now," he said and went off to bed. I poured myself a drink and sat in the big chair by the window, staring out across the Valley. I sat there most of the night.

The big Christmas tree stood like a white-bedecked heavenly visitor, crisp as December's chilly child, overseeing the Valley. Looking out at that scene and the reflection of the fireplace dancing in the window, my mind began wandering.

It darted back to the only other period of conscious living I could remember—to the quiet, knowing times: It's here that high school crushes live and die. They aren't practical. Funny what high school crushes can do. I wondered how long could I go on? How long do utterly impractical things live? "Well, now at last I've nailed it to the wall," I thought, "and it can't escape. This is the end. We'll never have another Christmas together. No chance. No way. This is it." Slowly, my heart heavy with sadness, I got up and went to bed. Tomorrow was Christmas.

N I N E T E E N

I awoke early to the sounds of the children opening their presents. I joined them, putting on as good a front as I could manage. Robert was doing the same. We all trooped down to the playroom to show him his surprise present—a pool table. Then I went back to bed so that I'd be in better shape for dinner. Cooking wasn't my job; cleaning up was. By the time Mother and Uncle Ken arrived, the kids and Robert had made the entire Christmas dinner.

Well, that dinner was a disaster. Robert hardly spoke except to deliver some nasty remarks and the kids and I concentrated more than necessary on our food. The tension was like barbed wire, and Mother must have thought something awful had happened. But she said nothing.

The signs were familiar to her, as I had run to her before when things got too much and I couldn't take any more. But each time she'd sent me back after a pray, saying things would work themselves out and they had.

Finally dinner was over. I was doing the dishes when Robert came in and made another of his extremely nasty remarks. I can't recall what it was exactly, but it was the last straw. I smashed the platter into bits and ran to Thomas' bedroom. I was hysterical. Mother came to the door and stood staring, absolutely stunned by my behavior. After I calmed

down a bit she said very quietly, "Get up, Daughter. Let's go home."

Her words surprised me. At last, I told myself, she realizes what I've been going through. We went home.

Once inside Mother's house I flung myself onto her bed and fell into a fit of sobbing while she left me alone, letting me get it all out of my system. Neither of us heard the front door open.

I had the feeling I was being watched and I turned to see Robert standing in the doorway with a disgusted look on his face. I suddenly realized how love can turn to hate, pure hate. I let out one great, enormous shriek that brought Mother to the bedroom.

"Robert, go home," she said quietly. Without a word to either of us he turned and left.

What was the next step? I couldn't go back, that was sure. Divorce? That word had never entered our vocabulary, yet I knew I was at the end of my rope. Self-preservation was my only motivation at that point. I couldn't even help the children until I got hold of myself.

I told Mom to tell the children that I would be back as soon as I could straighten everything out and not to worry too much. I knew I had to get away; Robert would be back. So I ran to Connie and Beryl. Beryl put me on a plane to Hawaii to stay with wonderful friends there. Christobel caught a plane direct from a New Year's Eve party (and almost got picked up as a hooker with her black satin skirt split up to there) to join me. She found me still bawling and a mess.

I hadn't slept much at all. I tossed and turned and the word *divorce* kept looming, but when I considered it I felt I might as well ask someone to tear my right arm out at the socket.

Finally, instead of wailing to the Lord, I got down on my knees and prayed in earnest. The Lord said,

> This separation is of Me. I care more about your growth than you care about anything in this world. You two have not grown forward but, yea, backward and are destroying each other. I love him as I love you, and I have a

222

work to perform in each. So know this separation is of Me. And see, through all thy troubled, yea, grievous path, have I not thrown rose petals, yea, strewn them on every side? Peace. Peace. Peace. Trust me.

I smiled as I thought of my rose petal friends and with the greatest relief I fell asleep for twenty-four hours straight.

The next morning I called our lawyer, Sam Zagon, in Los Angeles. He finally said that Robert agreed to the divorce. "Fine," I said. I couldn't believe he would give up so easily. "Now I want everything split right down the middle, everything."

"That's fair," he replied. "I'll draw up the papers right away."

"And have Robert sign them."

"Okay," he said, and I made preparations to go home.

Well, not exactly. I couldn't go home, so I went to the Eagle's Nest, where Thomas had stayed when we were in Chicago.

Robert came down to see me the next night. He couldn't believe I would go through with a divorce. He looked drawn and haggard and said he hadn't been sleeping. "I guess I haven't been very good to you lately. Please, honey, I'm sorry. Don't do this," I remember him saying. He was actually shaking and there were tears in his eyes. I really couldn't answer him. I simply let him know I intended to get a divorce as soon and as quietly as possible. We would split everything fifty-fifty and let the children choose with whom they wanted to live.

All my clothes were still at the house, where I'd left them the night I took off, so I was now faced with going back for them. My lawyer arranged for Robert to "quit the property" while I went back for my belongings, to avoid a confrontation. Thomas, Tracy, and Buck were there and, although I'd talked to them on the phone, it was just wonderful to be able to hug them again.

I assured them that I wasn't going to make things ugly by fighting for them, that they could choose for themselves. "I'm going to live at the Eagle's Nest until it's all settled," I told them, "and you can come with me if you want to or stay here with Dad. This is all such a terrible mess and the only thing we can do is be where we feel most at home, and I just don't feel at home here anymore."

Tracy chose to go to the Eagle's Nest with me, but Thomas wasn't quite sure what he wanted to do. During the time I'd been away, Robert softened and started working on Thomas. For one full year he hadn't spoken a civil word to the boy and now all at once he wanted him. Thomas didn't want to make his decision then, he preferred to give it more thought. That was just fine with me, I told him. The right thing to do under the circumstances.

Buck had no such problem. As I went about gathering up my belongings, he trailed after me, crying, "I want to live with my Dad." He adored his father and in his eyes Robert could do no wrong. When he turned sixteen, he had the same problems Thomas did, but at ten he was still Daddy's boy.

When I went into the bedroom to get my clothes, I saw Robert's message to me. There on the bed, on my side, was a great big black funeral wreath. I burst out laughing. People I've told this to think that was horrible, but I thought it was hilarious. I called Thomas and Buck and told them to go downstairs and bring me a cue stick and the seven and eight balls. I laid the cue stick on Robert's side of the bed and then put the seven and eight ball on either side of the handle on the pillow. Seven was his football number, the eight ball was what he was behind, and the cue stick symbolized where he'd spent most of his time during our last year together. That was my message to him, and I heard later that he laughed when he saw it. It was the only funny part of the divorce.

The next morning Sam Zagon told me that Robert refused to sign the papers and had gotten his own attorney, and that I would have to do the same. There was to be a fight. (That was more like Robert.)

My new attorney was totally anti-Robert Waterfield. He immediately had our assets frozen to Robert, claiming misappropriation of funds. Robert's lawyer said that was like calling him a thief and in a countersuit stated that Robert wanted custody of the children because I was a drunk. Robert told reporters that I was too drunk to cook the Christmas turkey. My kids roared with laughter when they read that in the newspapers. "Mom never cooked a turkey in her whole life," they declared, "drunk or sober." All of this was strictly legal manipulation. Robert and I both knew it, but the public didn't and the newspapers had a field day. My drunk story made worldwide coverage. I knew, because I hired a clipping service and presented Robert with a huge scrapbook after the divorce was over, saying, "This is my reward for living with you for twenty-three years." Then I leaned forward and said quietly, "That's a little like the pot calling the kettle black, isn't it?" He simply answered, "Well, honey, all's fair in love and war."

Back in the Eagle's Nest with Tracy, Thomas came over to talk to me. He put me through a long question and answer session about the whole situation. Then he made a few more visits, each time asking different questions. He was judging and wanted answers, not evasions. And I accommodated him. I laid it out flat for him every time. On his third or fourth visit he just stood looking at me for a long time before saying, "If I come down here, where would I sleep?"

My heart leaped. "We'll get you a bed, don't you worry. The important thing is that you've decided where you want to live." So now I had two of my children with me. Buck had elected to stay with Robert. I understood.

The Rams' doctor talked Robert and me into seeing a psychiatrist, although neither of us thought it would do any good. We went separately, of course, and I only twice. By that time I had hired a private detective because of all the bad publicity. I was advised to get myself some weapons with which to fight back. The detective had given me proof of Robert's record of infidelities. Robert felt that it was perfectly okay for a man to fool around, but it was not okay for a woman to do the same.

At the second session with the psychiatrist I told him that Robert and I never had any problems whatsoever with our sexual relationship. I never held out on him. In that department we were perfectly compatible. So why, I asked the doctor, had he found it necessary to indulge in other women?

The psychiatrist's answer was simple and discouraging. "They're notches in his belt," he said easily, "like a gunfighter. These affairs don't involve love. They're nothing more than notches in his belt to mark his conquests." Terrific, I thought.

The divorce was proceeding with its usual slowness and the battle still raging, when at last we were summoned to court. I was really apprehensive about the whole thing. In fact, I was terrified. Don't ask me why.

I turned to the Lord and prayed. One important message gave me the strength and courage I needed:

> Why do you stand at the gate trembling? Gird up your loins like a man. Go forth and meet the enemy on his own grounds. Know ye not that I have provided you with weapons forged in the fire of Truth? Why do you stand weeping like a fatherless child? Know ye not that I am your father and your father's father? Before the worlds were, I was. Go forth and meet the enemy, for your sword was forged with Truth and can split the bowels of Hell. It shall defeat the world. Yea, flesh. Yea, the Devil. And all which I have promised shall come to pass, sayeth the Lord.

Armed with that, I went into court on the appointed day. When Robert came in, he slid into the seat beside me and muttered, "Well, this sure is a goddamn degrading and humiliating end you've brought us to."

I stared straight ahead and shrugged my shoulders. I didn't say a word in reply, but I was thinking that it was our marriage that had become degrading and humiliating. If something's true, then face it. I didn't give a damn about what the Joneses thought or about keeping a fairy tale going for the public.

Robert's attorney didn't show up, so the whole thing was postponed and we were told to go home to wait. We finally reached a point where our attorneys stopped talking to each other. I didn't know which way to turn.

It was Christmas 1966 when I left home, and our divorce wasn't granted until July 1968. It was a long time with nothing of real importance happening except waiting. And drinking. Almost anything at all served as a reason for me to get smashed, and of course I couldn't accomplish anything. I was no help to myself or to anyone else.

Someone once described my mother and me as "do-gooders," and at the time I didn't think it was a very nice term. Later I realized that there are some people who by nature help others, and I was raised to do just that. I started out helping four siblings, having my mother as an example, and as long as I had a solid base of operations, like a happy marriage, it was what I liked doing best. As I became older, it became a way of life.

Now, finding myself incapable of doing that, I knew something was radically wrong with me. Scared to death about the divorce, I couldn't help anyone, including myself. So . . . I drank.

Tracy was now sixteen and she was feeling the divorce more keenly than any of us realized at the time. She became stubborn, uncommunicative, and most difficult to live with. We had a few run-ins, because during that entire period she was not at all helpful. On the contrary, she seemed to be going out of her way to be obstructive. I don't remember what kicked it off—maybe I've blocked it from my mind—but one morning, fed up with her behavior, I gave in to a black rage and hollered, "Why don't you go and live with your father?" Her eyes grew very large and round, and without a word she went out of the house, got into her car, and drove to Robert. What had I done? I allowed my own frazzled nerves to take over and lashed out like a demon at that poor child. It was too late for self-recrimination, so I thought that perhaps she needed time with her father. I certainly couldn't have been easy to live with.

She lived with Robert for a while, but that didn't seem to work either. He was constantly worried about where she was—babysitting or with some guy? Finally, Tracy ran away.

Thomas took off in his car, and when he found her she told him that she was on her way up to Big Sur, where she intended to live by herself. Thomas talked her out of that and brought her back home to see if I could help, but she kept silent. I talked and she just stared straight ahead. I told her how much I loved her and how difficult I knew things were for her and that I couldn't bear it if she went away. I apologized over and over for what I'd said. Then the dam broke and she started to cry. She cried and cried and got it all out of her system and we held each other as tightly as we could. At last she said that she wanted to stay with me. I was so relieved that I started to cry.

Things settled down for the rest of the year. The kids were in school and the lawyers were still not talking to each other. I was told that matters were at a status quo, legal talk for dead end.

TWENTY

Christmas 1967. A full year had passed since I'd left Robert, and I became very sentimental and blue. I didn't know what to do with myself, so I took Tracy up to San Francisco to visit Christobel. But it didn't feel right. We'd always been home at Christmas with our family. So I phoned Robert and asked him if he'd like to spend the holidays together. He was very pleased with the idea, and when I told him what time we'd be arriving he said he'd meet the flight after the football game.

I felt much better after that call. At least the kids would be together, and if we adults could manage to keep ourselves under control, it just might turn out to be a decent Christmas.

The day of our flight back to Los Angeles turned out to be a miserable stormy one and our flight was canceled. That should have told me something, but if it did, I wasn't listening. I booked the next flight out and phoned Robert at the Barrel to advise him of the change in our arrival time.

"What are you talking about?" he replied in a slurred voice. "What plane? I don't know what the hell you're talking about." The Rams had lost the game and he must have been absolutely boiled, because he kept repeating that he didn't know what I was talking about.

Fighting back the tears, I grabbed Tracy's hand and held onto it for dear life all the way back to Christobel's house. Christmas, our very favorite time of year, was totally screwed up. Our family was split in two, the divorce was dragging on and on, Bucky was with Robert, Tracy was in San Francisco with me, and Thomas was in Los Angeles. I was really feeling sorry for myself. From my well of misery, I called my sister-in-law Pamela, who had a beautiful gift of interpretation, and asked her to pray for me. She prayed in tongues and got a message. The Lord certainly was tuned into my giving in to despair, because I was answered very firmly:

> It's not your birthday, it's Mine. It's time to think about why I was born, not you. Have I been with you so long and you know Me not? Have you been in the furnace alone, Shadrach? Would you be with the world and seek peace in pills and solace in a bottle? I have said I will give you peace. I have encircled thee with My arm. Clothe thyself in the armor of God and know in Whom ye believe. Then ye shall know peace and love. I have brought thee out of Hell and I shall not let thee return.

Well, that was that, as far as I was concerned. I simply had the Christmas blahs, letting my emotions rule again. My Heavenly Father sure knew how to jerk me up, however.

I phoned my lawyer to let him know where I was, and he advised me in no uncertain terms to come down to Los Angeles for Christmas, because if I stayed away from one of my children at this time, Robert could give out the story that I'd left my son alone on Christmas. He would have a ball with that one.

"Okay," I said to myself, "Tracy and I are going home to Thomas and the family in the Valley, and we'll all be together to celebrate the Lord's birthday." And that's exactly what I did.

Nineteen sixty-eight, according to my numerology book, was a Six Year, a good one for me—a personal year, a year for family, for romance, and for helping someone who would need me. For the past year and a half I'd been no good to anyone, I'd been receiving help instead of giving any, so I firmly resolved to get it together and prepare myself for what I had to do.

My first New Year's resolution was to stop drinking, until the trauma was over anyway. Another important decision was to get all of us under one roof in a proper house, instead of the cramped quarters of the Eagle's Nest. I decided to buy my brother Ken's house, now that he had left the compound. We'd be close to the family, and my kids would be with their cousins. It was perfect.

Because of all the work that was needed to put the house in shape, it would be a while before we could move into it, but that didn't matter so long as I knew it was waiting for us. The problem was raising the money to pay for it. Kevin Pines and Jerry Shaw had moved to Los Angeles, and one day, while I was talking to them about the financial bind I was in concerning the down payment on the house, Jerry turned to me and said he would lend it to me. Just like that.

I'm not sure of the exact amount, but I think it was somewhere around $25,000. Kevin and Jerry were lifesavers to me. Not just for the money but, what was more important, their moral support—I could always count on them to make me laugh when I most needed it.

I saw a lot of those two. They were to be of tremendous help to me later in my life too. Jerry's check solved the immediate problems. I used it for the down payment and then got started on the house.

The rest of my social life was a big nothing. Patti Gilbert, whom I knew from Chicago, was a born matchmaker. She couldn't stand anyone being alone and kept insisting I meet new men. I needed something to boost my morale she said. Patti was constantly phoning to say she had a bachelor whom she wanted me to meet. I gave in to two or three of her "morale-boosting" dates, but they turned out to be duds. Then there was one man she especially wanted me to meet who was in town doing a play with Gloria Swanson. But by then I'd had it up to here with her dates, so I said, "No more!"

It's awfully hard to start dating again when you've been married for so long. I'd had about all I could take, so back I

went to the lonely life of waiting for the divorce to become final.

Then came that terrible day I shall never forget. I was at home when the phone rang. Tracy had swallowed an overdose of sleeping pills at school and was in an ambulance on the way to the hospital. Thomas was with her. I tore over to the hospital as fast as I could, thinking all the way, "Oh, dear Lord, it can't be true." I was shocked and terrified. "Why, why, why?" I kept on asking myself, then praying that she'd come out of it all right. Praying that it was some kind of mistake, some kind of accident, anything but a suicide attempt.

Tracy had never taken a sleeping pill in her life. That was a lucky break, for if she ever had, she would have known how quickly they work. As it was, she had popped the sleeping pills into her mouth just before entering her classroom, thinking she'd finish class and then go out to her car to curl up in the back seat. She hadn't wanted to do it at home.

Well, it didn't work out that way, thank God, because right in the middle of class she zonked out and slid off her seat onto the floor. Her startled teacher immediately called an ambulance and notified Thomas, who went with her to the hospital.

As soon as she was out of danger, I phoned Dr. Christian, the psychiatrist I'd been seeing (Mrs. Browning had moved), and told him what had happened. He had already seen both Thomas and Tracy earlier.

"Bring her in to me the moment she's released from the hospital," he ordered.

I did as he said, and when I got Tracy there I left them alone to talk it out. When they finished talking, Dr. Christian called me in and let me have it straight.

"Well," he said, "she wants to do it again. She's going to keep trying. That means she can't go home. She's got to be someplace where she can be watched all the time and helped. I know a good sanitarium not too far from your house that specializes in just Tracy's sort of problem—a place mainly for young people. And I'll still see her every day."

During all of this Tracy had barely spoken, only a few words that indicated nothing about how she felt about the matter. She hadn't completely closed us out yet. She was silent while Dr. Christian phoned the sanitarium, and I hadn't the slightest idea what was going on in her mind.

When the arrangements were made, I drove Tracy home to get whatever things she might want to take with her. Thomas helped pack her things and then, without warning, he grabbed her by the shoulders and began to shake her. "Why did you do it, Tracy?" he shouted. "What do you think Mom and I would do if you killed yourself?"

Poor boy, he was desperately trying to tell her he loved her, but all he could do was yell at her. She must have gotten the message though, because all at once she began to cry. I took Thomas by the arm and pulled him away. "Come on, Son," I said, "Tracy's got things she must work out, and she's going to need all the help we can give her."

He understood and watched as we drove off. I got Tracy to the sanitarium and turned her over to the nurse in charge and then stood in the lobby staring after her as she was led away. I kept staring even after the swinging doors hid her from my sight.

Back home I phoned Robert to tell him what had happened and then began to pray harder than I had in a long time. The Lord heard my prayers and answered—still He was my strength:

> Like an injured sailor with an open wound and they poured salt upon it. Though it looked like adding pain, yet the salt water is healing. Yea, it is being healed. As a child who cried and will not be comforted. Stretch forth your hand and she shall take thy hand and it shall be a binding together of hands by Me. But be thou steadfast. I am thy Rock, and nothing, no nothing, shall snatch you out of My hand. Ye must be steadfast.

I knew what all that meant. Steadfast was the keyword all right, and that's exactly what I was going to be.

I was at Tracy's side every single minute, day and night, that regulations allowed, but still she didn't talk to me. In fact, I got the feeling that she didn't particularly like me being with her, that she wished I'd leave. But I didn't.

Robert came to see her and was filled with anguish and fury and wanted to pick her up and take her out of there. That, of course, would have been the worst thing anyone could have done. He couldn't bear seeing her like that, yet couldn't find the words to comfort her. He was so distraught and helpless that he visited one more time and never came again. He couldn't take it.

Neither could I, but I forced myself. I continued coming afternoons and evenings. Thomas came too. Many times. Dr. Christian told me a point had been reached where he thought that he, Tracy, and I could have a talk session together. He warned me, however, that she was still in a bad state of depression.

Well, that "talk" session was strictly one sided. The doctor talked and Tracy was silent, staring and unreachable. This went on and on and on until I just couldn't take it any longer. Out of frustration, fear, and worry, I blew my top.

That did it! Tracy turned those enormous blue eyes of hers toward me, and I watched them fill with tears and flood over. She couldn't stop crying. I felt terribly guilty, but the doctor said it was the first time she had cried since she'd entered the place, and he considered it a good sign. A beginning. Then he told me that he thought I shouldn't see her for a while.

That was hard for me. Not seeing her was worse than seeing her in the condition she was in. All I could do was see those huge tears streaming out of her wide, unseeing eyes. I kept thinking of her locked up in that room, cut off from those who loved her. But I also had to admit that those who loved her had been the cause of what happened.

It was not an easy thing to admit. The shock of the divorce, the uprooting, the emotional tearing apart, having to make choices, all that had done this to her. I sat at home and prayed and read the Bible and waited. Waited for what? A miracle? Perhaps.

One chilly, rainy night I had a fire going and soothing music on the hi-fi. I was sitting there hypnotized by the flickering flames in the fireplace. All of a sudden I became aware of a soft sound, a movement I couldn't identify. I turned and saw the glass door to the room begin to slide open. There, with huge, frightened blue eyes and wild and wet hair stood Tracy.

"Honey, what happened?" It was all I could manage, I was so astonished by her sudden appearance.

"I came home, Mom." It was the first time I'd heard her really relate to me in all those weeks. "I climbed over the wall and ran home."

I went to her and gathered her in my arms and brought her close to the warmth of the fire. I held her for I don't know how long. Then I got her into a hot bath, wrapped her in a warm towel, and gave her something hot to drink. I knew I had to phone the sanitarium. I explained to Tracy that they'd be frantic when they discovered her missing, and she agreed that I call.

When Dr. Christian spoke with her, she listened in silence to all he had to say. He told her that she could spend a few hours with me, but then I had to bring her back. He impressed upon her the importance of completing her treatment, assuring her that it wouldn't be too long before she could come home for good. He sounded very promising and she took him at his word and a few hours later went back willingly with me.

The following day Dr. Christian told me that Tracy running away was a very good indication. That's what he had hoped for. That was why he didn't want me to see her. Now she wanted to come home on her own. The will to live was exerting itself.

Not long after that Tracy was dismissed and came home to the new house. Of course, she had to continue seeing her doctor for some time afterward, and since she wasn't allowed to drive, I had to take her. Oddly enough, this proved to be one of the most maturing experiences in her life. She told me that all during her time in group therapy she observed her fellow patients, learning from what she saw and heard, and that plus her private sessions with the doctor all contributed to making her very adult. She no longer read the exterior masks of her fellow mortals, but looked to the interior. I'd just as soon talk to Tracy today as any friend I have.

She didn't want to return to the Van Nuys school where she'd taken the pills, so it was decided that she go to a boarding school. Both she and her doctor agreed that it was important for her to live away from home, so that she could be more or less on her own, have her own sense of responsibility, and not be too closely involved with her parents' problems. As much as I hated to have her go, I saw the wisdom of the decision.

During the time Tracy was in the sanitarium, Robert and his attorney had cooled down considerably. They suggested both sides should come to some equitable agreement if for no other reason than for Tracy's sake. Robert did not want to hurt his daughter. I was for that, yet the divorce proceedings still dragged on and on.

During all of this I had to go to New York to attend a WAIF conference. There was no way I could avoid going, even though I didn't particularly feel up to it. New York and WAIF reminded me of Bill Kirk, who had joined the migration to the West Coast. Bill had left ISS to take over the job of heading the Motion Picture Relief Home in Los Angeles.

It was while I was in New York that my desperation to have someone help me with the entire mess of the divorce reached its peak. Late one night, when I couldn't sleep, the answer came to me from out of the blue. Bill Kirk! He was indeed the one person I could depend upon who would be able to find out what was necessary to clear this whole thing. Why hadn't I thought of him before?

When I returned to Los Angeles, Bill went right to work planning strategy. We went to my attorney's office, and I'll never forget the scene. Bill wanted a list of what I should get if we went to court. My attorney tried the same routine he'd always pulled on me. He strode up and down, ranting and raving about what a greedy bastard Robert was and how he didn't deserve to get this and certainly wasn't going to get that and on and on. Bill Kirk just sat there and took in the performance without saying a word. And when the lawyer ran out of breath, Bill said ever so softly, "Yes, but you see, what we want to know is, should we go to court, what will *you* ask for?"

Bill and I had decided earlier we would get a list out of my attorney that I would then personally take to Robert for approval so we could get the ball rolling. These two lawyers had been going around long enough with all those legal she-nanigans and had succeeded only in increasing their fees and not in getting the damned divorce settled.

After a bit of stalling, the lawyer gave up, because you just can't get around Bill Kirk, the personification of pa-tience. Bill never got mad and didn't stomp and rage like the lawyer did; he merely asked the same question until he got a straight answer.

Having been forced into a corner, the lawyer began rat-tling off his demands: "Well, I want this and I want that and. . ." And Bill would softly interrupt with, "Just a minute, I'm writing it down." That poor lawyer looked as if he were about to explode.

When we finally left the office, Bill said to me, "Now Jane, I want you to put one thing on that list that you don't really want."

"What for?" I asked, puzzled.

A small smile crossed his lips. "Because when Robert's lawyer objects to these demands, as he's bound to, and says that you're asking for too much, you will have that thing to give up."

Believe it or not, that's exactly what happened, and it worked. Bill Kirk was the first person to get anything accom-plished after a whole year and a half. Robert and I sat down alone in my kitchen and came to our agreement. And that was at last that.

It was agreed that I would get the Newport Beach house with a mortgage, and Robert would get the house in the Val-ley with no mortgage, because he'd been living in it for over twenty years and I knew he couldn't face the prospect of moving. I'd gone through so much in the beginning getting Robert to move onto the hill, now that he was settled in so deeply, it would take a major earthquake to get him out.

The settlement was agreed upon, except for some land in Malibu we had bought during the happy years when we had planned on building the perfect dream house. I told Robert I would give up that property and instead take another parcel we'd bought for investment on Woodman Avenue in the Valley. It was zoned for apartments, and I was thinking I might design and build some there. Robert agreed but thought that this was worth more than the Malibu property, so he insisted on something extra thrown in to make up the difference. By this time I was so tired of all the haggling that I told him he could have whatever he wanted as compensation. He chose the oil stock we'd acquired and I agreed. It was like a game of Monopoly.

So that was the end of our marriage, a marriage which had lasted for nearly a quarter of a century. And there's no denying that we had had many years of our own brand of happiness.

People have often said, "Why did you put up with him if he was such a bastard?" But, you see, I found him attractive and challenging. If that doesn't explain it, maybe this will help. If you find Paul Newman, Steve McQueen, or George C. Scott attractive and worth fighting for, you'll understand Robert and me.

Robert was sexy, dynamic, opinionated, extremely bright, witty, and as stubborn as they come. You either find that kind of man irresistible and exciting or you don't understand him and can't tolerate him for a moment. And I'm no dainty violet either, in temperament or mouth. Believe me, I can be a bitch. So we deserved each other. Although I often felt I was fighting a losing battle, he once astounded me during an argument when he hollered, "Honey, you know, sometimes you seem ten feet tall. Back off!"

When my kids saw *The Lion in Winter* they laughed, "Mom, Dad would definitely have had you banished to a castle, but he'd have always brought you home for Easter, too."

I saw another good example of Robert and me in *The Prisoner of Second Avenue* on Broadway with Peter Falk. I nearly died laughing and was falling in the aisle. It was my own darling, crabby, impossible husband up there on the stage, and I don't need to tell you I was the wife. As a matter of fact, I was getting divorced at the time, so it was especially poignant, sad, and funny all at the same time. Those had been the good years and they were wonderful, but when everything went wrong, it went to hell in a basket.

TWENTY-ONE

While I had been in Chicago doing *Catch Me if You Can,* I had received a letter asking if I'd be interested in playing a character role in a film called *Born Losers.* It was an independent picture to be directed by Tom Laughlin, who was to become famous with *Billy Jack.*

The role was dramatic with only one really great scene. I was to play the mother of a teenaged girl who had been raped by a gang of motorcyclists who take over a small town. It was my first character part, and I was eager to have a go at it. I had once asked Shelley Winters, who should know, how to go about getting the kind of fat parts she got instead of those stupid things I was always being offered. Her advice was good. She told me to find a great script with a great part, get it to a good director who cares, and then do it. Do it even if it's totally out of character for you, and in the meantime do small parts that are different.

So I grabbed Tom Laughlin's offer, because it fit the bill to perfection. He didn't have much money to work with—it was a really low-budget film—and he had to use unknowns for the young parts. He intended to use stars for the parts of the parents but, as it turned out, I was the only "name" he could get. So when the film was released it was my name

up there in big letters, even though I only had that one good scene.

I loved working with Tom Laughlin. As Shelley said, he cared. He discussed my character with me and made me really see and understand her. If I could have worked with other directors like him, and done bigger parts like that one, I would have been happy.

As soon as I finished working on *Born Losers,* I went back to Chicago to do a play called *Here Today,* a move that was to change my life. This time I decided to stay out at the theater complex in the country only during rehearsals and once we opened I would move into Chicago proper, where I would have some diversion. The management supplied me with a car so it would be no trouble getting back and forth each night.

I'd gotten the script early and Tracy had gone over it with me as she always did, so when I arrived for rehearsals, I was feeling great. I looked great too.

My leading man, Roger Barrett, was six foot three, well built, curly haired and wore horn-rimmed glasses that made him look quite studious. He gave me the once-over as I'd never experienced before, and I've had plenty of that treatment in my day. He actually made me nervous. After the usual introductions, we got down to business and had a first reading of the play.

While we rehearsed *Here Today* during the day, Roger played in *Tom Jones* at night. Even though I was impressed by what a good actor he was, I couldn't see this professor type as the riotous squire of *Tom Jones.* I made up my mind to catch him in the play.

My birthday was approaching, and Roger surprised me after rehearsals one day by asking if he could buy me a drink for my birthday, so off we went. Mine was water and lemon; I still wasn't touching booze. I learned that he had been a minister for a short time because his father had been one, then gave that up and became a college professor teaching English literature, and then gave that up to become an actor. He was very intellectual, bright, and charming and had one of the most beautiful, deep speaking voices I'd ever heard. He earned a lot of money with his voice doing what's called voice-overs for television commercials.

I let him do most of the talking during that very pleasant hour, our first alone, and was sorry to see it end. Then Jerry Peters, my birthday buddy from home, and I went to the theater to see *Tom Jones*. I was completely flabbergasted by Roger's performance. Of course, he wasn't wearing glasses, but he did things up on stage that were in no way like the actor I was rehearsing with. There was nothing at all in his portrayal that even slightly resembled the professorial man I knew. I was truly astonished by his talent and his change of pace.

Two days later we opened. After the first night's performance I was in my dressing room removing my makeup when I overheard Roger complaining about the problem of getting back and forth to the theater from town. When I saw him a little while later, I asked him if he'd like to drive my car to and from the theater, since I also lived in Chicago. That way he'd have a ride and I wouldn't have to try to find the theater every night—we were miles out of Chicago. He thought it was a great idea.

During the long drives to and from Chicago we would talk. The more we talked, the more we learned about one another; and the more we learned, the more we got to like each other. As those nightly journeys continued a real affection started to flow between us. Despite the fondness, I felt I was being cautious about relationships, and so I began putting him through what I hoped was an unnoticeable third degree.

"Do you like sports?" I asked as casually as possible.

He thought about it for a while and then, with the same casualness, said, "Well, yes. I guess I do somewhat. I went to a football game a couple of years ago, no, I think it was a baseball game. Anyway, I went. And I, uh, bought myself some popcorn and I think I spent more time watching the people around me than I did the game." He laughed, "I can't even tell you who won or lost."

I could have kissed him. I continued to hit him with little innocent questions like that to find out more about him, and his answers were always the right ones.

In discovering how many people Roger and I knew in common, I found that he had dated Patti Gilbert for a while when she lived in Chicago. Then he confessed to me why he'd stared so at me when I'd walked into rehearsals that first day: It seems that back when Patti had been trying so hard to fix me up with dates and I'd finally yelled quits by the time she came up with the third, Roger had been that third. He had been in Los Angeles working with Gloria Swanson.

We laughed about what a shock it would be to Patti if she knew we had met anyway and that we were doing exactly what she had wanted us to do, date on a regular basis.

The play ran for four weeks, and by the time July rolled around, we had been together every possible minute. Roger kept saying, "I don't know what's the matter with me. I've never been like this. I've never been a hand holder, but I just can't keep from hanging onto yours."

It was true. No matter where we were, at dinner or with friends, our fingers were entwined. It was as if he were afraid to lose me. And I knew just how he felt, because I felt the same.

The time had arrived when we had to face the situation that had been thrust upon us, so I muttered something like, "Well, what happens now?" I couldn't meet his gaze when he said, "You know damn well what happens now." And one thing led to another and I remember thinking, "I don't believe this. I just don't believe this." I was so happy that I was in a state of shock.

Over dinner one evening, while we were discussing mutual friends who were getting married, I happened to mention that if I ever got married again, I would like it to be in October. Roger threw me a look and said he didn't think we could wait until October.

His words took me by surprise. It was the first indication he had ever given that he was thinking of marriage where we were concerned. By the time the play closed, we knew we were going to get married. In an absolute daze of happiness, I flew back to Los Angeles while Roger stayed on in Chicago to tie up the loose ends. I couldn't remember ever being so happy. Here I was with a man who loved the same things I did—the same music, the same kind of art, the same kind of thinking—and was in the same business. Someone I could talk to about everything under the sun, and who would talk to me. Someone who would read poetry to me in that beautiful voice and who would dream with me about all the things we would do together—the plays, the trips, the kind of life we would build. It was almost too much to bear. How could I be so lucky?

So the date was set. August 25. As Roger had said, we couldn't wait until October. I rushed around getting things in order. Fred Robertson, another birthday buddy, loaned his beautiful apartment to us, since I couldn't see taking Roger to the compound and immediately plunging him into family. I wanted his introduction to be a gradual one, with meeting the children at the top of the agenda.

Driving out to the airport to pick Roger up, I could barely keep a steady thought in my mind. There was so much I wanted to show him, the house in Newport Beach, the land where I planned to build apartments. And there were all my friends I wanted him to meet, and I wondered what the children would think of him. Would they like him? Of course, they would. How could they not? Roger was the most likeable man in the world.

Then there he was. We drove directly to Fred's apartment, where we spent the night together, just the two of us.

The next morning Tracy came over to meet Roger. I was on pins and needles—I wanted so much for her to like him. After introductions, they sort of felt each other out while I watched nervously. Then, as we started out the apartment, Roger held out his hand to Tracy, and without a second's hesitation she took it. The two of them walked to the car together. She liked him! I was to find out soon after that she was absolutely mad about him. The same went for Thomas when they met. Unfortunately, Buck was with his father, so he didn't get to meet Roger.

After a round of parties we got down to the business of

planning the wedding. Roger had been married years before and his wedding had been a small one, and mine to Robert certainly hadn't been much, so we agreed that this one would include everybody we knew, and I really think it did.

The invitation list was enormous. All, and I do mean all, my friends were on it: the Hughes gang, Vincent and Mary Price, Bob and Dorothy Mitchum, Richard and Pat Egan, Patti Gilbert and her husband Hank Saperstein, Bill Kirk, Connie and Beryl, and of course the crew—the two Pats, Margaret, Alberta—and just about everyone's relatives. Then there were all of Roger's friends, including Reggie Gardiner and his wife. It seemed like half of Chicago was there, and the list kept on growing. Verrill and Cristobel even sent out invitations to people we didn't really know but who had taken out ads in the WAIF book. They must have thought I was mad. I wanted to kill those two. But the excitement had them dingy.

It would be a big wedding, all right. The ceremony was to take place at the Beverly Hills Presbyterian Church, and the reception at Della's (now Mrs. Eric Koenig) Beverly Hills home.

It was to be a Mexican affair, and a dear friend of mine, Suzi Brewster, designed the gowns that Christobel, Tracy, and I wore. They were made of heavy raw silk with mirror embroidery and in the wildest colors imaginable. My dress was that kind of shocking pink that hurts your eyes, and over it I wore a marvelous milticolored jerkin. Perched on my head was a little pillbox hat, and around one ankle was a gold chain with tiny bells on it. Matching sandals completed the outfit. All quite wild and very colorful.

In contrast, Roger wore a beautiful Edwardian white suit and a gold-embroidered vest with a heavy gold chain and gold and topaz cross hanging down his chest. He was big enough to get away with anything and had the flair to do it. The church decorations carried over the colorful motif I wanted. Gene Callahan, who'd won Oscars for his set designs, used orange, pink, purple, and yellow flowers and brightly colored ribbons all over the place. The whole church was simply bursting with color. It was unbelievably lovely. With all that brightness and Mexican music, it was no doubt going to be smashing.

Howard Hughes, whom I hadn't seen or heard from in years, sent giant baskets of flowers and a huge box with an enormous bow on it, so big that Roger and I had to get up on a chair in order to reach and untie the ribbon.

"I bet it's one of his airplanes," Roger cracked.

It turned out to be an octagonal Spanish coffee table with a hibachi sunk in its center. We loved it. It was so thoughtful of Howard; I was really touched.

It was a beautiful day to get married. Fred Robertson was doing our hair that morning and had already finished with Tracy's and Christobel's and was just starting in on me, when Billie Paul, now Billie Bloom, and Babs Allen came in to supervise.

Thanks to them, Fred and I were fifteen minutes late getting to the church and we found ourselves locked out! I guess to make sure that fans wouldn't mob the place, once everyone who was supposed to be there had gone inside, the doors were locked. But they had forgotten one thing: the bride!

Fred and I desperately began pounding on the heavy doors. Anyway, they suddenly realized that I was not among those present and finally the doors were opened, and that's how the blushing bride entered the church for her wedding—late!

Christobel and Tracy stood up with me, and Paul, Roger's brother, and John Himes were with Roger. My brothers Tom, Kenny, and Jamie were ushers and Wally sang for us. He sang beautifully, and I learned later that Rudy Vallee was so impressed that he arranged for Wally to go out on the road with a musical show.

The reception afterward was such fun that Roger and I didn't want to leave. He was seeing so many of his old friends as well as making new ones that we could have stayed there listening to that wonderful Mexican music, eating that great food, and drinking that marvelous champagne pretty close to forever.

The only thing Roger and I didn't have in common was the amount of sleep each of us needed: Nine hours was my minimum and six hours was his maximum. We decided that he would get up first and go for a long walk on the beach and a swim until I finally came to life. So the first morning

after my wedding, well before my nine hours were up, I was shocked into wakefulness by this huge bear in a wet bathing suit falling on top of me.

"No," I mumbled, "You can't wake me up. I've got to sleep. I'll be sick if I don't sleep."

"No you won't," the bear murmured in my ear. "I was swimming out there when suddenly it came to me that I was married. Actually married, and to you, and I'm the happiest man in the whole world and I had to come and tell you."

I woke up—fast!

The press, wrong as usual, broke the story that I'd divorced Robert Waterfield one day and married Roger the next. Not true. I'd started the divorce proceedings a year and a half before I met Roger. Those tireless gossip mongers knew very well that for a year and a half I'd been alone.

Being married to Roger was a whole new experience for me. With him, if I ever looked the slightest bit troubled or down in the mouth, he would say, "Okay, now, something's wrong. I want to know what the problem is. Something's bothering you and we're going to lay it right out on the table and examine it."

So, whatever it was that was bothering me was brought out in the open, then we'd discuss it and get it over with. There aren't many people who are able to do that, who don't go on pouting when their feelings are hurt in some way. Roger had gone through a great deal of analysis and felt that it was a total waste of precious time to do anything other than "have it all out in lavender," as he put it. Confront it, get it out of the way, and forget it. He was so right.

Life with Roger was very uncomplicated. He was the opposite of any man I'd ever known. If you asked him a question, you got a straight answer. I really don't think he knew what it was to lie. He couldn't be bothered with anything but the truth. He just laid it out flat. There was nothing devious about him. He should have been a psychologist or a counselor of some kind, because he loved people and loved helping them. He was constantly getting himself involved with friends' problems when they came to him. I was always fascinated by the way he handled people.

We started making plans for the future. We were going up to the snow country for a real wintery Christmas, then after that to Florida where I had a commitment for a television show with Jackie Gleason. So we would have snow and sun to start off the new year—terrific!

We talked about plays we would like to do together and resolved to seriously start reading as many as we could to find just the right ones for us. Then an offer came for Beryl and me to go to England with our act. Connie had married Del Courtney and retired. Since Roger had never been to London, we thought it would be a marvelous opportunity. There was so much I'd seen there and wanted to show him. My only condition was that we had to go as soon as possible. I wasn't going to let anything interfere with our plans for Christmas.

Beryl and I tried out a new act in a club on Ventura Boulevard and it went off fine, so we got ready for England. Roger and I had taken Tracy to a boarding school in Ojai, California, where she was very happy, so she didn't mind at all when we decided to take Thomas with us to England, leaving her at school.

Thomas, at this point, was into music and played a real mean set of drums. Although we had a regular drummer with us, there was one number where Thomas could sit in and do a solo. He was thrilled. As for Bucky, he was still with his father and I hadn't been able to arrange a meeting between him and Roger. I really felt bad about that.

We arrived in London where we had a few days before beginning our tour in Wales. Roger took Thomas out that afternoon and bought him a beautiful tweed suit, because Thomas was going to meet his natural mother and sister the next day. The press was already hounding us. I can't say I wasn't nervous, but I felt Thomas was ready. Florrie Kavanaugh hadn't seen him since I'd taken him to America, and it was really a touching reunion for them both. He was all grown up with long hair and a tweed suit—quite a change from the fifteen-month-old toddler she'd given to me.

That meeting in London made us all very happy. The Kavanaughs were so proud of him. And so was I.

Unfortunately the mattress we had in London sagged badly and Roger's back began acting up. He had a chronic back problem and always went to a chiropractor to get it adjusted. We tried to locate someone who could give him an adjustment, but were unable to. It bothered him so badly that I tried talking him into returning home, but he wouldn't hear of it. He wanted to stay with me and there was no talking him out of it.

"We've just been married," he said, "and it's too soon to be separated. Besides, this is my first trip to England and there's a lot I haven't seen yet."

Then we went off to Wales to begin the tour. It proved to be one large, crazy mess. We were alternating shows at two clubs an hour and a half apart by car, so we had to dash from one club to the other. It was exhausting! Roger came with us to both shows at the beginning for a few times but soon gave it up. Early each morning he'd go sightseeing in the countryside, but I was too bushed from all that running in between shows to go with him. Instead I slept. Much as I would have liked to sightsee with him, I couldn't possibly make it with those two shows at night. So he had to be on his own.

He'd always be with us for the first show, then while we went out to do the second one, he'd go back to the hotel and arrange a gorgeous supper to be waiting for us when we returned exhausted and starving to death at 2 A.M. He'd eat with us and recount all that he'd done and seen that day.

Roger was blessed with an insatiable curiosity. Life for him was one great big interesting experiment. He would always talk to people during his wanderings and then tell us about them. He was a vital and fascinating man with an inquiring mind and an unquenchable thirst for knowledge.

During our stay Roger went mad, just absolutely mad, on a huge shopping spree. He bought all sorts of things until finally I had to cry halt. "For heaven's sake Roger," I exclaimed, "Christmas is just around the corner and if you don't stop all this mad shopping, there'll be nothing left to get."

But he just laughed happily and said, "I don't care. Christmas is today and every day for us."

The shows went well in the places which were properly booked, and Thomas played the whole show even better than the hired drummer, but he finally had to go back to school. Beryl and I really missed him. One place we were booked into was a country pub with one electric light hanging on a string and nine or ten people lined up at the bar wondering what on earth those girls in beaded gowns were doing. Roger had to go back to London for our paychecks half the time. Take a tip: Never go with a booker who isn't ready. But it was my fault. I had insisted on "now." Eartha Kitt was playing to packed houses in the same town in a proper club. We all got together at the hotel in the afternoon and she took Roger to her show one night.

When we finished that fiasco, there was one more week in proper clubs and then we were through. Beryl headed home instantly, but Roger and I returned to London. Roger's back was still acting up, a constant nagging ache. Since we couldn't find a chiropractor, we finally settled for an MD, but he didn't do much. He just rubbed some oil into Roger's back and put a heat lamp on it, which didn't help at all. Roger needed an adjustment desperately and there was no one around to give him one. We had been in England for eight weeks and his condition was getting worse. The time had come for us to get back to New York and have him taken care of properly once and for all.

The first thing after our arrival in New York we went to my chiropractor there. Roger's spine by now was like rock, immovable. It had been out of line for so long that the muscles around it were in constant spasm, and the doctor couldn't do a thing with it. The pains were radiating across Roger's chest and into his arms, making any movement excruciatingly painful. The doctor was concerned because the vertebrae that touched the nerves going to the heart were involved, so he sent us to a heart specialist for a cardiogram to see if any damage had been done. Thank God, it showed nothing wrong with Roger's heart, but he was advised to go home and check into a hospital.

In the middle of all this we were contacted by a producer who asked if we'd be interested in co-starring in a

forthcoming road company of *Hello, Dolly!* Roger was so excited at this opportunity that he insisted we stay on in New York long enough to read the script and do the singing tryouts.

Well, poor darling, here he was with this simply gorgeous voice of his, but he couldn't for the life of him carry a tune. So it was decided that he'd talk the songs like Rex Harrison did in *My Fair Lady*. We were both so thrilled about doing the tour, we decided that instead of dragging our asses around the country by plane from stop to stop and sleeping in dreary hotel rooms, we would buy ourselves a motor home and travel in that.

Roger was even more excited about the tour than I was because he so loved to work. "I'm a real nut for work," he warned me when we decided to get married. "That's something you've got to understand right up front. I have to work. If you don't want to work any more, that's okay with me, but I have to."

So now we were going to work together and travel together in our motor home and I was delighted. But first things first. It was back to Los Angeles to find out about Roger's back.

Despite the fact that the pain had eased, I was still worried about Roger. I knew how tricky that condition could be. I kept on at him about checking into a hospital, but he refused. So I nagged about it until we came to a compromise. He'd go to a doctor and have tests done and also go to my local chiropractor, but he would not stay in a hospital unless the doctor in Los Angeles insisted. Positively.

Well, he got the works all right—a complete and thorough physical. Once again the electrocardiogram gave him a clean bill of health. That left the chiropractor to adjust his spine and relieve the pressure, which, as we both knew, was the root of his problem. But this chiropractor, too, was unable to move Roger's spine at all. It was locked in, hard and tight as a rock. He gave Roger a muscle relaxant to take the following morning so his back muscles would be relaxed enough to allow an adjustment the next day.

That evening we had dinner with Kevin and Jerry. We talked for hours about our plans for a snowy Christmas, the trip to Florida for my television show with Jackie Gleason, and the *Dolly* tour in our motor home. There was so much ahead of us, so many things to be done and shared and enjoyed. Roger and I went to bed that night feeling wonderful about everything.

Usually, Roger would awaken hours before me, but the next morning was different. When I awoke, he was still in bed beside me. He got up once and then went right back to bed again. I was concerned both by that and by the way he looked.

"What's the matter, honey?" I asked.

"I think I'm getting one of my migraines."

He had been plagued by headaches on and off for years, but this was the first one he'd had since we'd met. "Could it be coming from your back?" I asked. "You know, some nerve being pinched?"

"It could," he agreed. His face showed the pain he was in. I remembered when my back was giving me trouble, I'd lie on the floor on my stomach and have someone push down hard on both sides of the painful vertebrae, and it would give some sort of temporary relief. I suggested that to Roger.

"Come on," I said, as I helped him off the bed, "lie down and we'll see if we can at least get rid of your pain until we make it to the doctor." I figured that and the muscle relaxant should do the trick. I pressed hard on his spine and it relieved some of the pain.

"Oh, that feels much better," he sighed. "It really feels good." Then he got to his feet, put on his robe, and sat on the edge of the bed looking as though the move exhausted him. He looked terrible. The pain had returned, but he looked different this time, pale and drawn.

I knew something was horribly wrong, so I ran to the phone and called the doctor. "Something's terribly wrong with Roger, Doctor," I said. "You must come over. Now!"

I turned to tell Roger, who was still sitting on the edge of the bed, but before I could even open my mouth, he let out a terrible great roar of pain and fell backward onto the bed. I was in a state of shock. I couldn't believe what I saw before

me. I couldn't believe that this could happen. It was a nightmare that I'd wake up from in a minute. It wasn't real. It wasn't, it wasn't, it wasn't!

But it was. And I wouldn't wake up from it. Not ever. My Roger was dead. He had gone while I was standing there at the phone. He left me just like that. I couldn't do anything besides stare in disbelief, fighting the awful truth that was there in front of me, the undeniable truth that couldn't be wished away.

I ran wildly from the house and across the lawn, screaming, "Jamie! Jamie!" at the top of my lungs for my brother.

The next thing I knew, my family was with me back in the bedroom, standing helpless and disbelieving. Roger looked so peaceful and so beautiful, as if he had never felt the terrible, excruciating pain that had pulled that awful sound from him.

I don't know how long we stood like that before I at last found my voice. "Please go away," I said softly. "All of you. Please, please, go away and leave me alone with him." They did.

Then I lay down alongside him and patted his face and talked to him. I lay close to him and remembered. Remembered how he'd done all that shopping in London way before Christmas and how he'd said, "Christmas is today and every day for us."

I looked at his beautiful face and remembered how I had wanted to be married in October, and how he had said we couldn't wait that long. How right he was, because if we had waited, we wouldn't have had these three and a half wonderful months together. How strange—his pre-Christmas buying spree, his insistence on getting married as soon as possible, as if everything had to be crowded into a short space of time because there wasn't much left. Had he instinctively known something? Had he sensed what couldn't be thought or put into words, something in a part of the mind we know nothing about? Who's to ever know?

TWENTY-TWO

The actual sequence of events is still blurred by shock and pain and disbelief. At one point, I do recall, Thomas came back in and stood at the foot of the bed, tears streaming down his face, looking at Roger.

"Mom, how could the Lord have taken him when he loved you so much?"

I had no answer for him. I had no answer for myself.

The doctor came and signed the death certificate, which stated that Roger had died of a massive blood clot that caused an acute coronary occlusion. Roger was forty-seven years old. I will always wonder whether the vertebrae that were out had affected the nerves leading to his heart and put too much strain on it. If they had been adjusted would everything have been all right? Would that have saved him? I'll never have the answer.

All I knew was that it was November 18, 1968, the day his life ended and mine came to an absolute and total dead stop.

The funeral. Everyone who came to the wedding came to the funeral. Everything was taken care of, but I went around like a sleepwalker. My eyes were open, but I don't remember seeing. Kevin and Jerry picked up Thomas, Tracy, and me. I just looked unseeingly at everyone. All these people

who had shared our happiness at the wedding were now going up for a last look at their friend.

I didn't wear black. I just couldn't somehow. I did put on a black velvet hat that Roger had bought for me in London and black gloves, but my dress was a pale shade of blue. Thomas and Tracy stayed close while Kevin and Jerry each grabbed my elbows and clung to me for dear life.

There were many flowers all over the place. Howard Hughes sent a pair of huge lavish stands of white roses and orchids, each about nine by twelve feet to the mortuary, as well as a great big basket of white roses to the house.

At last, with Kevin and Jerry guiding me, I walked out of the funeral parlor, got into the car, and went home. Everyone in the world seemed to be at the house, and I was greeting them and walking around in a daze. But I just wasn't there. I really wasn't. That wasn't me wandering around and talking to everyone. Margaret and Alberta were there and Alberta said something like, "My God, they must have her so sedated she's in never-never land."

Was I in never-never land? Probably. I would have liked to have been there, that's for sure. Never-never land had such a good, safe sound to it. In any case, I wasn't sedated. I didn't have to be. I was literally stunned out of my mind.

Sometime during that period I had copies made of our wedding pictures and wrote on them that Roger was the most wonderful thing that had ever happened to me. I mailed them to everyone who had been to the wedding and the funeral. I'd thanked them earlier for their wedding gifts, and now I was thanking them for the flowers, the notes, and for standing by me.

I did all of that under perfect control.

During that time, of course, I prayed. Prayed nonstop. Most of it was, "Why, why, why?"

Then my sister-in-law Jackie got this message for me:

> I shall touch thy heart this day, my beloved; thou art precious unto Me. I hold out My hand and wait for thy grasp. Yea, I am with thee always. Yea, I am; thou hast lost nothing, for nothing is lost in Me, for all is eternal.

For I, thy God, know the appointed time and shall
ye *deprive* Me of My appointed ones? Do ye not know
that some spirits leap over the wall for their spirit's need
is greater in heaven than on earth?

Rejoice, O Daughter of Zion. Rejoice that My will
be done.

The Lord was still on top of the situation. He had given
me those words to hang on to. I read and reread them for
months to come.

Della Koenig, who'd had our wedding reception, insisted that I come home with her to Mexico City. A change
of scene was in order, she said, to get away from all my
memories. I could be home for Christmas. I just acquiesced
and did anything anyone told me to do. I was like a zombie.
I really thought that I was losing my mind.

Della was studying painting at the time, and one day,
when I guess she couldn't stand the way I was any more than
I could, she dragged me off to her art class. Her teacher was
a wonderful woman as well as a wonderful artist, and the
first thing she did when she saw me was prop me up on a
high stool, toss a huge colorful shawl over my shoulders, and
start a portrait of me. I didn't care. At least I didn't have to
talk. (Della had wanted me to wear a gray satin gown of hers
and stand by a mantle. My ego rose high enough to balk at
that: No one was going to paint a typical "lady of the house"
portrait of old J. R., even if I never saw it again.)

The teacher's name was Irene de Bohos Sebastian and
she was like a miniature Anna Magnani. It was fascinating to
watch this vital lady work, and for a few hours each day I
was able to watch, listen to symphonic music, and think un-
disturbed about Roger. I wanted to remember every tiny thing
about him. It had to last me the rest of my life. All I wanted
to do was think about him, to remember what he'd said, the
sound of his voice, that fabulous voice. I'd look at his pictures and letters hundreds of times, memorizing everything
so I'd never forget.

When it was time for me to leave, Della presented me
with the portrait Irene had painted. I was totally surprised.

What a good friend Della was in times of happiness and sorrow. I found out over and over again how many good friends I really had. God knows I was no good to them, but they simply weren't going to let me sink if they could possibly help it.

I still have that painting. The Widow Barrett is in green slacks, a bright flowered shawl, and boots, perched on a stone wall in the woods, and she goes with me everywhere, from house to house. A memory.

On the way home I knew I'd have to spend my time unstructured. The strain of having to fit into anyone else's program was unbearable now. Maybe forever.

And then, before I knew it, Christmas was upon us. I had lasted until Christmas. Kevin and Jerry were going to a Christmas Eve party and insisted that I come along. It made no difference where I was physically. Mentally and emotionally, I was still somewhere where nothing could get at me.

It was a big party at actress Marilyn Maxwell's house and lots of people I knew were there, but I just sat quietly by myself in a corner and started drinking for the first time in 1968 since Roger died. In no time I was smashed. Rock Hudson came over and started talking to me. I could hear the empathy in his voice, but I couldn't manage to answer him at all. I just wasn't there.

On Christmas morning I finally walked into my house all alone and cracked wide open. The dam inside me burst and a sob from my depths rose to a shriek. I remember wandering aimlessly through the house, screaming at the top of my lungs, "No! No! No! No! No!"

I screamed and screamed that impotent rejection of the truth. These were my first tears since that black November day. That was the start of my years in hell. Just pure hell. I don't remember anything else of that Rogerless Christmas.

Back in October when Roger and I were planning our tour, I remembered that I was entering a Seven Year, which is likened to the Sabbath. I wondered then how I was going to be touring all over the country with a play in a Seven Year, which is supposed to be a time of rest and contemplation with little or no activity and as little human contact as possible.

Well, that's exactly what did happen for me after all in that year, despite our plans. I did nothing. I stayed alone and preferred it that way.

Time is so mixed up in my mind about that period that it's almost impossible for me to remember just what I did when. I had signed to do that television show with Jackie Gleason in Florida, and now everyone, family and friends alike, was insisting I go. I took Christobel. There again things are vague. All I can recall of that time is that I got the flu and never did get to do the show. I was so sick I just couldn't move.

Then, it turned out, the Los Angeles chapter of WAIF was considering holding a ball on the cruise ship *Statendam,* the ship I had gone to Hawaii on with Esther. The owner of the Dutch Line invited me to join their current Caribbean cruise and check out the ship and its possibilities for the ball. At first I said no. "I can't face all those people," I told Christobel. "I just can't."

But when it came to the choice of going back to Los Angeles or going on the cruise, I couldn't bear the idea of going home, and so to continue running away I accepted the cruise as the lesser of the two evils.

I was hardly sleeping at all during this time, and that, plus my terror at having to mix with a boatload of people, was really turning me into a nut case. I'd lost all my self-confidence and was sure I'd never be able to perform before an audience again. Sam Vine, a marvelous hypnotist, made a tape for me that took care of both those problems. I played it at night while I was in bed, and it not only put me in the proper attitude for sleep, but also gave me a posthypnotic suggestion that I could do whatever I wanted to do, even perform before an audience and enjoy it. Sam really saved my sanity.

It was a simply wonderful tape that I played and played and it worked. I even gave a show on the ship the last night out when I didn't really have to. I began sleeping well and even enjoyed the cruise.

On the whole, that cruise was a big help. I was keeping busy, I was on the move, and I was sleeping for a change. And I wasn't doing too much thinking, which was just the medicine I needed then.

On the last leg of the cruise, we went through the Panama Canal and up the west coast of Central America to Acapulco. After Acapulco we headed up to Los Angeles and that was the end of the cruise. And the running away. I was home and I didn't want to be.

There was nothing there to hold me together but memories. And drinking. I was doing a great deal of that and everyone was going crazy trying to keep me away from it. Drinking and staring at walls were all I was interested in doing. I did manage to perform the necessary everyday things, however, trying not to think while doing them. The business of life-must-go-on is bewildering, painful, and often nonsensical. I found it completely impossible. Where to start? And how? And why?

I fell into a deep depression for the first time in my life. I now realized how Tracy felt in the hospital when no one could reach her. How had she survived this totally hopeless state of being? I couldn't look ahead. There was no future to look for, just this engulfing abyss of self-pity. I just didn't give a damn about anything or anyone. Worried friends looked at me as though they were sure I'd never get back on my feet. I had been to some of them a tower of strength, and now they were seeing that tower crumble.

I don't know what they were thinking, but they acted as though the world were coming to an end. Well, mine sure as hell had. I just wanted to drown myself in booze.

Everyone tried to help, even people I hadn't heard from in years. I received lots of letters, one in particular from Marjel Delauer, who'd been married to Bob Delauer of the Rams. I hadn't seen or been in contact with her for maybe ten years. She wrote reminding me how I had once helped her when she was loaded down with some very serious problems. She recalled how I lectured her to "stop being an ass and start praying." Now here she was telling me the very same thing, offering me the same comfort, reminding me that the Lord still had a plan for us all just as I'd reminded her so long ago.

It helped—for a short time anyway. I would be all right for a time, and then wham! I'd be gone again—drinking and staring at the walls.

Occasionally I tried going out to visit friends, but for the most part I stayed home. I went on that way until I couldn't stand it any more. I asked one of my gal friends, Kelly, to move in with me. She was having her own set of problems at the time and she grabbed at the idea. The arrangement worked out fine and things got a little better. Kelly and I decided to rent the Valley house and move to the Newport Beach house. Now for a change I could stare at the back bay instead of walls. I loved the water.

I kept busy staring and, of course, drinking. It all got too much for Kelly, and when she couldn't stand it any longer she somehow got me to a psychiatrist who lived not far away. I was in a terrible state of depression by then. Now I had a psychiatrist as well as Kelly and the rest of the world trying to keep me from the bottle, but I wasn't listening. I wanted to crawl in a bottle and die.

The psychiatrist kept harping at me to admit that Roger wasn't the perfect human being I felt he was. I felt the whole thing was ridiculous. I knew damn well why I was so depressed and miserable and drinking, and I told him so. I felt that I had been given my second chance at happiness with Roger and that I'd never again find anyone like him, and so I would never be happy again. That was the reason. No sense probing.

Finally, I decided to buy a boat. I had always wanted one, but Robert had always put his foot down. Now that I was answerable to no one about what I wanted to do, I saw no reason why I shouldn't have one. I spotted the one I knew I just had to have. A catamaran cruiser. It was like a floating apartment and cost $52,000. I bought it.

The house had its own dock, and Kelly's boyfriend was around all the time to take care of the boat and run it when

we all wanted to use it. We took trips to Catalina, Long Beach, and Santa Barbara and had lots of fun on that boat. It also kept me occupied, which was, in a way, therapy. We decorated it inside and out in Mexican colors of course.

I put green outdoor grass carpeting on the top deck, added outdoor chairs and a barbecue and even a phoney orange tree in a pot in one corner. It had all the comforts of a real patio. My decorating certainly wasn't Yar, but I didn't care. I named the boat *The Outlaw*.

However, all this constructiveness in no way cut in on my drinking, and I still had my fits of deep depression despite the therapy offered by the activity. No matter how hard I tried to keep my mind on the boat and decorating it, I knew what was eating at me, and so nothing really worked for long. On top of that, Kelly, who surely meant well, was behaving more and more like my keeper and it was driving me nuts, until one day I just exploded and hollered at her.

"Look," I screamed, "I feel like I'm living with a goddam jailer and I've already had that with Robert Waterfield! If I need a boss around to tell me what to do and how far to jump, I'll advertise for one!"

So she left and I was alone again. But it felt good. Pat Alexander, my old modeling pal, came down and spent a few days. Her husband was overseas and we caught up on all that had happened in our lives. We were forty-nine now.

I spent time walking along the back bay and I began to notice little, insignificant things that were happening to me of which I'd been totally unaware for months now. Somehow appreciation for things of the senses was stirring. One night I woke up at 3 a.m. and sat quietly, nibbling, thinking of Roger. These are the words I wrote:

DEALING WITH THE DEVIL
(or One Up on the Adversary)

Chocolate, nuts, candy mints do not make up for your
    absence.
But the knowledge that I can enjoy them is comforting.
The nice feeling of being tired, but not distressed.
The calm of sleepy awareness is nearer heaven than I've
    thought possible.

We're satisfied with such little things when stress pushes
us too far, too much, too soon.
Relativity becomes so obvious—
Thank God they've let me down for a while.
My thumbs still move—my tongue can grow wet when
left in its bed of saliva.
Everything's working up to par—patient doing nicely.

The air is balmy—the city quietly filled with night.
That truck is much quieter than the last one.
This cigarette tastes much better than before I fell asleep.
My mind can comprehend two plus two equals four and
not even stagger.

God is in His Heaven and all's well, I've checked it out.
Now back to sleep.
I love you, Jane, honey, now back to sleep.

Quickly before the boogeyman gets you. Back to sleep!
Sleep! Sleep! Sleep!

The depression was slipping away, praise God.

TWENTY-THREE

I was offered a cameo, which is a bit part, in a picture called *Darker Than Amber*. I thought it would give me the chance to do another character part, but *Darker Than Amber* wasn't the vehicle. The small bit I did was left on the cutting room floor. I wanted to get a crack at parts with some depth to them instead of the sexy ones I'd always been handed. I didn't care if I looked like hell, as long as I could get a chance to A-C-T. Well, it didn't turn out that way, and the less said about that cameo, the better. It was the last film I ever did, and I was very unhappy with it.

The truth is that, more often than not, I've been unhappy about the pictures I've been in; that is, the final results displeased me. Working on them was always a ball. I loved working with the people.

I loved being on the set and I loved the "family" feeling of the studio, and of course my wonderful crew. In other words, I loved the actual work, it was the results that were disappointing.

Play rehearsals were marvelous, with everyone working together toward the same goal, but once a play opened and ran for a couple of months, it became absolute torture for me to be tied to it night after night. I need change too much, and time to do nothing at all.

Jane Russell (signature)

The films that didn't displease me and which I especially enjoyed doing were _The Fuzzy Pink Nightgown, Gentlemen Prefer Blondes,_ both _Palefaces,_ and _The Tall Men._ Other than those, I got little artistic satisfaction from my work. Howard Hughes was a good and fair boss, but he lacked the artistic taste to do the kind of films I really would have liked to be in, with parts I could get my teeth into. He wasn't the man I needed if I was to have developed into a serious actress. So I really have no idea how far I could have gone in films.

As for the publicity, I went far all right—no arguments there—but, except for comedy, I went nowhere in the acting department. I worked with directors like Raoul Walsh and Howard Hawks, whom I adored, both experts at action films, and I did my best work with them, but I never got to work with what is called a "woman's" director, men like William Wyler and George Stevens, men who did those wonderful Bette Davis and Crawford and Hepburn pictures. I would have given my eyeteeth to do a picture with George Cukor, but such opportunities never came my way. William Wyler wanted me for _Friendly Persuasion_ with Gary Cooper, but I was already committed to something else then. That could have broken the pattern. I was definitely a victim of Hollywood typecasting.

If I could do a story that involved kids or that had something to do with God in our lives, I'd jump at the chance. But unless something meaningful comes along, I'm perfectly happy doing what I'm doing.

I don't think I would have been very successful had I started in pictures today. The first time a producer would have come up with a nude scene, I'd have gone back to the ranch. I'll admit that pictures were too Pollyannaish and unrealistic then, but today too many producers are going for skin and violence just for shock value, and I think it's sad. In the forties and fifties, ingenuity in a story line was used to capture audiences.

The studio machine kept stars alive then because it was in the studio's best interest to sell their product, but today's stars are really only as good as their last picture. It must take a great deal of knowledge (or good advice) and determination to stay on top today. You will see actors turn in an excellent performance, but if they don't get offered another good vehicle, they quickly fade from view. I'll venture to say that agents have come into their own.

Some of today's movies are marvelous, of course, and the technology just keeps on getting better and better. If Meryl Streep, Robert Redford, Jane Fonda, Barbra Streisand, Paul Newman, Robert De Niro, or Dustin Hoffman is in the cast, you know you have a fair chance of seeing something worthwhile—but, honestly, my favorite picture from the last few years is *On Golden Pond*, with two stars from the thirties and forties.

Television is turning out stars—but it too has a publicity machine. Stars are told pretty much what to do, as they were in the major motion picture studios.

My life has been full of "as it happened" coincidences. Like everybody else, I've done my share of banging on doors that stayed locked no matter what I did, but it seems as though I've had more than my share of doors that suddenly flew open without any effort on my part. Every time it happens, it amazes me.

Two doors—a man and a play—opened for me almost together in late 1970, two years after Roger had died. I met the first man I felt I could be interested in at a WAIF ball in Detroit: Father Paul Mills. He was a very handsome clergyman who worked with addicts in a drug rehabilitation center. Detroit and the San Fernando Valley are a long way apart, so after our few dates in Detroit and many phone calls to the Valley, he decided to come out for Christmas. He was a charming, well-educated Irishman, and we talked for hours, mostly about helping others. It was the first nice Christmas I'd had since my divorce. But when he had to go back to Detroit, we couldn't figure out how we could be together more often.

Then suddenly I was signed for a month's engagement in my old standby *Catch Me if You Can* at the Meadowbrook

Dinner Theatre in New Jersey. As it happened, Haskell Gordon, a pixie who has an acid mouth and who was an old buddy of Roger's, had also been cast in the play.

The management asked me to come to New York a week early to make some television appearances publicizing the show. That was fine with me. Grabbing the opportunity, I called Paul, who arranged to fly in from Detroit so we could spend a few days together before the play started. I wouldn't wish a long-distance love affair on *anyone*.

Arriving in New York, I started my rounds of the television studios, appearing on several shows, including David Frost's and Dick Cavett's. I damn near didn't make Cavett's, but "as it happened" was working and I did appear as per schedule after all.

Haskell, who was in New York too, kept urging me to see the musical *Company*. He said it was a great show and I really mustn't miss it. After Paul arrived, we arranged to go, the three of us. All during *Company*, Paul kept nudging me. "You could do that part," he whispered. "You'd be sensational in it." I shushed him. A few minutes later, "I can just see you doing it, Jane, you'd be great!"

I sat there loving everything, the book, the music, the role of Joanne that Elaine Stritch was playing so beautifully. Joanne was a woman who laid everything right out for you: no mincing around. She was the kind of gal I love—honest, very tuned into what was going on around her. And there was so much wit in the part. But talking about me playing the role was like running around looking for the Sugarplum Fairy. Elaine *had* the role and, by the kind of performance she was giving, she deserved to have it.

When the play was over, Haskell wanted to go backstage to say hello and congratulate Elaine and Larry Kert, the male lead, and that whole marvelous cast. I don't ordinarily go backstage unless a really close friend is in the cast, but Haskell kept insisting, so the three of us went together. While we were there, Ben Strobach, the stage manager, came over with a big grin on his face.

"I can't get over your turning up like this," he said. "I

was supposed to contact *you.* Hal asked me to see if you'd be interested in doing *Company,* replacing Stritch."

I stared at him.

"See?" Paul was nudging me again. I was in shock.

"Didn't I tell you?" Haskell said, grinning.

Ben could see that I was speechless, so he finally started explaining. Hal Prince and his staff, who were in Boston getting *Follies* ready to come to New York, just happened to be watching the Cavett show the night I was on. They had been searching for a replacement for the Broadway cast of *Company,* since Elaine was scheduled to go with the road company. I don't know what it was that Hal saw in me as he watched that interview, but he had turned to his staff and said, "What about her?"

Gathering my brains together, I told Ben to call my manager, Kevin Pines, and gave him Kevin's number in California. Once in a while I decide to do something without discussiong it with Kevin first, which makes him furious, but I figure it's good for him. I'll admit there have been times I've regretted going ahead on my own. But not this time. Not with Broadway involved.

Kevin remembers it quite well:

What I didn't dare tell her was that she had to audition. Not because of temperament. She can be the most exasperating female on earth, but never because of temperament.

I'd seen the instant I laid eyes on her in New York that she was concerned over the now and then nature of her affair with Paul. Auditions are damned important, but Jane can get broody and I was afraid telling her in advance would twist the strings even tighter.

"We have to go so you can meet Prince," I told her. "How do I know whether you'll like him or not? You may hate him. You may not want to work with him for one minute."

She bought it. But all the time I knew she was going to have to sing and also to read lines for them. A pro-

ducer has a right to check those things out. On the other
hand, while I have the courage of my convictions about
Jane, I didn't want to add to the pressure she was obviously feeling.

On the plane headed for Boston, I kept trying to
prepare her without giving the show away.

"Jane, what if they ask you to sing. . . ."

"Oh, they won't."

"Yes, but what if they do? Maybe you should be
thinking of a couple of songs you'd like to do."

"No. They won't ask me to do that."

"But they might. Just to get your range. You know."

"Don't worry about it. They're not going to."

Okay. Miss Know-It-All knows it all.

"Uh, why don't we look through the script, Jane?"

"What do we want to do that for?"

"Well, they might want to get an idea of how you'd
read the part."

No, she didn't want to do that either. We talked
about this and that and I began to worry whether I was
doing the right thing.

We arrive at the airport in Boston and I haven't
succeeded in preparing her at *all*. She's edgy.

Now Miss Russell decides she has to eat! She needs
to lose *pounds*, but she has to eat. There's a sandwich
and candy and nut place next to the theater and we go
in there, me with visions of her getting up to sing with
a mouthful of nuts and spraying the whole damn orchestra pit. I start to carry on, becoming somewhat
flamboyant, trying to get rid of some of the pressure.
She's suddenly doing her Miss Tranquility number. She
does that, you know. Every once in a while, at the
damnedest moments, she'll get fatalistic, figures it's all
up to the Lord. Then I *really* want to kill her. Not that I
don't believe her when she taps her shoulder and says,
"There, Kevin, He's right there." But *He* doesn't have
to go out there and do His number.

She has a sandwich with bread, of course, which
doesn't add to my joy. When we get to the theater, we
sit in the very back, watching the end of the *Follies* rehearsal.

Now I find a new worry. Will that feeling of
"Broadway Theater" freeze her up? Rehearsal finishes

and the cast leaves. There's just Hal Prince and Stephen Sondheim and Michael Bennett and a few others, all sitting down in front. Ruthie Mitchell, Hal's assistant, comes over.

"Are you ready to sing, Miss Russell?" she asks pleasantly.

"Do what?"

"Sing for us."

Jane turns and looks at me.

I shrug off the ice. "Go ahead, Jane, baby." Nodding and grinning, "Go ahead."

She gets up without so much as a twitch and goes to talk to the pianist. I can't tell whether she's playing Indian, which she's capable of, believe me, or whether she's as cool as she looks. Me, I'm on the hot line to the Lord. I don't know whether He's on the other end, but I'm saying my piece anyway.

Jane climbs up on the stage wearing the new black suit I'd assured her any housewife would be proud to wear. But I must say, with the big black fur hat, she's made the whole outfit *some*thing. She really has great flair and a sense of what will work for her. She moves across the stage on those gorgeous long legs, looking *great*.

They had several rifle mikes set up at the front of the stage and Jane calls out, "Are these on?"

"Oh sure," somebody yells back. "They're on."

Well, they weren't. She sang, staying in range of those dead mikes even when she was moving around as they asked her to do. She sang a couple of songs, filling the theater with her voice. And when they asked her to up a key to brighten the song, she did that easily. You know, everybody sits back and says, "Oh well, what can a movie star do? Without retakes and cuts and splicing and dubbing, they're dead!" Well, she showed them. She looked great and she sounded greater. Then they asked her to read with the stage manager feeding her cues from that damned cold script.

Let me tell you, when a stage manager reads with you, he gives you *nothing*. Whatever there is in the scene, you have to find for yourself and bring alive *by* yourself. Well, Aunt Jane laid back her ears, stretched out those long legs, and *ran*! Everybody applauded and

carried on. She shocked them! When she finished, Hal
Prince came over to me apologetically. "Kevin, how do
we know?" he said. "Unless we see it for ourselves, how
do we know?"

I was going to kill Kevin as soon as I came off stage, but
Hal was being wonderful and saying that we should stay over
and see *Follies* that night. It was a marvelous show. But I could
never have done it, not night after night. I'd get too depressed. I told that to Kevin. I don't think he knew what I
meant. It's hard now, looking back to that time to remember
at all. I was still devastated over losing Roger and I was un-
bearably lonely. I was so happy to have found Paul, but he
was in Detroit and it was a mess trying to get together. I
suppose I was pretty vulnerable at that point in time.

Kevin and I went backstage to see Mary McCarty, who
was in the show. I had worked with her in *The French Line*
and I wanted to tell her how much I enjoyed her. Alexis Smith
had been great in the show and I congratulated her. She was
rather cool. When we left the theater I suddenly realized that
I hadn't seen Mary.

I felt terrible. Between Alexis and my one track mind, I
could have offended Mary, a woman I loved and whom I
wouldn't hurt for the world.

We went back to the theater, only to learn Mary had already left. Fortunately, a couple of the chorus boys were able
to suggest where she might be.

Kevin and I raced to the nearest bar, close by the Shub-
ert. There they were, Mary and Dorothy Collins and Ruthie
Mitchell and Hal Prince, sitting at a table together. Kevin and
I joined them.

Something happened between us that night. They were
so friendly and easy, all of them. Great vibes, as my kids
would say. I was able to open up to Hal about my fears. He's
a very warm kind of person. He talks with a husky catch in
his voice that's very attractive, and has a marvelous sense of
humor. I suppose he can get irritable and cross when he's
putting a show together, but I've never seen him that way.
He is a darling man whom I learned to love.

I told Hal that the idea of appearing on Broadway was damned spooky. What was really worrying me was our schedule, only two and a half weeks of rehearsals. All my life I'd thought how great it would be to have three whole months to prepare something, the way new Broadway shows begin. While you don't rehearse much in picutures, except for musical numbers, you can do retakes for as long as the director's patience and the budget will allow.

Hal tried to reassure me. I wasn't to worry, everything would turn out fine. Then he said, "You don't remember meeting me before, do you? I took you and Jeanne Crain to the Brown Derby years ago with Alfred Vanderbuilt." He was right. I didn't remember, but it must have been while Jeanne and I were making *Gentlemen Marry Brunettes*. Hal went on telling funny stories on himself and we all laughed and reminisced.

I felt so much at home with those people. It felt like family. The theater really can be that way, you know, a special kind of family. I think we were all on the same wavelength sitting around the table that night, open and relaxed and trusting, truly *liking* each other.

Looking back, that was a very important "as it happened," my missing Mary at the theater and joining her at the bar instead. Otherwise I wouldn't have seen Hal and Ruthie till rehearsals for *Company* started and we wouldn't have gotten to know one another beforehand. This may have been one thing that made a big difference later, because I was to strain their affection more than I had any right to. Luckily for me, Hal was never *just* a producer and director, or our relationship could never have stood the pressure I placed on it.

Back in New York I went to see *Company* again. I started realizing how damn complicated it really was. Hal's office sent me the music so I could begin studying the score.

Since I was going to be appearing at the Meadowbrook for a month, I figured it would be worth the trouble to look for an apartment to live in; with the *Company* role to follow, I'd be in New York for eight months, so it made even more sense. After searching and searching, I found a beautiful, large

unfurnished apartment with a terrace and a view of the Hudson River. Best of all, the apartment was only two blocks away from the Alvin Theater, where *Company* was playing.

There was only one thing wrong. It was on Eighth Avenue, not exactly the best part of New York. After I moved in I found that pimps and hookers also live and work on Eighth. There was quite a contingent of them in my building.

Soon after I moved in, Bob Mitchum phoned to say hello while he was in New York on his way to Europe. I told him about the apartment and the interesting neighbors.

"Well," he said in that gentle, devastating way of his, "how do they like *you*, honey?"

Bob has a way of turning everything upside-down and somehow giving it another, funny, marvelous perspective as a result. He is a gorgeous person.

Other show business people lived in the building too, writers and so on, but none of *us* owned fancy cars with glass domes and the Cadillacs out front. Those belonged to the pimps.

Kevin was so appalled at the apartment; he was as close to incoherent as he'll ever be. I should live on the East Side, he shouted, and get a car and driver to take me to the theater, do the movie star bit. Kevin worries about image, but I'm not sure whether it's his or mine. Fortunately, he had to get back to California, so I didn't have to listen to him too long.

I started my month of traveling back and forth to the Meadowbrook, doing *Catch Me if You Can* there. At the apartment, I would read the *Company* script, trying to find the key to Joanne's character. The lines seemed meaningless, just words on paper. They might as well have been a string of names picked out of the Manhattan phone directory. And Sondheim's odd-metered music was even worse. I would listen to it over and over and over again. But no matter how hard I tried, I couldn't begin to learn it. Although Sondheim numbers are not just simple, ordinary pop tunes by any means, I should have been able to learn them. But my head would not work. I started getting really scared.

I was having even more trouble sleeping than I usually did. When I'm under pressure or doing any kind of continuous stage work, I need more than nine hours of sleep. I don't mean *want* more; I mean *need.* I simply can't function without sleep. It happens to be the way I'm made. I had my eye shades and earplugs, of course. I can't sleep without those, even in the darkest, quietest room. But while they shut out the light and sound, they couldn't do anything to stop the wheels that kept turning in my head. Or the knot twisting in my stomach.

One night I didn't make it to the Meadowbrook. For the first time in my life, I missed a performance. I'd worked when I was exhausted, when I was sick, when my guts were knotted over what was happening to my marriage with Robert, even after Roger's death. I'd gone out there and smiled and sung, acted happy and carefree, read my lines. I'd made it. Somehow, I'd always made it before. But not this time.

Someone phoned Kevin in California.

Kevin:

> I found Jane crying. Everything was wrong she told me. Everything in her life. She was worried about her children, her responsibilities, her lack of ability to manage her own financial affairs. She couldn't cope with anything. She couldn't even *think,* she said, let alone memorize material. It broke my heart to watch her.
>
> Maybe the most important thing of all was the emotional upheaval she was going through with Paul, who is really a fine man, a very decent guy. Kind, very straight, in some ways like Roger. She was so desperate to have someone who was her own. Without that, it seemed as if she had no base, no foundation.

Kevin stayed on with me in New York and we got me pulled back together again, at least enough to go on with the play at the Meadowbrook. The apartment was still the way it was when he'd left, empty except for beds and some odds and ends. Usually I love fixing up the places where I'm staying, but now, who had time to think about furnishings? And the way I was feeling, who cared?

After three weeks I was still getting nowhere with the *Company* book and score. I would try and Kevin would do his best to help, but I simply couldn't concentrate on anything. I must have been crazy to accept. I'd get out there on stage and go through something I'd already lived through once in Toronto. I couldn't, I *couldn't* go through that again. It was insane to think I could do it. I'd never make it. Not with two and a half weeks, not with two and a half *months* of rehearsal time. Not even though I wanted to play Joanne in the worst way.

Catch Me finally closed. I had some time before rehearsals for *Company* started. I had to get out of New York I told Kevin. Maybe if I got away for a while I could get my head working again. I'd visit some friends in Detroit and see Paul. Talking on the phone was never satisfactory. Maybe seeing him would make the difference.

Actually, I was running scared and I think we both knew it. All I could think of was Toronto.

It was 1965 or 1966. That much I've managed to forget. I was in New York doing something or other and let myself get talked into doing the musical *Pal Joey* in Toronto with only one week to prepare. It's hard to understand the backbreaking work involved in putting a musical on stage unless you've been in one. In prior musicals, I'd had a month to learn the book and score before rehearsals started, but I went into *Pal Joey* replacing someone who'd had some kind of emergency. I must have been out of my mind to agree to do it. I had never seen the book, didn't know the score, *nothing,* and had just one week to learn everything, rehearse, *and* open! Insane.

In our one week of rehearsals we had three different directors, one after the other. And we had three different choreographers. One after the other. Each one of those six people changed everything, the dances, the movements, all the business. Instead of working on the book, we kept having to learn new moves, new routines. Who had time for lines? And the songs, forget it!

"Don't worry about it," they'd tell me when I'd bitch. "You already know 'Bewitched, Bothered and Bewildered,' don't you? The rest'll be a cinch."

Sure it would.

I knew that song from Sinatra's great record. There was only one small catch. "Bewitched" has three choruses, and in *Pal Joey* I had to sing all three. Frank, however, had taken the first eight bars out of one chorus, the second eight out of another, and the third out of still another. That's something that's done frequently when a show tune is adapted for a single record. And those were the lyrics *I* knew.

There we were in that perfectly beautiful Royal Princess Theatre and none of us knew what the shit we were doing *at all.* I'd have given half the world to get out of that show. But I couldn't. Finally I made the stage manager listen to my complaints. I had to have the beginnings of my lines written on that enormous stage, clear from one side to the other. I had them written on napkins, tables, on my forearms. I had lines written on the palms of my hands, on the toes of my shoes, on my purse. I had lines written *everywhere.*

On opening night Joe Bennett, who played Joey, came to me. "Are we really going to *do* this, can't you *stop* them?" he begged. Poor Joe didn't know what he was doing either after three choreographers changed his dances completely. "We *can't* open, Jane. There's no way! It's ludicrous!"

But open we did, right on schedule. On stage I felt as if I were swimming in a lake of glue. I'd stand there frozen, my mind empty, and Joe would do his best to cue me in a way that would remind me of my lines. Through every scene. Every act.

And then it was time for me to sing "Bewitched." I opened my mouth, and heard the lyrics that came out of me automatically. *Sinatra's* lyrics, the ones etched into my memory. I stammered trying to find my way back.

It was ghastly. From beginning to end. We must have looked like a bunch of clowns stumbling through our dances, fumbling lines, bumping into each other, forgetting crucial business, misplacing props, all in full view of an appalled audience.

After the show, the whole cast felt sick. A lot of the kids stayed up all night, hoping against hope, waiting to see the reviews. I never read my own reviews anyway, not since Howard Hughes wouldn't let me read the ones for *The Out-*

law. So I went to bed. Why torture yourself? I knew what they'd be like without reading one word.

I heard about them anyway, of course. The critics slaughtered us. They must have sat up all night squeezing their brains to spew out words that were horrible enough.

The day after our opening, I had to appear on all the local television talk shows to publicize the play. I went on and told the world exactly what happened. I told them about the lines that were written on the stage. I guess all the people who bought tickets after my exposé came to see this funny show where nobody knew what the hell they were doing.

I was so frustrated in that show, I was in agony for the first four days. There was no way to escape the humiliation. Each night, I had to go through it. Again and again. Stepping out on that stage was like submitting yourself to torture you dreaded but knew you had to endure. At each performance I wondered, "How bad will it be *this* time?"

The third night on stage I started into "Bewitched" for what seemed like the millionth time. Wrong! *Again!* I turned to the orchestra pit and shouted.

"Hold it! I'm going to get this damn song right if it's the last thing I do! Start over!" I began the song again, walking across the stage and pointing to my chalked cues as I sang. When I finished the number, the audience laughed and screamed and applauded. They thought that was just marvelous. I didn't. It's bad show business, for one thing. But more than that, there I was, one of those "film actresses who really can't do much, you know"—and proving it in spades.

Never in my life have I been so glad to have an engagement end. Except it never really ended for me.

It was with me in New York. It came with me to Detroit. There, instead of getting better, things got worse. There was really no place I could go where I could escape my fear. Toronto haunted me. I was carrying it with me wherever I went.

And nothing went right between Paul and me. Maybe nothing could, the way I was feeling. Again, I couldn't sleep. I'd lie in bed wide awake. Finally I'd get up and start drink-

The blonde and the brunette.

Mr. and Mrs. Roger Barrett.   Mr. and Mrs. John Peoples.

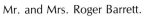

The WAIF children in Korea.

From horror *Pal Joey* . . .   . . . to glory *Company*.

Our trio: Beryl, Connie and Jane.

Isn't she lovely? Typical 40s publicity.

The French Line bathing suit. The bikini I *wouldn't* wear!

The one-piece I did wear in *The French Line*.

My nightclub act at the Sands Hotel, Las Vegas.

Catch Me If You Can on the dinner theatre circuit.

Playtex TV's bra lady.

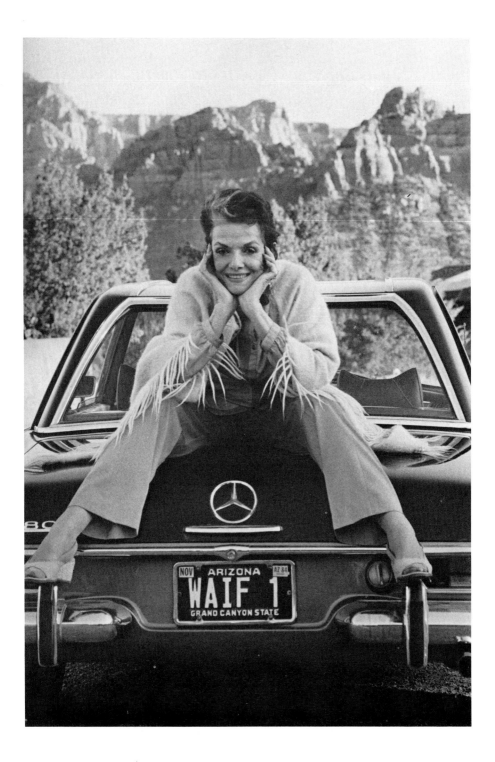

Sedona: Home, sweet home.

"The Yellow Rose" with David Soul and Sam Elliott.

Big bad John and big bad Jane.

ing and pacing back and forth, up and down, have some more booze. Finally it all came together and closed in on me.

Kevin:

The minute I heard Jane's voice on the phone from Detroit, I knew. I'd felt disaster coming when I had taken her to the airport. She'd had two or three drinks there and that worried me, because she still hadn't really gotten back on her feet yet from the time she'd missed her performance at the Meadowbrook. I didn't want her to go, but there was always the chance that seeing Paul would help. Anything that would help her was fine with me. Anything.

Ever since Roger's death, the particular loneliness she lived with became worse, became terrifying for her. I have never yet seen a star, *anybody,* who hasn't paid a goddam big price for being singled out to be a public personality. Every damn one I've seen around the business has paid for the privilege of being called STAR. It's like a heavy mortgage, a life-time mortgage. As long as you're a star, you never get the damn thing paid off.

I could hardly understand what she was saying. She was frantic, babbling, crying, incoherent. There was no talking to her. She wouldn't, maybe couldn't listen. I kept trying but I couldn't reach her. So I said, "Okay, yes, fine, Jane." I was to get her out of the contract with Prince. She couldn't, she just couldn't hack it. I should close the apartment. Sublet it, whatever. We'd go home to California. That much was clear. She was saying a lot more, but nothing that made any sense. Like half the time she was talking, but not to me. I was more than a little frantic myself, but I knew that nothing I said was getting through.

Several minutes later, the friend she'd gone to see phoned me, concerned, frightened, unable to handle Jane at all. I was really torn. But finally I said to get a doctor, put her in a hospital, I don't care what you have to do, just get her some competent professional help, we've got to get her back on her feet again no matter *what* it takes, no matter how long.

For two days, I lay in that bed. Dying. There were bars on the windows, a heavy mesh screen guarding curtains that were closed so that I couldn't see out. A loudspeaker blared constantly. Noise always drives me crazy. I would try to sleep and that damn thing would shout and I'd jump. They had taken away my clothes, my purse. I was in the psychopathic ward. Believe me, psycho wards are just that. For crazy people. If you *aren't* already, they can make you crazy fast.

I finally saw the doctor and told him that I had to get out of there or I was going to go stark raving mad. He thought I was in no shape to be released. I explained about the lights and the noise. I knew he couldn't do anything about them, but if he could just stop the staff from waking me up all the time . . . . That improved at least.

I realized it was a rib that was so painful I couldn't lie on it or turn over. I told one of the attendants. After a while I was taken to the lab for an X-ray. They found nothing wrong, they assured me. About six months later, my back was bothering me and I had another X-ray taken. I learned then that a rib had pulled loose from my spine and there was a quarter inch space between my spine and the rib. It's that way for good now. I guess the hospital people were afraid if they told me, I'd sue them.

I had heard of a place where Marilyn Monroe was taken one time when she was very upset. The attendants, the whole damn hospital staff would come and peer into the glass in her door, staring at her like she was some kind of a strange bug in a cage.

I wanted to get *out* of there. I kept asking and asking, but the doctor explained that I could only be released to someone responsible.

Kevin:

> Looking back, it's easy to see where I could have made things pleasanter for her. I had no idea what that goddamn room was like, about her rib, things like that. Now I can see that she was falling apart all during her Meadowbrook engagement, little by little, under my eyes

But I didn't know these things at the time. And I did what I thought was best for her.

In the meantime I had to take care of her affairs in New York. I called Prince's office. He was in Europe at the time, but I arranged a meeting with Carl Fisher, Hal's general manager, and Ruth Mitchell. I had heard that Ruth Mitchell was a tough lady, that she had been a lady stage manager, and you know what *that* means, Kevin, baby. She was anything but tough. She was divine. I'd known Carl for many years. He's a sweetheart. A very gentle man in addition to being a gentleman.

Still a contract is a contract. The Prince office could hang Jane out to dry. They had cause to bring suit against her if they wanted to. I walked in to talk to them feeling as if it was the demise not just of her career, but of my personal friend.

But I had to tell them the truth. I felt they deserved to know why she was backing out. And I didn't want them to think she was a temperamental Hollywood lady, because Jane isn't. I was counting on their faith in her and their genuine interest in her.

As I talked, I started crying. I couldn't stop. I was facing the fact for the first time, really letting it into my guts, that she was having an emotional breakdown.

I could *feel* their compassion in that office. It's something I'll never forget. They released us from the contract, and they both did their best to put me back together again. Then I returned to that damned apartment to arrange to get rid of it and to tie up some other loose ends for Jane.

I was furious and desperate. I tried to pray, but even that didn't work. I was alone. Totally alone. Forsaken.

I rang for a nurse and asked for something to read. I had to do *something* or I was going to go mad.

The nurse let it slip that Paul had been calling every single day and leaving messages. I hadn't even known that he knew where I was! I asked her why the hell I hadn't been called to the phone. She mumbled. I'd been sleeping and they had orders not to disturb me. This still didn't explain why I hadn't even been *told*.

Among the bunch of magazines they brought me was a little book by Norman Vincent Peale. For days I had been thinking things like, "Lord, You got me in this place. I had the chance to do that play but was too afraid to do it, so You must have me in here for a reason." Then I opened Dr. Peale's book and certain sentences literally leaped off the pages at me.

> This is the day the Lord hath made. Let us rejoice and be glad in it.
>
> I sought the Lord and He answered me and delivered me from all my fears.
>
> Try, really try. Think, really think. Believe, really believe in Him and thus in ourselves.
>
> Lean awhile upon the windowsill of Heaven and gaze upon the Lord. Then with that vision in your heart, turn strong to meet the day.
>
> In quietness and trust shall be My strength. Drop all your problems into a pool of quietness. Be still and know that I am God.

It really seemed as if that book had been meant for me for that moment, right then when I needed it most. Well, I sat there and bawled and bawled and bawled, like a baby. Dr. Peale's thoughts were all things I had known, but they were so appropriate, it felt like a loving, understanding hand was being stretched out to me. And I could pray again.

I grew calm. The fight inside me had stopped. And I didn't feel alone any more.

I started to laugh, "Lord, I knew You had me here for a reason." I said to myself, "All right, dumb ass, the Lord opened up this door on Broadway for you. He'll give you the strength to go through it."

That very afternoon, when the doctor came to see me, he told me that he'd received a couple of phone calls from Father Paul asking about me and wondered if the three of us could have a talk.

Paul came the very next day. I've never been so glad to see anyone in my life. He's a very straight guy. Paul said he didn't know where our relationship was going: Sometimes it was fine and sometimes he was plain scared to death. He thought if I could do the play, it would be good for me in a lot of ways. The doctor said he needed to find out if I *should* go back and do the play first. I smiled. I knew he was wondering if I could hack it.

The three of us sat around and talked everything out. Our relationship, the play, my fears, everything. When it was all laid out on the table before us, the doctor said, "Well, now, what if you and Paul don't work out, will you still do the play?"

"Whether we work out or don't work out," I replied calmly, "I'm supposed to do the play, so that's what I'm going to do. That is, if they'll still have me."

He studied me for a long time before answering. Then he said, "I think you're ready to leave." Then he smiled. "In fact, you can go right now if you'd like."

If I'd like? I could have kissed that man. In two seconds I had all my things together, grabbed Paul by the hand, and we dashed out of the door and ran all the way to the exit like a pair of kids. I didn't look back.

TWENTY-FOUR

Paul and I had a marvelous time together before he put me on the plane for New York. I phoned Kevin and told him if he hadn't closed up the apartment yet, not to, and that I'd do the play if Hal hadn't found a replacement.

Kevin went back to the Prince office. "Well," he said, "Miss Crazy has decided she *can* do the show after all." They told him they'd love to have me, but it was up to Hal Prince, who was still in Europe. When Hal returned to New York, he and I met to talk. I explained about my experience in Toronto and being so afraid of a repetition of *that* scene on Broadway.

Hal smiled. "I knew. I knew exactly what you were thinking," he said. "And I knew you'd come back and do the play. Honey, we didn't even *look* for a replacement for you."

What a man!

We went to work. We started with rehearsals for the dance routines and the musical numbers first. Ethel Martin, who had danced with Jack Cole, worked with me alone. I am always amazed how someone like Jack or Ethel not only memorizes long, complex routines for each individual and for each number, but also knows exactly where everyone is supposed to be at every moment during those complicated, interweaving ensemble numbers. When I reached the point where I was moving around pretty well on my own, I joined the rest of the new kids in the cast. I saw them struggling and learning and forgetting and relearning, just like me, I thought it would never get put together by opening night. Everybody was trying so hard, but there was so much to learn and so little time. By the end of the day, everybody's fanny would be dragging.

A musical is lots and lots of hard work, but the worst part is worrying, "Am I ever going to learn it?"

In one number I had to come in singing after nineteen bars. "Just count it off," they told me. No *way* for me to do that. I'm not talking about tempo. Tempo, I understand. That's the beat, something you feel in your blood, in your guts. I never have any trouble with beat. But forget counting.

While I was doing *Gentlemen Prefer Blondes* with Marilyn, Jack Cole came to me once about a dance number she and I were doing together. We'd rehearsed and rehearsed, but when we were finally ready to shoot the scene, Jack was still worried.

"Look, Jane," he said, "Baby's always a little offside. So you're going to have to hit it right on the nose. Don't wait for her. You *hit* it."

That wasn't any problem for me and the number looked fine on screen.

But counting out nineteen bars is something else. I knew I'd have to get it by ear, which is the way I learn everything. And I did.

Kevin came to see every single bloody rehearsal. The kids in the new cast were a great bunch, and we still write to each other, but at first they couldn't figure out what this fool in the white safari clothes was doing there. I think they finally decided Kevin was my Jewish mother come to put me on the stage. He was always there, watching in the wings, turning up at my elbow whenever I wasn't on the stage, acting his funny, outrageous worst to keep us all laughing and loose. Everybody ended up falling in love with him.

I still couldn't seem to get a handle on the character I

was to play. Hal wasn't around during those first rehearsals and I didn't know what to do. It helped to watch Elaine in the part though. I can always pick things up and learn by watching someone else. Other Geminis tell me they do that too. For one thing, seeing Elaine helped me find the guts to be as blatant as the part required. I wasn't trying to copy her. That's really a useless thing to try, even if it worked, which it doesn't.

Finally Barbara Barrie, who was from the original company, said something that gave me the key I was searching for.

"It's a group of people who don't know each other," she said. "And everybody's being terribly polite to everybody else. Joanne's a person who has no patience with idiots. She comes in and sort of takes over."

I figured, all right, Joanne's a takeover kind of gal, I know how to do *that*. I'd done it enough in my own life, God knows.

It wouldn't have been so rough if we'd had more time. But I felt like I was always hurrying to finish one thing so I could get started on the next. Nothing could be left out, it was all important. I kept racing to get it all done. It seemed like the only time I wasn't running, I was either in the john or asleep. But in my head, I was running even then.

Then we had a problem with my costume. The woman who was doing the clothes for *Company* didn't have any idea of what to do with me. That's happened to me before many, many times.

During the fittings, she'd mentioned opaque stockings. She wore them herself, black ones, and she had put them on Elaine and thought she was going to put them on me. I drew the line there and said no, I wanted very sheer black hose.

Kevin and I were in my dressing room when the finished costume was delivered. I put it on and came to stand in front of the mirror to see what I looked like. What I looked like was Ernest Borgnine in drag.

The skirt, for one small thing, was far too long and far too wide on me, even though I'd *told* her. With my long legs I look best in skirts so tight other gals couldn't even walk in them. In that costume my legs looked like two straws sticking out of a bale of hay. But worse than that, the dress had no style, no chic, *nothing.*

The woman ended up making a second dress. *More* fittings. It wasn't much better than the first. Unfortunately, most of the stills that were out in front of the theater were taken with me wearing the second outfit. Something had to be done. Then, three days before we were to open, Hal saw it on me. He took Kevin aside and said, "Go out and buy her a dress."

Kevin and I raced around New York and ended up at Bergdorf Goodman, which carries Pauline Trigère clothes. I adore her. I tried on a black crepe dress, cut beautifully, and it was absolutely divine. It was also very expensive, but we bought it. Then Annie Miller recommended a shop where she'd just ordered stage jewelry for her role in *Hello, Dolly!* The shop was able to make up glittery junk jewelry for me in a hurry, so running into Annie, who's bubbly and a walking tonic, paid off in two ways. The costume problem was solved.

All I had to do now was open.

Our first performance before an audience was for fellow actors, and the house was jammed. That can be a nightmare, since they're all in the business. But even though they tend to be overcritical, you know they're rooting for you—and if you're good, they *love* you. Well, we were good, and they *loved* us.

After opening night the original company split in two, with one group going on the road with Elaine and the other staying in New York with Larry Kert. We new ones worked hard trying to learn everything and kept together and helped one another. We had to, we were all in the same boat. The veterans kept to themselves for the most part, hardly talking to the new kids, and, except for Larry, it was the coldest atmosphere I'd ever experienced backstage. From the reports coming back from the troupe with the road company, they were having the same problems: The original cast members formed a sort of clique and were bored to death with the show, and except for the new members of the cast, there was little or no enthusiasm.

Then, after our official opening, the reviews came in—those desperately needed, hard-earned, and sweated out reviews that meant life or death for a play. Mark Twain once said, "When your actions speak for you, don't interrupt." Well, I certainly agree, and though I've never been one to blow my own horn, I must say, I never have done anything I've been so happy about as overcoming my fears and doing that show. The Lord gets all the credit for my part in the show and for the reviews. They were the best things that ever happened to me professionally.

One of the reviews read, "When Jane Russell launches into 'The Ladies Who Lunch,' her big solo in the second act, you realize that she is still a force to be reckoned with. And that this debut may very well mark the beginning of a whole new career for an actress whose celebrated attributes up to now seems to have been only her cleavage." And another, "It's hard to define Stardom in a generation that doesn't seem to produce it, but out there on that stage you saw it in Miss Russell."

I had never been so happy with myself as I was then. The weeks of rehearsal had gone by in a big blue haze. I'd been hot and then cold, afraid and then confident, but I'd come through and was thrilled that I had. Thirty years after my debut as an actress in *The Outlaw*, when I didn't know a camera angle from a cameraman, I had opened on Broadway and received rave reviews. As Mom would say, praise the Lord.

I decided that since I was going to be in New York for all of the six months, I would write to Carmen to see if she'd like to come and stay with me for the length of the run. Her answer by return mail said that she could, and I was thrilled that we'd be living together. When Carmen arrived we got going in earnest with the apartment. The J. P. Stevens Company decided to decorate it for a publicity story. It looked just great. Flower boxes all in bloom filled the terrace and gave it the feeling of a real California apartment. I really felt at home there.

Life, for a change, was good and fun filled and productive. Everyone came to see the show. Tracy, who was attending college in Prescott, Arizona, came with a boy she was going with. My Mom came, and one way or another the whole family got there. Surprisingly, even Robert came. He and Hamp Pool were back in New York for the funeral of Dan Reeves, who had been the owner of the Rams. The apartment was always filled with friends, and I was constantly occupied with one thing or another.

Carmen supervised the shopping and the cooking with our Jamaican housekeeper. Paul came for a visit and stayed with us until it was time for him to return to Detroit for his master's degree in sociology. As for our relationship, it developed into a steady friendship.

It was a very wonderful time of my life. About this time, Kevin wangled a fabulous contract for me with the Playtex bra people to do their television commercials. They were tastefully done and it seemed like a natural. I've been doing them ever since, and it has served to keep me not only financially secure, but also in the public eye.

My fiftieth birthday came up during the run, and Kevin threw a wonderful surprise party at the Spindletop Restaurant. A hundred and eighty people came, including all the kids in *Company* and all our friends who were in New York. Even ol' Fred Robertson flew in to share "our" birthday. It was a ball, a birthday I'll never forget.

My mother was very, very impressed with my Broadway success, much more so than she'd been about doing "pictures," which to her wasn't quite the real thing. After all, she'd been a stage actress when she was young and knew what that was all about. So when she and Aunt Ernie visited New York, she understood and was proud of me.

For the first three months I loved doing the play, but the next three months were like having my teeth pulled. I was counting the minutes until I could go home. When the play's run was over I rushed back to the Valley to my friends and family.

TWENTY - FIVE

Taos West, the name I'd given the apartment complex, was finished when Carmen and I got back to Los Angeles, and we moved in. The result of all the work my brothers and I had put into it was as beautiful as I had dreamed it would be. The overall effect was that of a big Indian-Mexican hacienda, and I just loved it.

Carmen stayed with me for about six months and then I was once again on my own. I'd planned those apartments with an eye to privacy, and that's exactly what I had, which is grand if you have someone to be private with. But if you're alone, you could go bananas, and I was on my way.

A few days before New Year's, in December 1972, Bayeux invited me to Santa Barbara, where his sister, Benny, and Mom Kellogg were throwing a party. I grabbed at the opportunity for two reasons: One, I had always loved Santa Barbara, and every time I went there I hated to leave; and two, it was a great chance to get myself out of the rut I'd gotten in.

I arrived the day before New Year's Eve and was so relieved and happy to be there that I got myself so drunk I almost didn't make it to the festivities. I sobered up enough the next day to say to Bayeux, "I've always wanted to live up here, but something invariably got in the way. Don't you know someone in real estate who can take me out to look at houses?''

I was back to my favorite hobby. The day after New Year's I was out with a real estate agent looking at houses. I saw one I adored. It was close to 100 years old and was right next to the Miramar Hotel in Montecito. It was casually furnished with beach house furniture, had huge beams on the ceilings, and a big fireplace was set back into one wall of the living room. Best of all, you could see the ocean from the garden and upstairs bedrooms. And when you walked the floors creaked. Marvelous!

"I'll take it," I announced firmly and sat right down to make out a check to clinch the deal. Both my brothers Tom and Ken thought I'd gone out of mind. Tom had done some really lovely things to my apartment and couldn't understand why I would want to leave it. How could I get him to see that I was lonely as hell in it and preferred living in Santa Barbara near Benny and Bayeux?

I won't say that I was never lonely there too, because I was. But it was somehow better being lonely there than it was back in the Valley. What I couldn't escape in either place was going to bed by myself every night. I just didn't like it. As I've said before, I was born married. It seemed to me that all I had been doing these years, except for the months in New York, was wander around in search of a home. Now that I'd found it, dynamite wouldn't get me out of it. I even got myself a dog, a lovely big German shepherd.

After a while I started dating. There were three nice bachelors I saw from time to time, but nothing much came of that. Much of my social life consisted of seeing all the friends I had in and around Santa Barbara. I saw a lot of Merilyn Garcin, who was divorced from her husband Bob, and was going with a very nice guy named John Peoples who lived up in Santa Maria. So while I did manage to keep busy, I was still going to bed alone in that big house, and I was still lonely.

Benny came over one night when I was feeling particularly blue to have a pray, as we often did. She had gone to chapel when she lived in the Valley. We joined hands on my bed and began to pray, when all at once Benny boomed out, "I will give you more than a dog to love."

And I said aloud, "When, Lord, oh, when?"

When I'd gotten my dog I had said to myself, "Well, I guess I'm going to be one of those little old ladies with a dog and live this way for the rest of my life." Now, praise God, I was finding out that the Lord had other plans for me.

I did *Mame* in San Francisco and Chicago during this period and I loved it. San Francisco was close enough for a bunch of family and friends to come, and again we had a ball. Jerry Shaw, my director buddy, said I related to my nephew in the play better than any Mame he had seen thus far. I think every actress in town had done Mame at one time or another.

I also was able to purchase my house and had my brothers send up my furniture. It didn't take long to be completely settled in. Everything was working out just fine. I had my house where I'd always wanted it, I had my friends nearby, and I had my dog. But there was, as yet, no one who was my very own special fellah.

John Peoples was six feet two. He had been in the U.S. Air Force for twenty-four years and was now a retired lieutenant colonel involved in real estate and investments in Santa Maria. He was originally from Texas and had a hilarious mouth. He'd come up with sayings that would either shock his listeners or have them rolling on the floor with laughter. There were no two ways about John. He had the most original and expressive ways of describing things.

I had spent almost a year living quietly in Santa Barbara straightening myself out, and all during that time John Peoples was just a friend who stopped by once in a while. He had broken up with Merilyn some time before. One day John called from Santa Maria.

"What are you doing?" he asked, a note of melancholy in his voice.

"Nothing special," I replied. "Christobel is down from San Francisco and we're just sitting around. Why?"

"Oh, I don't know," he said, "I'm kind of at loose ends and wondered if I could come on down."

Knowing John, I wasn't sure he'd show up, as something was certain to come along that would divert him. By 10:30 P.M. I figured I was right, and we all went to bed. I was just falling asleep when he arrived. He came upstairs, sat on the edge of the bed, and we talked about nothing in particular. Then, without any warning whatsoever, he leaned over and kissed me.

Well, to say I was shocked would be the understatement of the year. I think he was too. He stayed at the house a couple of days, and we were never out of each other's sight. It was obvious that we had fallen in love. Just like that.

I didn't know what to think. We went to a play and after the performance John took me to the country club, where it seemed as if everyone was there: Meg and her husband Tom, Mom Kellogg, and Benny. They kept staring at us because we were either sitting and holding hands or dancing or laughing together as though we shared some private joke. Benny's comment was, "You two look like a pair of matching bookends."

After John went back to Santa Maria, I was walking on air. It had been a perfectly wonderful few days.

John had been married twice before, once early in the service and once after, but he'd spent years single in between. He had one son, Dude, twenty-four, with whom he was very close. He came from a large family, his parents having loads of relatives, and he was one of five sons and had a twin sister. So he was as used to large family groups as I was.

I'd always prayed for a man who would know all the ins and outs of business and who'd be able to handle what money I had and would have. Well, John Peoples was all of that.

Our first kiss was on December 1, and by the time December 25 rolled around I was pretty sure of what I wanted. John had to go to Texas for Christmas, because his son was coming in from Georgia where he lived and John couldn't disappoint him. So we would be separated for the holidays: John would be in Nacogdoches, Texas, and I would be in Santa Barbara with my mom and the kids.

"I'll call you on Christmas morning," were his parting words. Before he had a chance to make that call, I checked with an astrologer friend of mine and had my dates all worked out in advance. When John phoned, I greeted him with, "When would you rather get married, January 31 or April 20?"

Long pause. Then he said, "Are you proposing to me?"

"Yes, you big fool!" I hollered into the phone. "What do you think I'm doing? Now answer me, which date do you want?" He didn't bother answering that question. "I'll be right home," he said and hung up. *Home.* That's the word he used.

The wedding date was set: January 31, 1974. And I was happy, in love, and secure for the first time in seven years. I went blithely ahead with the wedding plans, and the closer that day came, the more nervous John became. But I thrived on it.

John is a very informal man and hates dressing up. Around the house he usually wears loose-fitting caftans and can't wait to get out of his going-out clothes and into one of his caftans. Aware of this, I got an idea.

"Guess what we're going to do, honey," I said.

"What?"

"We're going to be married in caftans. You'll feel more comfortable."

"Okay," he laughed.

I started planning at once. He and I would wear green caftans; his would be velvet with gold braid down one side. Everyone taking part in the ceremony would also wear caftans, two in royal blue and two in turquoise. When I told John of my color scheme and asked what he thought of it, he came up with one of his typically John Peoples cracks: "I think we'll shine like a new nickel in a goat's ass."

John's brother-in-law, Walter, flew up from Texas a week before the wedding for his fitting, but, insisting that Texas be represented, he announced, "Ah'm gonna wear mah cowboy boots and spurs and mah cowboy hat with mah caftan, and ah don't care what anyone says." And I said, "Great, it'll be marvelous." And he did just that.

John and I decided to keep the ceremony intimate and have only the wedding party present. Tracy, now twenty-three, came, and Buck, eighteen, showed up with a half-grown beard in the grubbiest looking hippy outfit he could find. But I was glad that he had come, that he wanted to be there.

The wedding ceremony was just beautiful, and afterward we all went over to Mom Kellogg's for the reception. Many of the people present I'd never met before. It seemed as if half of San Francisco was there. My old friend Babs and her husband, Quentin, flew in from Colorado, and since Quentin was a flyer like John, it was instant friendship between the two. The next day we all took *The Outlaw* for a cruise to Catalina. John had learned to navigate and it was honeymoon time.

With the festivities over, John and I settled down to being married and mending each other's lives. John has been fantastic with my kids. Even when they resisted at first, he went right ahead doing the positive thing, and if they failed to react in the way he thought they should, he actually cried. He may act like a bear, but he's really a big pussy cat when it comes to children.

As the kids got to know him, they returned his affection. They also know by now that if they bring him into any of their plans, he's going to try to be so helpful that he ends up taking over the whole project. It's become sort of a family joke, because they now plot and plan behind his back and say, "How are we going to do this or that without Papa John finding out about it? Because if he ever does, he's going to take over and shove us on down the road." John blows off a lot of steam hollering at them, but he's always there whenever they need him.

It was about that time my twenty-year contract with Howard Hughes expired, and so I had no more money coming in from that source. True, I had the Playtex commercials and some real estate, but the eighty-unit apartment building that should have been making a profit wasn't. My brother Tom was managing it and was too soft-hearted. From a financial standpoint, the place was going down the drain.

No sooner were John and I married, I had to go out on the road again in order to pay the taxes on the building. So Kevin got me a booking to do *Catch Me if You Can* at the five Chateau de Ville theaters, each about an hour or two outside of Boston. It would be a five-month run. I told John that if I was going out to work, I was not going alone—I was sick of that bit. So he agreed to come along. Again the choice was either to stay in Boston and drive out to each theater every night or to move each month as the play moved. We chose the latter.

John got a real taste of show business and loved it; he liked the other actors in the company and had a ball around them. A couple of days before a move, he would be out scouting the town we were heading for, finding a place for us to live in and making sure everything was in order for my arrival. Then he would move us in. He was the best advance man any show ever had. Anything arranged by John Peoples always worked out without a single hitch.

By the time we returned to Los Angeles, he already realized that moving around like gypsies was not the life for us, so he sold the Oxnard and Studio City houses I owned and began looking into how the apartment building was being run. I wanted to sell that too, but John suggested waiting. He was thinking about handling it differently. And while he was still thinking it out, we went out on the road once more with *Catch Me if You Can* in Dallas and then in Ohio. Then home to Santa Barbara.

One evening in the early spring of 1976, John and I were sitting in our living room quietly watching the news when suddenly they announced that Howard Hughes was very ill and was being rushed to a hospital in Houston, Texas. I was terrified for him. Why hadn't he been there a long time ago? It was said he had a kidney ailment. I felt sick and ran to the phone to call Nadine Hanley, his right-hand girl for some thirty or forty years. Surely she'd know something. I knew she hadn't really seen him for years either, but she was in touch with the men who were with him and they must know something. She didn't know any more than I did.

Finally the word came that Howard had died en route. My God! How could they have waited so long to get him some real help? What had really happened? I knew he was stubborn, but if any of his old guard had been there, they wouldn't have listened to him. He would have been in a hospital long before. Howard had the ability to forge lifelong friends; I knew many of them and knew they wouldn't have let him die. They'd have laid down their lives for him. Where were they? But none of them had seen him in years. I wish to God I'd been there. I'd have outshouted him and anyone else and he would have been in a hospital on a kidney machine.

The news hounds were on the phone as soon as they heard he was dead, the bastards. I couldn't tell them a thing. I hadn't seen the boss for so long I literally couldn't remember the last time. What had happened to my darling boss all these years? It wasn't odd that I hadn't seen him. He often disappeared for months at a time, but there was always a twenty-four-hour number you could call and a message would get back eventually. I hadn't had any reason to call, but many of the others, like Nadine and Walter Kane, a Hughes employee, couldn't get any word back, even on important messages. It was very strange and weird. I suddenly thought of all the rumors that had been flying around: rumors about his death, that he'd been kidnapped, all the long hair and nails stories. And I knew it was not the Howard I knew. Months ago I had talked to Jean Peters, his ex-wife, and she had told me not to worry about "Uncle Howard," that he was just fine. Now, I was sick and sad and angry. What had happened in between? Someday we'll know, but in the meantime I felt desolate.

I thought back to the first time I had ever seen Howard and what he had been in my life, how he had changed it, what a good friend he had been, how loyal and "as good as his word." I loved him.

John finally made his decision regarding the apartments. "The whole thing is ridiculous," he began. "Your money should be making money for you instead of you having to keep going out and adding to it. So you're through working as of right now. Unless you find something you really want to do, you're through with this grind. Okay with you?" Was it ever! No one had ever said to me I didn't have to work since I'd been eighteen years old.

So we went back to Los Angeles and immediately bought out Tom's share of the apartment complex, paying for it in part by returning the house on the family compound that I had bought years before. Now Tom had everything except Jamie's house. John and I took over one of the apartments and the first thing he did was raise all the rents, which put the place on a profitable basis for the first time. He plunged in and worked very hard around the apartments making the place better. He would know he was doing the right thing if we came out of it with a profit.

What can I say about John Peoples? Well, he's wonderful and marriage to him brought my life into kilter as it hadn't been for years. I'm miserable alone. I close up and life has no sparkle. I'm really two different people: one kind when I'm married and another when I'm not. With my marriage to John, no one had to guess which I was. One look was all you needed. John is a very special sort of man, and a real individualist to boot.

There are some wonderful things about John Peoples that make life so much easier for me. My friends are his friends and are always welcome at our house. None of my women friends dash away when John comes driving up as they did with Robert. And if we want to have a party and invite everyone we know, we do just that and have a ball. While we don't have show business in common, John takes charge of the business end of it for me, such as arranging bookings, travel, hotels, and all of that. And he's good at it.

One of the main things I adore about him is that he's perfectly ready to make changes in our life, such as moving or getting into the car or a plane and going somewhere different. Robert Waterfield used to think it over and over from all sides until I'd get so hogtied I no longer cared if we went or not. John, on the other hand, is as active as I am.

Although he can be impossible when he's ill, and I have that little cross to bear, I have to admit that he has his as well. Like my cooking.

Just as he couldn't change himself into a good patient, I couldn't change myself into a good cook. It's a long-standing family joke: "Jane can't even hard-boil an egg successfully." Once I tried to refute that charge. I was on a diet and decided to hard-boil a dozen eggs. I put them on the stove at about midnight and then settled down with John to watch the "Late Show."

"Remind me to turn off the eggs," I said.

"Okay," he muttered, "I will." But he didn't. The film ended, we went upstairs to bed, and I was awakened in a couple of hours by a god-awful smell.

My first thought was that they must be burning garbage over at the Miramar, but I saw that all was peaceful next door. I went back to bed, but couldn't fall asleep, since the smell was getting stronger. It seemed to be coming right into the room. I awakened John.

"Whassamatter?" he mumbled.

"Breathe in," I ordered. He looked at me as though I'd gone mad.

"You wake me up in the middle of the night to remind me to breathe? Haven't I been doing okay up to now?"

"Breathe in," I said again, "deep."

He did and almost exploded. "What the hell is that stink?"

"That's what I'd like to know," I replied.

Suddenly his eyes opened wide. "Oh, my God," he exclaimed, "the eggs!" He leaped out of bed and flew down the stairs with me one step behind. I was almost knocked over by the smoke that was coming up the stairs. We could barely see a thing in the kitchen. Thick smoke was pouring out of that big pot on the stove.

Of course. The water had boiled off and the eggs had exploded, leaving pieces stuck to the ceiling, the refrigerator, and the walls. The pot itself was a charred hulk. It took us the whole next day to clean the kitchen and get the pot back into working order. Needless to say, it's in everyone's interest to keep Jane out of the kitchen.

Life with John and Jane is a happy and slightly crazy one. A large part of our life is our children. As far as John is concerned, our children and their welfare are of the utmost importance and consideration. And things were going well for them. Thomas had gotten his band together and was playing in a club in Prescott, Arizona. Tracy was in love with one of the musicians, Jim, and was quite serious about him despite Thomas' violent objections. Dude also was doing well and back in Texas now. Buck had quit school and was working for the Beverly Hills Parks Department and then later as a mechanic in a garage. Buck and his Dad had reached the same impasse Robert and Thomas were in just before the divorce. Things were not exactly peaches and cream for them: Buck rebelled and Robert roared. I didn't get to see nearly enough of Buck.

Robert and I had set up a trust fund for the kids at the time of our divorce. Thomas and Tracy bought houses. Buck bought cars. He had gone through all of the money in a little over one year, by which time he was nineteen. He had just enough left to use as a down payment on a four-wheel-drive pickup truck that he used for weekend hunting trips.

One evening Buck went out on a blind date with the sister of a girl he'd gone with some time before, and that date grew into something more serious. Pam Hudson, a cute brunette, was soon to become Mrs. Robert Waterfield. Buck was nineteen-and-a-half and she was seventeen and still in high school. They were both very young, but also very much in love, and we all hoped that this would help settle him down.

Then John and I received a call from Tracy announcing that she and Jim were going to Las Vegas to get married despite Thomas' objections. She had also called her father, who by that time had remarried, but he said he would not attend her wedding. She asked if we would.

Of course I said we would. I wasn't going to let my daughter get married without me. So we flew to Las Vegas and took Buck and Pam with us. It was a mess. Thomas was so against the marriage that he didn't come and had already fired Jim. Some of the band arrived looking like hippies. John and Jim had an argument at the bar, but Tracy did get married, and John and I flew back to Los Angeles and Tracy and Jim went back to Prescott. The tensions were enormous.

Now I had two of my kids married off, and I prayed that all would go well with them both. I felt pretty good about Buck and Pam but had serious doubts about Tracy and Jim. Then my sister-in-law Pamela received a very important message for me from the Lord that I've kept with me throughout all the changes which have taken place in my kids' lives, the joys, the tragedies, and the new commitments. I will never forget the message:

> I have not made thee a mother hen that should sit upon her nest and count her eggs. So why sit ye there cackling? Have I ever sent ye anywhere that ye have not wanted to go? Still you are cackling, and hear what I have to say unto thee. Thou are not a brood hen.
>
> With the wind whipping through your mane and your nostrils flaring, ye stand a proud, free horse upon the plains of this life. Ye will not be broken. Neither will ye run with the rest of the mares, following some stallion after his every whim. I have made thee a free spirit. I did not choose at random for thy children. I prepared a womb for them and gave them unto thee. Fear not, neither in the night wind nor in the heat of day, for I am with thee. I am with thee always. Ye shall see great things in them. Ye shall see through their eyes. Ye shall be with them in all things. I have many things in store for them. They shall learn and ye shall learn. There shall be changes in them and ye shall see them. Hold tight, speak softly, and hear the still small voice that shall speak unto thee in turmoil and in conflict. Keep thyself that I may be near thee and give thee peace, for many things shall be done and many things accomplished. I have sent thee and I have sent them with thee. Gird up thy loins like a man. Ye are My Son. Be a faithful watchman over My children for I shall require an accounting from thee.

Well, the Lord sounded pretty tough and I couldn't be sure why. I felt that something was coming up that would require me to "gird up my loins like a man." I knew whatever it was, the Lord was warning me. He would be with me, so I stopped worrying and let myself be content with my life and with my children.

TWENTY-SIX

John had taken over a fish processing plant in Santa Barbara. He figured it would be a perfect setup for Buck, and when his son Dude came to live in California, John turned the plant over to the two boys to run.

Buck and Dude hit it off from the start and were just mad about each other. They even began referring to one another as "my brother." They worked fifteen hours a day and showed a profit. John was overseeing the operation, but the boys were doing the work: They took huge trucks down to the dock when the fishermen came in with their catch, weighed the fish, then loaded them into the trucks and transported them to the plant, where the workers would fillet them. It was all a gigantic operation that employed more than a hundred people. As soon as it got rolling, Buck and Pam swapped our cottage for an apartment of their own.

About a year after the fish processing plant had begun operating, some friends of ours came from Chicago to visit and we all went out to dinner, where I'm afraid I had too much to drink. I hadn't done that for a long time and the effect on me was bad. I awoke the next morning with a terrible hangover. It was ten o'clock and John had already left for Mexico on business for the plant. I felt ghastly and couldn't find a thing in the house to take—neither whiskey, which we no longer kept in the house, nor buttermilk, which usually worked for me. So I got in my car to make the trip to the market to get something.

I was pretty shaky, but I made it. But on the way home . . . WHAM! I didn't see what I hit until after I hit it. All I can remember was that as I left the freeway I looked to the right. There was no one in sight. The left was a blind corner from my Mercedes 280SL, so I inched out cautiously, saw it was clear, and then pulled out all the way. A red ten-ton truck came barreling down from the right, the beach side, which had no stop sign, and I hit him.

Shaking from head to foot, all I could do was sit there and cry. The young man who was driving the truck came over and sat next to me, trying to calm me. I wasn't hurt, but I felt miserable at what I'd done. The whole front end of my car was crushed and I was crying for that as well as from shock. I loved that car.

It was all a matter of lousy timing, because Santa Barbara was being used as a test area at that time by the State of California and the district attorney had started a crackdown on drunk drivers. So there I was, in the midst of all that, involved in an automobile accident. Never mind that it was half past ten in the morning; there'd been an accident and it was a marvelous opportunity to lower the boom on someone with publicity value.

Just as the patrol car arrived, my friend Jimmy Gawzner from the Miramar Hotel pulled up. It was all very calm and controlled, with the other driver being very nice about it all. His truck had suffered no damage except to the rear wheel, but he wasn't worried about that; he felt more concern for the "poor lady in the smashed Mercedes," as he referred to me. We agreed to each take care of our own damage and signed a paper to that effect. When the police began asking questions about any recent drinking, I explained I hadn't had a drink since the night before. The driver of the truck said that he would be willing to sign a statement that he had smelled no liquor on my breath. Jimmy said the same. Yet there I sat shaking and bawling from both hangover and shock.

The police wouldn't let go. They felt that they had themselves a drunk driving case, and so off to jail I went.

I put in a call to my attorney, who advised me that even though I hadn't had anything to drink since the night before, I should refuse to submit to a blood test. "You never know just how long alcohol stays in your bloodstream," he warned, "so it's better that you don't take a chance."

When I refused to take the test, the police informed me that I wouldn't be allowed to drive for six months. Then they proceeded to give me other tests, such as walking heel to toe or some such thing that I can't even do sober, some sort of game with my fingers which I couldn't understand, then touching the tip of my finger to the tip of my nose and counting backward from 100. That I could do. I was held at the police station for five hours, and when Buck came down to get me, he was told I was "sleeping it off." I didn't even know he had been there.

After a bit of hollering on my part I was allowed to phone my attorney again, and he was stunned. "You mean you're still there?" he exclaimed. "I sent Buck down to get you hours ago, and when he didn't call, I figured you'd been released."

Buck, in desperation, had called the Los Angeles airport and stopped John just before he boarded the plane for Mexico. John stormed into that jail and carried on as only he can, demanding to know who was in charge and who had done this terrible thing to me. Finally, all loose ends were tied off and I walked out to await my day in court.

Ironically, I was called to Los Angeles to receive the Humanitarian Award from the Motion Picture Society for my work with WAIF and then to San Francisco to attend a showing of The Outlaw given as a fund-raising affair for the WAIF chapter there. I went through the motions and tried not to think about my forthcoming trial, but it didn't help.

I woke up at four in the morning on the day of my date with the judge. I was a total wreck. I'd never in my life been on the stand and the whole thing felt like the Day of Judgement had come for me. The district attorney was determined to nail me as a test case and the judge was well known for being tough on "names." Great.

Jimmy appeared as my witness, but the driver of the truck was out of town that day. My lawyer was with me, as was John, who was so furious over the whole stupid affair that at one point during the proceedings he had to be restrained by Jimmy and a bailiff.

The upshot was that the judge found me guilty and sentenced me to ninety-six hours in jail, the sentence to begin immediately. I protested, requesting permission to at least go home to get some personal belongings. It was refused. I kept trying. The judge considered my appeal for a few minutes, relented, and we all went home. We sat around for a couple of hours and watched, of all things, *Gentlemen Prefer Blondes*. I could feel the tears welling up—to have to go through the humiliation of jail. Then as the appointed hour drew near, I packed a small bag with toothbrush, toothpaste, soap, cleansing cream, and stuff like that, and off I went to jail.

The women officers and the three other girls in the "dorm" were all very nice to me, and that made things a little easier to bear. I was explained the rules, told when mealtimes were, and shown how to operate the one-unit combination wash basin and john. Breakfast was served at half past six, but you were awakened an hour before in order to clean up your cell. Half past five in the morning? Me, who never gets up before ten? Lunch was brought up to the cells and consisted of sandwiches, fruit, and coffee. Dinner was served in the dining hall at half past three and then it was back to the cells. Naturally, by eleven, when the lights were turned off, you were so damn hungry you could die. The girls advised me to hold back some of my lunch and eat it before going to bed. It was good advice and I was very grateful for it before my four days were up.

The dining room was a long, bare room with stainless steel tables and little, round stools attached to them. The time allowed for eating was all of fifteen minutes, so the food had to be gulped down if you wanted to eat at all. The food was so-so, good and bad in turn, but at least there was always a huge urn of either coffee or tea, and we could take a pitcher of it back to our cells.

I was only to be in for ninety-six hours, but the other girls were in for a lot longer. How many of us have ever been in jail? What do we know about it? What thoughts do we have, if any, about those who are behind bars? Those girls became my friends and companions for all of four days.

We talked a lot together, and for the most part the conversations dealt with men and mothers. I never gave much thought before about how much mothers can influence their daughters. I knew that mine did, but mine is an exception. What about the ordinary mothers? The uncaring ones or the downright bad ones? What about their influence? Meeting those women in jail and spending all those hours in conversation taught me a lot. I learned that those poor girls needed something, and it wasn't jail. It was help with a capital *H*.

Visits were twice a week and I got two of them. John came both times and was terribly upset to see me there. He was in far worse shape than I was and with tears in his eyes said he'd gladly do thirty days himself instead of my doing four. I had to cheer him up and I assured him I was fine and got him talking.

He filled me in with family news and how the fish business was doing and how Pam, Buck, and Dude were getting on. I was delighted with all the good news he gave me, but what did disturb me was the fact that our telephone hadn't stopped ringing since I'd been jailed. Reporters were calling from all over—New York, Los Angeles, London, everywhere—all wanting a story. That kind of publicity I could have done without.

When I had been sentenced, the judge had told me that a city supervisor had received the same punishment I was getting for the same offense. He wanted me to know that even a government official was being treated as I was, in case I felt there was any bias against me. What the judge didn't take into account, though, was that the supervisor's story never got out of Santa Barbara, whereas mine made New York, London, Tokyo, and Rome. When I got out I toyed with the idea of making a scrapbook of all the rotten publicity I'd received and sending it to that judge, asking him if he really thought the "punishment fit the crime." But I also kept thinking that although I didn't deserve to be punished this time, I sure had deserved it other times, so . .

While I was still in jail, reporters were driving poor John crazy, following him all over the place trying to get a statement from him. One daring fellow chased after him with a camera into the Miramar Hotel. That was the last straw. John turned to the guy and in his own inimitable style said, "That camera of yours had better be made of chocolate or something you like, 'cause if you use it, I'm gonna shove it either down your throat or up your ass."

Needless to say, the photographer took off in a hurry. You just don't fool around with John when he's mad. John's reenactment of that incident, complete with gestures and the newsman's expression, did more for my morale than anything else. I roared with laughter right through the connecting telephone, and the other visitors must have thought we were crazy.

Four days is not, after all, an eternity, although at times it sure felt like it. What made it bearable were John's visits and the letters I received from Benny. One contained a message that Carmen had gotten for me. It said,

> Yea, true willingness is born when ye are the least willing—if ye stand and claim thy birthright. Claim the Lord over that which cometh between thee and thy God. For I say unto thee that that which is offensive unto thy God shall rise up before thee and separate thee from the peace which ye have known aforehand. And that is how you will know that this is that for which ye are in need of being cleansed.
>
> Therefore, I say, stand where thou art. Attempt not to move in thy own strength, but stand where thou art, as the sin which doth so easily beset thee standeth in thy path to separate thee from thy God. And claim the Lord of thy life, and His Kingship over that thing—and make no move in thy own strength. And I say it shall truly have no hold over thee.

I spent the rest of that day in my cell pondering over the message. And I was still pondering that evening when all the others were in the main room watching television. I realized that the only times in my life when I had screwed things up were those when I was doing a lot of drinking. I could go along for weeks drinking just a little now and then and be fine, but whenever I got drunk, it was trouble. That had to be the "sin which so easily besets."

My day of freedom finally arrived and I was excited and at the same time a little sad at having to leave those poor girls. It's amazing how easily you can get to know other people who share your trouble. One girl made me a beautiful farewell card, artistically decorated and warmly worded; two others wrote equally warm notes, and I still have all of them.

Then at last came my moment of departure. The police captain plotted out the whole operation like a commando raid so I could avoid the ever-hovering "gentlemen" of the press. He gave out the time of my release as an hour later than it was set for and arranged for Buck to be at the rear entrance of the jail in his pickup. John was strategically stationed in front, in full view of the newsmen. The captain had been driven mad by those reporters, and it gave him great pleasure to outsmart them.

At the last minute the game plan was changed, and while the police kept the press occupied in front, John drove around to the side entrance, where I sneaked out and flung myself flat onto the back seat of his car. We tore out of there with tires screeching, and I'm sure there hadn't been so much excitement around that jail in a long time.

John and I headed home and Buck soon caught up with us on the freeway and drove alongside. When we got to the back door, Buck and his jailbird mother threw their arms around each other and laughed in hysterical relief that the nightmare was over.

John sold the apartments at a large profit and invested the money, making good his promise that I'd never have to work again if I didn't want to. All the emotional and physical strain had taken their toll on both

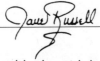

of us, so one day he suddenly said that we were going to get away by ourselves. He wasn't going to get any argument from me on that score.

Wahnono was up near Yosemite, where John had once owned a cottage. We rented a place up there and it was just heavenly. We took long walks through the redwood forest and went to charming little places in town for dinner. We had a fire going in the fireplace full-time, and it was as peaceful as could be, as well as honeymoonish and romantic.

One night, while sitting by the fireplace and talking about nothing in particular, both of us for the most part lost in our own thoughts, John suddenly burst out with, "Will you marry me?"

"You mean," I asked, "you want us to get married all over again?"

With a shy grin he said, "Well, I don't exactly remember the first time, and I think our marriage is something I should have some memory of."

I gave him a big kiss and asked, "Where would you like to go for this one?"

"Wherever you say."

I thought it over for a minute or two and then came up with a sudden idea. "Taos, New Mexico. I love the architecture there. I've never been there and always wanted to see the place. That's why I named the apartments Taos West."

"Okay," he agreed, "Taos it is."

We phoned Babs and Quentin in Colorado and they agreed to come down to be our witnesses.

Since we had already gone through all the necessary legalities, we'd have no problem with a second ceremony. The Episcopalian minister who presided called it a "rededication ceremony." So off we dashed to Taos, secure in knowing we were going to get married on a Sunday and have hotel accommodations as well, everything taken care of for us.

The wedding was lovely. I wore a beautiful new dress that John bought me and John didn't have a single drop to drink before the ceremony that time. Not one drop. This was a wedding John Peoples intended to remember. And he has and loves every single word of it.

It didn't take very long for the entire population of Taos to learn of the "John and Jane show" that was being held at the Episcopal Church, so when we arrived back at the ski lodge where we were staying, we walked into a marvelous surprise party given by the gang there, with champagne and all. It was a surprise end to a really surprise second wedding. When I married John Peoples, little did I know I'd be taking part in a replay, but both times are equally precious to me.

Then, our second honeymoon over, we headed back to Santa Barbara and our lazy, lovely life together.

T W E N T Y - S E V E N

Then something occurred that once again proved my faith in the Lord. Something that could have proven terrible. My mother used to talk to us in the chapel about God being love. She said that if we went into partnership with the Lord, we wouldn't be able to lie or cheat or steal or put anything over on our fellow human beings, because our hearts would be too full of love. We knew that the Lord would be grieved if we did wrong but that He would always be ready to forgive and help us get back on the track. There was no hellfire or damnation. We always felt the Lord's presence wherever we were.

For some strange reason I didn't want John to leave me on St. Valentine's evening in 1979 when he had to go to Los Angeles on business. He also was reluctant, but we couldn't understand why.

I went to bed very early that evening and planned to play tennis in the morning. It was a warm night, and in order to get some air into the bedroom I left the French doors open a bit. Those doors open onto the veranda, which was glassed in downstairs. I prepared for sleep with my usual nighttime ritual, begun during the years I had been running around the country doing my nightclub appearances: putting on eye shades to keep out the light and inserting earplugs to keep out the noise.

All secured and ready for a good night's rest, I crawled into bed and soon was fast asleep. Minutes later I was wide awake. Some deep inner sense told me that something was wrong. I removed the plugs and blinders and sat up in the darkness, alert, motionless, and listening for I didn't know what. Then I heard a tiny sound that affected me more than an explosion would have: a soft male voice murmuring, "Oh." Nothing else, just that one syllable.

I was absolutely frozen with fear. I could just make out a grayish shadow in the darkness as it slipped silently through the Fench doors and into the room. I watched with cold fascination as the shadow moved closer to my bed. I was quivering with apprehension but I tried desperately to keep a hold of myself. Screaming or calling for help would have done no good, since I was alone in the house and the nearest neighbors were too far away to hear.

I tried to swallow my fear and whispered softly, "Who are you?" No answer. Not a sound. I sensed his closeness and I went cold. Reaching out in the dark, my hand touched the side of his head. I felt short-cropped bristly hair. No one I knew had a crew cut.

"Oh, no," I moaned, "Oh, no," and turned and put my face in the pillow. With that I felt his weight on the bed and he leaned over and began kissing me across the back of my neck. I suddenly got very calm. I usually do in moments of stress.

"Look," I said, "You don't want to do this. You really don't. It will haunt you for the rest of your life if you do."

There was no sound from him, but he did stop the kissing. I went on talking, because my voice seemed to be keeping him passive.

"In the first place," I said gently, "this is the Lord's house and nothing bad has ever happened in it."

My voice remained soft and gentle and controlled. I went on, saying more or less the same thing. Then, all of a sudden, he flopped flat on the bed alongside of me, his head on the pillow.

I seemed to have no fear of this situation. I sat up straight and began to pray very softly, but aloud. I prayed and prayed and as I did, I slipped into tongues. I kept on in a language he surely didn't understand, and all the time he just lay there, motionless and silent. Then I stretched out my hand and placed it on his chest, which was bare, and said aloud, "Lord, You bless him. Bless him, Father."

I must have kept praying with my hand on his chest for five minutes, which is a long time to sit in the dark with someone who could very well be a killer or a rapist or a madman. I was getting no reaction from him, yet I knew I was having some calming effect, so I tried a new tack.

"Look," I said, still softly, "I don't know what you look like. I can't identify you. If you go out the same way you came in, you'll be perfectly safe."

I decided to take a chance and make my move. Ever so slowly, so as not to shake the bed, I slid off and tiptoed into the connecting bathroom. Once inside, I hurried out through the other door that led to the hall and then down the carpeted stairs to the paneled secret door that led to the den-office. There I crawled under the desk and pulled the telephone down to me. I was terrified of the sound traveling upstairs, but I dialed the police.

The cop on the other end kept asking me question, until I hissed back at him, "Listen, quit asking questions and get over here! The guy doesn't know where I am and I don't want him to find out by hearing me talking to you."

The police finally arrived and searched the outside of the house before coming in. I was still crouched under the desk, but since I'd heard nothing from upstairs, I was convinced the man had left. Then I accompanied the officers to the bedroom. I was right. He had gone. Once I realized it was all over, reaction set in. I started shaking like a leaf from a combination of relief and repressed fear.

When I related the entire experience to the police and told them how I'd handled it, one of the officers looked at me and asked, "Are you religious, lady?"

"I don't like that word *religious*, but I love the Lord, if that's what you mean," I answered.

"The reason I asked," the officer went on, "is that the very same thing happened to another woman recently, and she started talking about God too, and the guy left, same as yours did."

"Was she religious?" I asked.

He smiled. "When I asked her that, she said she'd been an atheist all her life but sure believed in God now." Then he laughed and said, "If this was the same guy, you two gals probably made a believer out of him!"

It would be the understatement of the century to say I was delighted when John returned the next day. He was furious that he'd been away. In a way I'm glad he hadn't been there, because the results would have been awfully bloody. As it turned out, my way was better: I had let the Lord handle it.

About that time Tracy wrote to announce that she was pregnant. The idea of becoming grandparents delighted John and me. We hardly knew Jim, as he was not about to get involved with "family"—shades of Robert Waterfield—but if Tracy was happy with him, we couldn't complain.

At long last things seemed to be on an even keel. Buck and Pam were together, Buck and Dude were working at the fish plant, and Thomas was doing well with his band. I invited Tracy and Jim to Santa Barbara for Christmas and planned a big old-fashioned family get-together, but at the last minute Jim decided not to come. He just disappeared. Tracy, seven months pregnant, looked all over for him and finally drove eight hours by herself all the way from Prescott, Arizona.

She arrived way after dinner, and we were furious that her husband had let her make that long drive alone in her condition. We found out that things weren't going too well in paradise. The marriage seemed to have gone along okay for a while, but the bad part was that they were constantly short of money. John asked Tracy if she'd like to stay with us and have the baby here. I think that was just what she had been hoping for, because she jumped at the suggestion. While it was sad that the marriage was in trouble, I have to admit it was wonderful having Tracy where I could be with her, watch over her, and share her experience. When the baby was about due to arrive, John and I drove Tracy to the hospital and I stayed to work with her as she did the breathing and exercises we had practiced.

Despite all the preparation, her labor went on too long and her doctor decided on a cesarean. When it was all over, John and I peeked through the glass of the nursery at our new grandson. Tracy decided to call him Jaime, an old Scottish name that has been in our family for generations.

Tracy stayed with us for several months, and it was wonderful having her and the baby around. Jaime was adorable, and John was the picture of contentment rocking the baby back and forth on his lap. This was a cozy, happy time for us all, but we knew it had to end, because soon Tracy would have to go back to Prescott to enforce whatever decision she came to. She never did get back with Jim, and eventually they divorced.

Not long after Tracy returned to Prescott, I decided that I didn't really want to remain in California. Like so many Californians, whether they admit it or not, the possibility of an earthquake was constantly on my mind. But there seemed no way we could plan on leaving Santa Barbara as long as the men were involved in business there. So I prayed, "Lord, if you want us to move, you'll just have to arrange it so we can."

Two things occurred that made our move possible. First, John sank our boat. Of course he didn't do it on purpose; I suppose he was just an unwilling instrument of the Lord. But she did sink!

We'd been making good use of that boat before and after our marriage. Often John went out with some of his fishing buddies and of course they'd get smashed and have a great time. One moonlit night he and some of the guys took it out with the intention of spending the night aboard. As it turned out, the ocean got very rough and one of the two engines started giving them trouble, so John decided to come on in on the good one.

Approaching the marina, he suddenly remembered that there was a huge sandbar at the end of the breakwater in

Santa Barbara Harbor. But it was too late. A monster wave came along, picked up the boat, and plunked her right on top of that sandbar.

I was awakened the next morning by a phone call from the harbormaster telling me what had happened. I dashed down to the harbor and saw our lovely boat sitting high and dry. The tide had gone out, leaving her beached in the middle of the sand. When the tow man arrived, I got aboard the tug to watch the operation from there. The tug pulled our boat off the sandbar and all the way up to the harbormaster's dock. It was there that John noticed that the boat was sinking. It seems that when she had hit the sandbar the screws had been driven right up into the hull and she had slowly been taking in water all the time she was being towed. Seeing what was happening, John panicked and screamed, "Get me off this motherfucker! It's sinking!"

Well, old John had left the radio on, so his words were broadcast over short wave for all to hear. He got himself fined for swearing over the air. They got him off just before *The Outlaw* went bubble, bubble, bubble right down to the bottom of the Pacific. With her went a television set, hi-fi equipment, lamps, furniture, clothing, just about everything. We had that boat furnished like an apartment.

That took care of one problem. The second thing that happened involved the fish plant. The city authorities suddenly noticed that the plant, which had been there for nine years before we took it over, was situated in the wrong zone and ordered it moved. John began looking high and low for a new location but couldn't find anything. The men were desolate at the prospect of closing down their business, which had finally gotten out of the red, but that's just what they had to do.

John was ready to go to court and fight it, but by then the boys had lost heart and said, "Let's just leave it, Dad. Let it go."

So we had no business and no boat and no reason to stay in Santa Barbara. I said to myself, "Well, I guess the Lord took care of that all right. So we're going to move."

I didn't have the slightest idea of where, or even if John would consent to move. I somehow had neglected to mention my idea to him or to Buck or Dude. I had a lot of convincing to do.

Pam and Buck decided to live on a ranch up in Ventucopa. It would be just the right sort of life for them, as they both hate big city living. That left John, Dude, and me, and we still hadn't figured out what to do with ourselves.

While in a state of indecisiveness, I suggested that we go to Prescott and visit Thomas and Tracy and see our darling grandson, Jaime. We did just that, and it was wonderful to see Tracy nicely settled in on her own and doing well.

One fateful day John and I decided to drive around the area for some sightseeing. We headed out to Sedona, which is only an hour's drive from Prescott. When we caught sight of that town, our mouths literally fell open in astonishment. There before our eyes was the loveliest sight imaginable: a town built at the bottom of a miniature Grand Canyon. Orange-red mountains towered on all sides, and it was just spectacular—the most breathtaking place I'd ever seen. And I recognized it instantly: We'd had a painting of it at the ranch in Van Nuys. I tore my eyes from the view and turned to John as he turned to me. He was the first to find his voice.

"Why don't we just sell everything and move here?" he said.

"Great," I replied.

He was kidding, but I was serious. For some time I had known we were going to move, and now we'd found the place. Sedona was, without a doubt, the perfect move, not only because it was so beautiful and peaceful and small-townish, but it was close to Tracy and baby Jaime and to Thomas.

What is my life like now? Happy and contented. I haven't worked in eight years except to do the Playtex commercials. They're easy and it's something I've always believed in—bras! It's fun to go to New York once a year with John and Kevin to catch the plays on

Broadway and see Hal Schaefer or Portia Nelson, who both live there.

We've lived in Sedona for five and a half years now. We ride bikes and play tennis and I keep busy with art classes, which I haven't had time for since I was in my teens. Sedona is full of galleries and artists and writers and people our age who want a quiet life among the beauty of the mountains. Around here I'm strictly Jane Peoples.

In 1977 WAIF left ISS to concentrate on children in the United States. There are now 500,000 children in foster care who need permanency in their lives. That's what we're concentrating on now. WAIF is getting more well known than ever and doing a wonderful job. We have adoption parties in connection with adoption agencies in many areas. The agency invites potential parents and the children available for adoption (most of them older or handicapped) to a park for a party given by WAIF. There they can play games, eat hot dogs, and get acquainted. The results are phenomenal. As many as thirty children can get adopted from one afternoon's effort. I wish we had groups in all fifty states to raise dollars, spread the word, change laws, and give adoption parties. WAIF has helped over 36,000 children find homes.

In Sedona, we get a lot of visitors: Jamie and Pamela from Van Nuys, old friends like Quentin and Babs from Denver, Benny and Bayeux from Santa Barbara, and even Richard Egan once when he did a play in Phoenix. While Richard's play was still running there, we got the surprise of our lives. Who should drive up to our house in a gigantic thirty-five foot motor home complete with wife and dogs, but Jack Beutel. We all went to see Richard's play and then brought him home with us on his day off. Richard, Jack, and I indulged ourselves in a wonderfully sentimental evening reminiscing about the "old days." Most of our talk was about Howard Hughes—how awful the rotten publicity had been at the end, his illness, the way he'd been rousted about, his terribly lonely death, and all that lousy legal squabbling over his money. We also talked about what a super-thoughtful man he'd been with us and all the others who had worked for him, a fact few people outside his employ ever realized.

Tracy remarried four years ago and we couldn't have been happier. Her husband's name is Kenton Foundas and he's Mr. Dependable, a Capricorn who works as a physiotherapist at the Veterans Administration Hospital. He's great with Jaime, and last year Tracy had beautiful twin girls, Sara and Andrea, whom five-year-old Jaime adores. He plays the clown and amuses them by the hour. I've never seen anyone beam the way John does when those kids climb all over him to kiss Grandpa—the big woolly bear.

Thomas and his friends have a new jazz rock group. They write lots of their own songs and sing great and the kids follow them all over Arizona. I think they're exceptional. He has no special girl—but he's next!

Buck and Pam split up while Buck was still in Cuyama working his beloved hayfields.

Robert Waterfield was hospitalized in intensive care in mid-March 1983. The kids all left their jobs and flew to his bedside; their wonderful, crabby father was desperately ill. On March 25, 1983, he died. It was the saddest time they ever had together, although everyone knew it was coming.

Ram football players, coaches, and friends from all over the country went to his wife Jan's to have a party after the funeral, which was what Robert wanted. On Easter Sunday, Buck, crying like a baby, took his Dad's ashes up to the Caliente (where Robert, Jackson, and Garcin used to hunt) and sprinkled them under the pine trees.

Mother moved from Pat Henry to me, then to Prescott to her oldest grandchild, Geraldine, and finally to Tom and Nola in Washington State. While she was with me she had her ninetieth birthday. John really outdid himself. His party for Mother was the biggest bash ever, and the entire family came—children, grandchildren, and great-grandchildren. It was just divine, and Mother was in seventh heaven. She did all her recitations for the kids and played the piano. John barbecued for everybody and was so pleased with his success that he began making plans for Mother's hundredth. She's ninety-four now and lives permanently in Washington near the Canadian border amidst the tall pines with Tom and Nola on another family compound made up of Henrys and Russells. She never stops praising the Lord for her health and all His goodness to all of us. She's absolutely right.

Ken and Lois have moved to Oregon to spend some time with their boys. Wally and Janet, his third wife, are in Nevada, and Jamie and Pamela are still on the only corner of the compound left in Van Nuys. Jamie's so stubborn he *won't* move. Carmen has a health food store in Elk City, Oklahoma, and we speak to each other at least once a week. Bayeux and Benny still live in Santa Barbara, and Christobel in San Francisco. There are lots of places for us to visit.

Pat, Margaret, and Alberta are scattered, but somehow we manage to get together once or twice a year. The high school four are still inseparable.

I've quit drinking anything alcoholic—or, as Shotgun would say, "laid it down for good"—so I'm as healthy as a horse. I hadn't done much drinking since our move to Sedona anyway, but each innocent little celebration eventually proved to be disastrous. Try this one on for size. After the first "Night of One Hundred Stars," the Jack Beutels and the John Peoples sat up until ten the next morning celebrating. After everyone had gone to sleep, I had a nightmare and "woke up" still in my bad dream. I got out of bed and wandered down the hall in my black nightgown to another star lady's suite. I wanted to warn her that the CIA was after all the stars in the show and to enlist her help in overthrowing them. I mean, really! She called a doctor, but somehow I managed to elude him and escaped to an upstairs kitchen, where I slowly came to and realized what had happened.

My poor husband, in the meantime, was awakened by the security guards. They searched for me in the lady star's suite. Hearing John's roar and noticing the blood-red murder in his eye, she pleaded with him, "John, you're not going to hit her, are you?" Incidentally, he never has. He only barks; he never bites ladies.

The lady star, by the way, was Liz Taylor, whom I'd met only once, briefly. No, Jane, you can't drink. My body chemistry has definitely changed. I used to be the one to take care of everyone else; now I can't even take care of me. So that's that.

As I lie in bed thinking back over my life, this is the prayer that comes to me:

> Lord God of Israel,
> For what am I asking? Why do I cry, "Where is God?" Is He not here—ever present? Surrounding me with ribbons of purple and cords of gold? Are not my feet led down paths of perfection while my eyes behold only the soft, pink clouds of heaven? Never seeing where my feet go—until after, as looking back on a long hallway saying, "There Lord? You took me there?"
>
> Thy ring sits lightly in my nose and Thy hand has, oh yea, such a gentle touch. Never to tear or mar, but to nudge gently. And I wish so much to please Thee—to be obedient—and am at once so lazy and slothful, so prone to lie down in green pastures, so tempted to put my face on a warm stone and dabble in the brook and never see Thy scepter of gold held forth—the crown You've promised—forgetting too often to look back on the carpet of scarlet where Thou hast led, until You turn my head, oh so gently, and say "See? This is where we have been. Take courage My daughter, My love."

The future? I want very much to continue painting. John has bought me a hilltop lot, so I know we are going to build a solar southwest house on it for our old age.

Last summer, Buck came to Sedona and helped John and Dude build spec houses (which I got to design), but suddenly Dude, the contractor, found just the right girl, named Pat, naturally, married her and moved to Lake Havasu City, Arizona. At the moment, Buck is in Santa Maria, California, near the Garcins, working in the oil fields. My kids are workaholics and always have jobs.

So, for a spell, everything is quiet, but once again I have a sneaky hunch that something is just around the corner. My old friend Patti Gilbert has a casting office and keeps coming up with offers. In 1984 I did two segments of the television series "The Yellow Rose" at Warner Brothers, playing Sam Elliott's wayward mom. It was time-consuming—but rewarding—and fun to be among 'em again.

Connie and Beryl, who had been working steadily alone, made noises about getting the trio together again. So we did a five-week cross-country tour to see if the public still liked our kind of music, the forties big band sound and swinging gospel. Well, those audiences were standing up when we left the stage, and it was a wonderful feeling.

We'll just see what the Lord has in store, but I know I have to stay on His path. It's too tough getting off it and I don't ever again want to hear Him say, "Your detours have been as in a maze."

F I L M O G R A P H Y

1943

THE OUTLAW (Howard Hughes) 103 minutes.□ *Producer:* Howard Hughes. *Director:* Howard Hawks (replaced by Howard Hughes). *Screenplay:* Jules Furthman. *Director of photography:* Gregg Toland. *Music:* Victor Young. CAST: Jane Russell *(Rio)*, Jack Beutel, Walter Huston, Thomas Mitchell, Mimi Aguglia, Joe Sawyer, Gene Rizzi. *(Note: THE OUTLAW was released only in San Francisco in 1943. In 1946, United Artists released it on a limited basis. RKO distributed the film nationally in 1950. Prints were also released in a 95 minute version and an uncensored 117 minute version.)*

1946

THE YOUNG WIDOW (United Artists) 100 minutes□ *Producer:* Hunt Stromberg. *Director:* Edwin L. Marin. *Screenplay:* Richard Macaulay, Margaret Buell Wilder. *From novel by:* Clarissa Fairchild Cushman. CAST: Jane Russell *(Joan Kenwood)*, Louis Hayward, Faith Domergue, Marie Wilson, Kent Taylor, Penny Singleton, Connie Gilchrist, Cora Witherspoon, Steve Brodie.

1948

THE PALEFACE (Paramount) 91 minutes.□ *Producer:* Robert L. Welch. *Director:* Norman Z. McLeod. *Original screenplay:* Frank Tashlin. *Additional dialogue:* Jack Rose. *Song "Button and Bows" by:* Jay Livingston and Ray Evans. CAST: Bob Hope, Jane Russell *(Calamity Jane)*, Robert Armstrong, Iris Adrian, Robert Watson, Jack Searle.

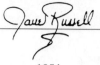

1951

DOUBLE DYNAMITE (RKO) 80 minutes.□*Producer:* Irving Cummings, Jr. *Director:* Irving Cummings. *Screenplay:* Melville Shavelson. *Story:* Leo Rosten. *Additional dialogue:* Harry Crane. *Songs:* Jule Styne, Sammy Cahn. CAST: Jane Russell *(Mildred),* Groucho Marx, Frank Sinatra, Don McGuire, Howard Freeman, Nestor Paiva, Frank Orth, Harry Hayden.

HIS KIND OF WOMAN (RKO) 122 minutes.□*Producer:* Robert Sparks. *Director:* John Farrow. *Screenplay:* Frank Fenton, Jack Leonard. *Songs:* Sam Coslow, Jimmy McHugh, Harold Adamson. CAST: Robert Mitchum, Jane Russell *(Lenore Brent),* Vincent Price, Tim Holt, Charles McGraw, Marjorie Reynolds, Raymond Burr, Leslye Banning, Jim Backus.

1952

THE LAS VEGAS STORY (RKO) 88 minutes.□A Howard Hughes Presentation. *Executive producer:* Samuel Bischoff. *Producer:* Robert Sparks. *Director:* Robert Stevenson. *Screenplay:* Paul Jarrico (uncredited), Earl Felton, Harry Essex. *Story:* Jay Dratler. *Songs:* Hoagy Carmichael, Harold Adamson. CAST: Jane Russell *(Linda Rollins),* Victor Mature, Vincent Price, Hoagy Carmichael, Brad Dexter, Gordon Oliver, Jay C. Flippen, Will Wright, Colleen Miller.

MACAO (RKO) 80 minutes.□*Producer:* Alex Gottlieb. *Director:* Josef von Sternberg. *Screenplay:* Bernard C. Schoenfeld, Stanley Rubin. *Story:* Bob Williams. *Director of photography:* Harry J. Wild. *Music:* Anthony Collins. *Songs:* Johnny Mercer, Harold Arlen, Jule Styne, Leo Robin. *Retakes supervised by:* Jerry Wald; *Directed by:* Nicholas Ray. CAST: Robert Mitchum, Jane Russell *(Julie Benson),* William Bendix, Thomas Gomez, Gloria Grahame, Brad Dexter, Edward Ashley, Philip Ahn.

MONTANA BELLE (RKO) 81 minutes.□*Producer:* Howard Welsch. *Director:* Allan Dwan. *Associate producer:* Robert Peters. *Screenplay:* Norman S. Hall, Horace McCoy. *Based on an original story by:* M. Coates Webster, Howard Welsch. *Music:* Nathan Scott. *Song:* Portia Nelson, Margaret Martinez. *In Trucolor.* CAST: Jane Russell *(Belle Starr),* George Brent, Scott Brady, Forrest Tucker, Andy Devine, Jack Lambert, John Litel, Rory Mallinson, Roy Barcroft. *(Note: MONTANA BELLE was filmed in 1948 by Fidelity Pictures for a Republic release, but in 1952, Howard Hughes bought it for release by RKO.)*

SON OF PALEFACE (Paramount) 95 minutes.□*Producer:* Robert L. Welch. *Director:* Frank Tashlin. *Screenplay:* Frank Tashlin, Robert L. Welch, Joseph Quillan. *Dances:* Josephine Earl. *Music:* Lyn Murray, Jay Livingston and Ray Evans, Jack Brooks, Jack Hope, Lyle Moraine. CAST: Bob Hope Jane Russell *(Mike),* Roy Rogers, Bill Williams, Lloyd Corrigan, Paul E. Burns, Douglas Dumbrille, Harry Von Zell, Iron Eyes Cody.

THE ROAD TO BALI (Paramount) 90 minutes.□*Producer:* Harry Tugend. *Director:* Hal Walker. *Screenplay:* Frank Butler, Hal Kanter, William Morrow. *Based on a story by:* Frank Butler, Harry Tugend. CAST: Bob Hope, Bing Crosby, Dorothy Lamour, Murvyn Vye, Peter Coe, Ralph Moody, Leon Askin, Jane Russell *(unbilled cameo guest star).*

1953
GENTLEMEN PREFER BLONDES (20th Century-Fox) 91 minutes. □*Producer:* Sol C. Siegel. *Director:* Howard Hawks. *Screenplay:* Charles Lederer. *Based on the musical comedy by:* Joseph Fields, Anita Loos. *Songs:* Jule Styne, Leo Robin. *Additional songs:* Hoagy Carmichael, Harold Adamson. *Musical director:* Lionel Newman. *Choreographer:* Jack Cole. CAST: Jane Russell *(Dorothy),* Marilyn Monroe, Charles Coburn, Elliott Reed, Tommy Noonan, George Winslow, Marcel Dalio, Taylor Holmes, Norma Varden.

THE FRENCH LINE (RKO) 102 minutes.□*Producer:* Edmund Grainger. *Director:* Lloyd Bacon. *Screenplay:* Mary Loos, Richard Sale. *Based on a story by:* Matty Kemp, Isabel Dawn. *Songs:* Josef Myrow, Ralph Blane, Robert Wells. *Music score:* Walter Scharf. *Choreographer:* Billy Daniel. *In 3-D.* CAST: Jane Russell *(Mary Carson),* Gilbert Roland, Arthur Hunnicut, Mary McCarty, Joyce MacKenzie, Paula Corday, Craig Stevens, Marilyn (Kim) Novak, Billy Daniel.

1955
UNDERWATER! (RKO) 99 minutes.□*Producer:* Harry Tatelman. *Director:* John Sturges. *Screenplay:* Walter Newman. *Story:* Hugh King, Robert B. Bailey. *Assistant director:* William Dorfman. *Costumes:* Michael Woulfe. *Music:* Roy Webb. *Song:* Louiguy, Mack David. *In Superscope.* CAST: Jane Russell *(Theresa),* Gilbert Roland, Richard Egan, Lori Nelson, Robert Keith, Joseph Calleia, Eugene Iglesias, Ric Roman, Max Wagner.

FOXFIRE (Universal) 93 minutes.□*Producer:* Aaron Rosenberg. *Director:* Joseph Pevney. *Screenplay:* Ketti Frings. *Based on a story by:* Anya Seton.

Music: Frank Skinner. *Gowns:* Bill Thomas. *Assistant directors:* Ronnie Rondell, Phil Bowles. CAST: Jane Russell *(Amanda Lawrence),* Jeff Chandler, Dan Duryea, Mara Corday, Robert F. Simon, Frieda Inescort, Barton MacLane.

THE TALL MEN (20th Century-Fox) 122 minutes.□*Producers:* William A. Bacher, William B. Hawks. *Director:* Raoul Walsh. *Screenplay:* Sydney Boehm, Frank Nugent. *Based on the novel by:* Clay Fisher. *Assistant director:* Stanley Hough. *Costumes:* Travilla. *Songs:* Ken Darby, José Lopez Alaves. *In CinemaScope.* CAST: Clark Gable, Jane Russell *(Nella Turner),* Robert Ryan, Cameron Mitchell, Juan Garcia, Harry Shannon, Emile Meyer.

GENTLEMEN MARRY BRUNETTES (United Artists) 97 minutes. □*Executive producer:* Robert Bassler. *Producers:* Richard Sale, Robert Waterfield. *Associate producer:* Mary Loos. *Director:* Richard Sale. *Screenplay:* Mary Loos, Richard Sale. *Choreographer:* Jack Cole. *Music:* Robert Farnon. *Costumes:* Travilla. *Gowns:* Christian Dior. *Assistant directors:* Basil Keys, Robert Gendre. *A Russ-Field Corporation, Voyager Production in CinemaScope, Stereophonic Sound.* CAST: Jane Russell *(Bonnie Jones),* Jeanne Crain, Alan Young, Scott Brady, Rudy Vallee, Guy Middleton, Eric Pohlman, Ferdy Mayne.

1956

HOT BLOOD (Columbia) 85 minutes.□*Producers:* Howard Welsch, Harry Tatelman. *Director:* Nicholas Ray. *Screenplay:* Jesse Lasky, Jr. *Based on a story by:* Jean Evans. *In CinemaScope.* CAST: Jane Russell *(Annie Caldash),* Cornel Wilde, Luther Adler, Joseph Calleia, Mikhail Rasumny, Jamie Russell, Wally Russell, Richard Deacon.

THE REVOLT OF MAMIE STOVER (20th Century-Fox) 93 minutes. □*Producer:* Buddy Adler. *Director:* Raoul Walsh. *Screenplay:* Sydney Boehm. *Based on the ncvel by:* William Bradford Huie. *Music:* Hugo Friedhofer. *Songs:* Tony Todaro, Mary Johnston, Paul Francis Webster, Sammy Cahn. *Sung by:* The Ames Brothers. *Costumes:* Travilla. *In CinemaScope.* CAST: Jane Russell *(Mamie Stover),* Richard Egan, Joan Leslie, Agnes Moorehead, Jorja Curtright, Michael Pate, Richard Coogan, Alan Reed, Jean Willes, Margia Dean.

1957

THE FUZZY PINK NIGHTGOWN (United Artists) 87 minutes.□*Producer:* Robert Waterfield. *Director:* Norman Taurog. *Screenplay:* Richard Alan

Simmons. *Based on a novel by:* Sylvia Tate. *Music:* Billy May. *Assistant director:* Stanley H. Goldsmith. *Costumes:* Billy Travilla. *A Russ-Field Production.* CAST: Jane Russell *(Laurel Stevens)*, Keenan Wynn, Ralph Meeker, Fred Clark, Una Merkel, Adolphe Menjou, Benay Venuta, Robert H. Harris.

1964

FATE IS THE HUNTER (20th Century-Fox) 106 minutes.☐*Producer:* Aaron Rosenberg. *Director:* Ralph Nelson. *Screenplay:* Harold Medford. *Based on a book by:* Ernest K. Gann. *Music:* Jerry Goldsmith. *Director of photography:* Milton Krasner. *Costumes:* Moss Mabry. *Assistant director:* Ad Schaumer. CAST: Glenn Ford, Nancy Kwan, Rod Taylor, Suzanne Pleshette, Jane Russell *(Guest star as herself)*, Wally Cox, Nehemiah Persoff, Mark Stevens, Max Showalter, Constance Towers, Howard St. John, Robert Wilkie, Dort Clark, Mary Wickes.

1966

JOHNNY RENO (Paramount) 83 minutes.☐*Producer:* A. C. Lyles. *Director:* R. G. Springsteen. *Director of photography:* Hal Stine. *Screenplay:* Steve Fisher. *Story:* Steve Fisher, A. C. Lyles. *Assistant directors:* Jim Rosenberger, Bob Jones. *Music:* Jimmie Haskell. *In Techniscope.* CAST: Dana Andrews, Jane Russell *(Nona Williams)*, Lon Chaney, John Agar, Lyle Bettger, Tom Drake, Richard Arlen, Robert Lowery.

WACO (Paramount) 85 minutes.☐*Producer:* A. C. Lyles. *Director:* R. G. Springsteen. *Screenplay:* Steve Fisher. *Based on a novel by:* Harry Sanford, Max Lamb. *Director of photography:* Robert Pittack. *Costumes:* Edith Head. *Music:* Jimmie Haskell. *Title song:* Hal Blair, Jimmie Haskell; sung by Lorne Greene. *Assistant director:* James Rosenberger. *In Techniscope.* CAST: Howard Keel, Jane Russell *(Jill Stone)*, Brian Donlevy, Wendell Corey, Terry Moore, John Smith, John Agar, Gene Evans, Richard Arlen, Ben Cooper, DeForest Kelley, Jeff Richards.

1967

THE BORN LOSERS (American International) 112 minutes.☐*Producer:* Don Henderson. *Director:* T. C. Frank. *Screenplay:* James Lloyd. *Director of photography:* Gregory Sandor. *Executive producer:* Delores Taylor. *Associate producer:* Jay Loughren. *Assistant director:* Paul Lewis. CAST: Tom Laughlin, Elizabeth James, Jane Russell *(Special guest as Mrs. Shorn)*, Jeremy Slate, William Wellman, Jr., Robert Tessier, Jeff Cooper, Edwin Cook, Paul Prokop.

1970

DARKER THAN AMBER (Cinema Center Films/National General Pictures) 97 minutes.□*Producers:* Walter Seltzer, Jack Reeves. *Director:* Robert Clouse. *Screenplay:* Ed Waters. *From the novel by:* John D. MacDonald. *Music:* John Parker. *Rated:* R. CAST: Rod Taylor, Suzy Kendall, Theodore Bikel, Jane Russell *(Alabama Tiger),* Ahna Capri, William Smith, Robert Phillips, Janet MacLachlan, Sherry Faber, James Booth.

1983

THE YELLOW ROSE (NBC Television) 60 minutes.□*Executive producers:* Michael Zinberg, John Wilder. *Director:* Harvey Hart. *Writer:* John Wilder. *Premiered:* Sunday, October 2, 1983. CAST: Sam Elliott, David Soul, Susan Anspach, Edward Albert, Cybill Shepherd, Noah Beery, Ken Curtis, Tom Schanley, Chuck Connors, Jane Russell. *(Note: Susan Anspach quit the series, and Jane Russell joined the cast to play the mother of Sam Elliott.)*

INDEX

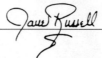